TESTIMONIALS

Readers who loved Bill Bryson's *A Walk in the Woods* will love hiking with minister Dale Clem. His writing is superb and, before long, we're in his mind, taking each arduous step with him as he and the colorful hikers he meets along the trail challenge not only the wilderness of the woods, but that of their entangled souls.

—Homer Hickam
Author of *Rocket Boys* and *Carrying Albert Home*

There is a Biblical precedent for spending time in nature and getting to know God in the wilderness. Dale Clem's reflections offer hope, humor, and insight on his spiritual journey, the Appalachian Trail.

—Jennifer Pharr Davis
Owner, Blue Ridge Hiking Company
Author of *Becoming Odyssa* and *Adventures on the Appalachian Trail*

***40 Days in the Wilderness* chronicles one pastor's journey to the deepest places of his heart as he backpacks the Maine to New Hampshire segments of the Appalachian Trail. Dale Clem reminds us throughout this poignant book of the importance of nourishing our souls by walking closely with God.**

—Rev. Debbie Wallace-Padgett
Bishop, North Alabama Conference, United Methodist Church

Dale Clem writes with honesty and humor about emotions one experiences on a long distance hike. The book is a great reflection of one's inner journey that occurs whether hiking 4 days, 40 days, or 4 x 40 days.

—Cathey "Mamma Bear" Leach, A

I am neither a hiker nor an outdoorsman, but Dale Clem is a friend and a wise, gentle, and thoughtful pastor with a great sense of humor, so I was eager to read about his 40-day journey in the wilderness on the Appalachian Trail. I laughed, I cried, and most importantly, I was drawn to reflect more deeply on nature, on God, on pilgrimage, and on the complex wonders of the journey of life, of death, and of life beyond death.

—L. Gregory Jones,
Williams Professor of Theology and Christian Ministry,
Duke Divinity School

As someone who has trekked along much of the landscape that Dale Clem describes, I loved the gentle humor of his encounters with other hikers and shared an intimate knowledge of the agonies and ecstasies along the way.... Whether you have backpacked in the Himalayas or simply stroll the mall, you will love and benefit from his inspirational and deeply moving account.

—Laurent A. Parks Daloz, Ed.D., Senior Fellow, the Whidbey
Institute, Co-author of *Common Fire*, and author of *Mentor*.

Dale Clem takes a walk in the woods, but he doesn't walk alone. He turns a hike into a pilgrimage with Christ, bringing along with him his congregation and those with whom he has ministered to and received ministry from over the years. Through his prayer and meditation, the Appalachian wilderness is transformed into a place of revelation and self-discovery.

—Will Willimon
Professor of the Practice of Christian Ministry, Duke University,
United Methodist Bishop, retired

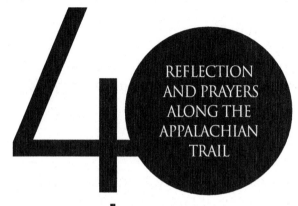

40

REFLECTION
AND PRAYERS
ALONG THE
APPALACHIAN
TRAIL

days

in the
wilderness

Dale Clem

Bardolf & Company

Forty Days in the Wilderness
  Reflections and Prayers along the Appalachian Trail

ISBN 978-1-938842-29-0

Published by Bardolf & Company
  5430 Colewood Pl.
  Sarasota, FL 34232
  941-232-0113
  www.bardolfandcompany.com

Cover design and interior layout
  by shawcreativegroup.com

For my wife Kelly, my steadfast rock,
daughters Sarah and Laurel, my hope,
my sister Connie, who
demonstrates perseverance

In memory of my daughter: Hannah,
my parents: Calvin and Joann Clem
my grandparents:
Jesse and Mildred Carter,
Andrew and Zana Clem

Robert Tucker, my scoutmaster,
and mentor and friend Michael Stewart

And for all scoutmasters,
and mentors everywhere!

Walking Prayers
(each line for 4 steps)

. . . .

Peace with every step.
Joy with every step.
Love with every step.
Grace with every step.
Smile with every step.
Community with every step.
Hope with every step.
Forgiveness with every step.
Strength with every step.
Jesus with every step.

. . . .

Praying for others
May she/he have peace with every step.
Joy with every step.
Love with every step…etc.

. . . .

Praying when facing difficulty
I can do all things with Christ who strengthens me!

. . . .

Jesus Prayer
Lord Jesus Christ, have mercy upon me.

. . . .

Prayer of connection
Peace Everywhere.

40

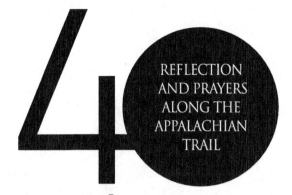

REFLECTION
AND PRAYERS
ALONG THE
APPALACHIAN
TRAIL

days
in the
wilderness

Dale Clem

Bardolf & Company

Prelude

I was around twelve when, on Christmas Day, my father, grandfather, and uncle took me down the railroad track to the family's woods for my first hunt. Each man had carefully instructed me on the use of my very own 4/10 shotgun, and I felt their eyes on me as I crawled through the barbed wire fence and dutifully answered their questions about gun safety. Apparently I passed, because at some point my grandfather instructed us to spread out from one another and slowly sweep through the forest and look for squirrel. As a link in this generational chain of males with guns in hand, I felt as though I belonged. Only years later did I understand that on that day I had been initiated into the world of men. From then on, when hunting season opened, I was my father's hunting companion, and we would spend most Saturdays hunting dove and quail. But our time together was more about training and watching our bird dogs than about bringing home a sack of game. And that time was also about something else, something even more powerful. In all our hunting and fishing adventures, my dad said few words, but it was clear to me that he felt more alive when he was united with nature. These experiences with my father brought home to me my own deep connection to trees, creeks, hills, and men.

It was the Boy Scouts, however, who introduced me to camping, and I loved the companionship, the outdoors, and the sense of independence I felt when heading off and being in the wilderness with them. At one point, I insisted our family camp together, and my mother and father reluctantly agreed. They watched skeptically as I set up an old canvas scout tent in the woods, a tent just large enough to fit the three of us, and Connie, my older sister, and Tippy, our dog. Since the sky looked like rain, I dug a good trench around the tent as the Scouts had trained me to do. But when the downpour of the Alabama summer thunderstorm hit, its power overwhelmed my defense and caused the tent to leak as the water rose.

After a miserable night, we loaded our soggy sleeping bags into the car. My mother was determined to never camp in a tent again.

Not long after, my parents bought a camper and a boat. My mother usually napped or read in the boat while the rest of us fished for bass, crappie, and catfish. We were always amazed when her line, unwatched and dragging behind the stern, caught as many fish as we did with our constant casting. I continued in the Boy Scouts and took my first big trail hike with them. I loved it—a hike on the Appalachian Trail from Georgia, near the border, to the Natahala Outdoor Center in North Carolina. I've always been grateful that the Scouts and my parents introduced me to the healing solitude of nature and encouraged me to explore creeks, fields, forests, and mountains.

I once read that the holiest people are found on the earth's highest places. Moses climbed Mount Sinai to meet with God and receive instructions, including the Ten Commandments. After his baptism, Jesus was tested in the wilderness for 40 days and successfully climbed Mount Temptation. Following his crucifixion and resurrection, Jesus and a few disciples climbed an unidentified mountain where Jesus was "transfigured" before them and they heard the voice of God. In the mythic imagination, mountains are liminal spaces—portals linking heaven and earth. When you are walking and climbing, you live in the physicality of your body, not just in your mind. Seeing the trail disappear into the unknown woods is an invitation to follow it. It uplifts the spirit to kneel on mountain-top overlooks and pray or simply gaze upon the vast expanse of creation. Climbing mountains in solitude may offer a path to listen with new ears to God. God may speak no differently in the mountains, but without the clutter, distractions, and pressures of everyday life, the receiver may be in a better position to hear what God is saying.

When the Boy Scouts introduced me to the Appalachian Trail, I was taken with the idea of one day hiking the entire 2100+ miles from Georgia to Maine. But my family and career and obligations as a minister took priority for many years. After I reached the mid-century mark, however, thoughts of hiking in the wilderness with the intention of praying for

40 days kept entering my thoughts. Forty is a number that keeps popping up in the Bible: Moses led the Hebrews in the desert for 40 years before they entered the Promised Land; Jesus spent 40 days in the wilderness; and Lent, the season of repentance and self-denial before Easter, is also 40 days. I was a 50-year-old father of two daughters, a husband, and clergyman who served the United Methodist church as a pastor, and had campus minister and missionary, and I could not get the idea of hiking in the wilderness for 40 days out of my mind.

Throughout history, men and women have received a call to leave their homes and families for a purpose unknown to them at the time. To Mary and the shepherds, it was angels who called them to leave. In Troas, Paul wanted to further his ministry in Galicia, but he was told "no" by the spirit and had a dream of a man begging him to come to Macedonia. He trusted that God had called him and immediately took a boat to Philippi, Thessalonica, and Beora (Acts 16:6-10). Jennifer Pharr Davis heeded the call to hike the Appalachian Trail after she finished college. After completing the trail, she had two more calls, this time to hike the entire length of the trail in a record number of days. The idea would not let her go. With remarkable tenacity, courage, and endurance, and the help of her husband and hundreds of supporters, she accomplished her goals. In 2012, she completed the hike in an unbelievable, record setting 41 days![1]

I myself had experienced an undeniable calling: to take my family to Lithuania and serve as missionaries. The call was so powerful that I could think of nothing else. It haunted my dreams as I slept and my thoughts while awake. My wife Kelly was not sure if it was a call from God or a mid-life crisis, but she went along anyway and our lives were enriched. This time, my call wouldn't let me go, either, but I felt torn. One voice kept telling me, "Only a religious fanatic would say, 'If Jesus went to the wilderness for 40 days of prayer and testing, why not me?'" Another voice answered, "Would God call anyone to do such a thing?"

Kelly's reaction was different at first, too. "When you have time off, we do things together as a family," she said. "It's selfish to do something just for yourself." Her words stung deeply, but she later amended them, explaining that she'd just thought that six weeks was a long time to be away. In time she came around to the idea and said she would back me 100 percent, and miss me terribly. She graciously let me go as a gift.

Explaining a call can be tedious and perhaps necessarily incomplete, so when others asked me about mine, I just said, "I want to section hike the Appalachian Trail from Maine to Vermont. It is the most difficult part of the entire trail, and I want to finish it before I get too old." This explanation was true, and it allowed me to avoid talking about my almost embarrassing call to piety and to avoid thinking about why I really wanted to go.

A hike, or pilgrimage, provides an opportunity for both an outer and an inner journey. The American mystic Thomas Merton wrote, "The geographical pilgrimage is the symbolic acting out of an inner journey. The inner journey is the interpolation of the meanings and signs of the outer pilgrimage. One can have one without the other. It is best to have both."[2]

For the young, leaving home is an expected part of life's journey. Once adulthood is established, however, what many people miss is a call to further growth, a maturing where we let go of our need to control, direct, and maintain power and status. At the end of *The Odyssey*, Homer's eponymous hero is called to make a second journey in his old age. After a lifetime of building his identity, it was time for Odysseus to let go of that self. This second journey doesn't come without pain. An image of a creature bringing a burning coal to touch the lips of the prophet Isaiah reminds us that spiritual purification involves scathing and wounding fire (Isaiah 6:6-7). Letting go of control and handing over that power to God is called a sacrifice because it's an act of giving up something that is important to us, and actions like that hurt. While I knew that I would be hiking and praying in Jesus' name, and knew that my intention was to change myself and become better able to further Jesus' mission and kingdom, I could not foresee how this would occur. I had to let go of my need for control and certainty and have faith.

And so I embarked on my journey in August of 2012.

I am grateful to the Monte Sano United Methodist Church for allowing me a six-week sabbatical for my perilous adventure. I especially appreciate Reverend Larry Millard and his wife Pat for volunteering to "shepherd" the congregation during my absence; and Reverend Kerry Holder Joffrion and Reverend Dr. Ed Soule, along with Rev. Millard, who filled in for me on Sundays.

I am also grateful to Jean Prevost, who helped me have a lighter pack and taught me how to dehydrate food; Roger Rinn, whose love of backpacking and the outdoors is contagious; Mike and Ruth Bentley, who offered wonderful hospitality to launch me on the trail in Maine; Jean Lovelace whose love and knowledge of the White Mountains of New Hampshire was helpful; Ed and Mary Bagley, who hosted me in their home in New Hampshire; my clergy brothers in my ICE (Institute for Clergy Excellence) group, with whom I feel privileged to travel and who continuously teach me; Michael Stewart, who died too young; and to Bob Blackwell, Ted Leach, Roger Thompson, Bill Blackerby, Bill Winters, Hughey Reynolds, and Michael O'Bannon.

I also want to express my appreciation for the fellow hikers and "angels" along the trail who showed up and helped me just when I needed it; and to those who kindly helped read this manuscript and offered helpful comments: Linda Hickam, Christel McCanless, Sara Norris, Kerry Joffrion, Loye Pine, Lue English, Judy Rich, Ruth Bentley, and R. G. Lyons; and to Chris Angermann for his excellent editing and for shepherding this book to publication.

And finally, with heartfelt gratitude and love, I give an unbounded "Thank you!" to my wife Kelly, who "kept the home fires going" while I was away. My daughters Sarah and Laurel continue to give me hope for the future and inspire me to be a better person.

Dale Clem
Huntsville, Alabama
2016

DAY

1

Perseverance

Mount Katahdin
Tuesday, August 21, 2012

"The Great Mountain" is what the native people in the Penobscot and Abennaki tribes called Katahdin in Maine, and on its summit the northern beginning and end of the Appalachian Trail (A.T.) lies. As a result, those wanting to start out hiking south from the trail's most northern point must first climb to the top of the mountain and then climb back down again. If they survive this, they can continue hiking the trail for more than 2,100 miles to Springer Mountain in Georgia. In Native American lore, the sacred mountain, named after the Creator, was both loved and feared, and given its nature, I suppose this was fitting. The native people would not approve of the great numbers of climbers who have braved its challenges. If given a chance, they would whisper to those brave enough for an attempt, "If you climb it, bad things will happen to you." But, according to Elder Arnie Neptune, the god Katahdin will lead humans who believe in him to their highest potential, if they also open their hearts and minds and listen.[3] Roy Dudley, a Katahdin guide and storyteller, has said that the mountain was home to a giant god named Pamola, who had wings and clawed feet. I hope he was benevolent.

In the town of Millinocket, when I had passed an antique store and asked the owner if he had any wisdom about climbing Mount Katahdin, he tartly replied, "Don't do it. I've climbed it nine times, and five of those times was to rescue hikers like you." I thanked him for the encouragement.

In 1846, when Henry David Thoreau decided to climb Katahdin, just getting there required braving an inaccessible wilderness. His group had to paddle canoes up rivers and across lakes and bogs to approach the foot of the mountain. Unlike Thoreau, I would be taking a shuttle

from the A.T. Lodge to the rustic Katahdin Stream Campground in Baxter State Park and would hike the Hunt Trail, which was first built by Reverend Irving Hunt in 1900. As Thoreau emerged above tree line in 1846, he didn't want to reach the top by following the same path as his companions, so he scrambled over the boulders, alone. He approached Katahdin as he had Walden Pond, to see what it could teach him. Thoreau wanted to "suck the marrow out of it" and live an original life. At the end of *Walden*, he wrote, "If one advances confidently in the direction of his dreams and endeavors to live the life which he has imagined, he will meet with a success unexpected in common hours." Thoreau described Katahdin as an untamed and forbidden place. "Nature here was savage and awful though beautiful."[4] Looking from the top, he quoted someone else who said that the effects of the lakes could be compared to those of a "mirror broken into a thousand fragments, and wildly scattered over the grass, reflecting the full blaze of the sun."[5] Thoreau climbed the mountain a second time in 1853 and attempted it again in 1857 but, due to a companion's illness, had to turn back. His disappointment is expressed in his book *The Maine Wood*.

When Reverend Doctor John Todd got to the top of Katahdin in 1851, he was glad he was alone because when he looked at the vast expanse he was overcome with emotion. He wrote, "You are communing with nature and nature's God and you feel as if you have no right to be here."[6] When Theodore Roosevelt attempted the climb, he lost his boot while crossing a stream and ended up making the ascent wearing moccasins. Mount Katahdin was the first wild and untamed place he had experienced, and it, along with the influence of his guide, Bill Sewell, planted in Roosevelt's mind the idea that such natural beauty should be preserved. Later, as President, Roosevelt made the conservation of wild lands for future generations a national priority. Among his many achievements was the founding of the U.S. National Park System.

I rode in the shuttle to the park with David and Karen. David is a friend and pastor in Birmingham who had already section hiked the A.T. from Georgia to New Jersey, and he was eager to hike a few weeks with me in Maine. Karen, whom we had just met, was a fearless middle-aged teacher who decided to exchange her classroom of fussy students for

David

mountains, mosquitos, and sore muscles. The ranger was an older woman who carefully entered our names in the register of southbound hikers and unceremoniously pointed out the daypacks for our use. She then indicated the floor space where we could leave our backpacks and told us that when we returned we would find our camp site number on them. We happily paid for the campsite, glad to have a place to spend the night in the park. I loved the idea of only carrying a daypack up the mountain, but the downside was that they smelled worse than the truck load of chicken manure I had spread on our garden as a kid. The body odor and sweat of the hundreds of hikers who used them was overwhelming. Although I was a little sad to leave behind my green GoLite pack, which I called the "Green Giant," I made a face, held my breath, and loaded the daypack with a first aid kit, flashlight, extra clothes, rope, water bottles, lunch, and a small bottle of merlot.

Dangling on the outside of the Green Giant were a red feather, a to-bacco pouch, and a shell—gifts from a priest in Alabama named Kerry, who is a good friend. Before I left home, she had driven up and handed me a gift nicely wrapped in a handkerchief. When I opened it up and was puzzled, she said, "You're the pastor, you'll know what to do with them." I held up the feather and she explained, "I found it on my walk in the woods and knew you were meant to take it on your hike. It symbolizes the other world, you know—the spiritual world, guardian angels, helpers, God."

Not wanting to come off as completely clueless, I contributed, "And the shell is the symbol of the pilgrim, rebirth, baptism and all that."

I touched the loose tobacco between my fingers and she said, "If you need some Native American Elder wisdom, make a little altar with rocks and sticks and sprinkle a little tobacco as a gift when you ask for help." Then she gave me a hug and was gone before I had a chance to thank her.

Kerry is the kind of person who just knows things and sees things that others do not. Some would attribute insight like hers to intuition or imagination, and maybe she is not that unusual; there have been many people throughout history who have a spiritual sensibility. But, she seems unusual to me. When there was a fatal high school bus crash in our city, Kerry was on her way to the hospital concurrently with the ambulances to meet the families and help manage the chaos of a grieving crowd. She listens to her dreams, has seen a ghost, and is always pondering what the spirit world is trying to teach through nature. If you are going on a dif-ficult and potentially dangerous trip, as I was, she is just the person you would want to have praying for you. I am not a superstitious person, and am generally suspicious of thinking that things have special power, but I do think there is power in rituals and symbols. So I took the feather and shell that she offered and accessorized my anonymous daypack with them. They attached nicely and looked great.

David chose a larger daypack and loaded it with a tin box that made a loud thump when it hit the bottom of the pack as it sat on the wooden floor. When I lifted his bag, it was twice as heavy as mine. I was curious and asked him about it, but he shrugged and I didn't pursue it. Karen chose a small pack that fit snugly underneath her bright blue raincoat. The black braces on both her knees showed under her khaki shorts. I was unsure about using walking sticks, but another hiker said that the sticks would help and that when I was scaling the cliffs and boulders, I should just toss them ahead. There was no special ceremony when we began our adventure—no cheerleaders holding up a big banner for us to burst through like at high school football games.

It was 7:55 a.m. when we took the first steps into the rainy morning and realized we didn't know which way to go. The ranger shook her head, pointed us to the trail, and added a warning: "Now remember, on top the weather can change in an instant." I had a camera and meant to take a photo of our first steps, but I decided to keep it in a plastic bag because of the rain. Already humbled, I tried to say the walking prayer I had learned from an introduction by Thich Nhat Hanh to Thomas Merton's *Contemplative Prayer*: "Peace with every step, joy with every step, grace with every step, love with every step," and added, "rain with every step." My hat and "Frog Tog" rain jacket and pants were saturated in twenty minutes.

I had started to prepare for my trip three months earlier by hiking a few miles with a full backpack and gradually increasing the distance and intensity to the point where I was hiking six to ten miles four to five days a week. I had fallen in the training and had the fresh wounds to prove it—scabs still decorated both of my knees. Hospitals give a yellow wrist band to unsteady patients warning "Fall Risk," and I thought I could've worn one of these bracelets the way I was slipping and tripping and catching myself with my walking poles. But I didn't care. The fresh smell of the evergreens was intoxicating. After years of longing, I was finally beginning my adventure. Ahead of me stretched an extended time to hike the trail and pray.

For about a mile the trail follows the Katahdin stream, and the sound of the tumbling, singing water was soothing and seemed to compliment my walking prayer mantra. The hike through the woods was

enchanting, but our pace was off because our feet, legs, and eyes were not yet in rhythm with the trail, and the distance took more time than we expected. My jaw dropped in amazement as some hikers with 2,100 miles under their belts lunged past us, their long strides in sync with the clicking of their poles on the rocks in perfect 4/4 time. They were sure-footed and unhesitating compared to us and our tentative steps. On the other hand, we began to meet hikers coming in the opposite direction who confessed that they had not made it to the top of Katahdin and had given up. The disappointment and shame on their faces was alarming. Of the 18 hikers we met, most had made it above the tree line but then turned back when faced with the challenge of climbing over the boulders in the rain and hail.

Karen looked at the sky and said, "It's going to clear up by the time we get there."

Nevertheless, my heart began to race when I realized I was about to emerge above the tree line. "Yeah, I made it," I said to myself, but I was shocked by the abrupt change.

Thoreau described this area as "rocks precariously lying or leaning on one another with cavities in between."[7] An icy chill replaced the comforting evergreen smell, and I was exposed to the fierce, pounding Canadian wind pushing me as I climbed on top of and over slick boulders. The wind's whistling sound filled my ears. The shaking evergreens, prostrated just inches off the ground, reminded me of street signs rattling during hurricanes. To keep my hat from blowing away, I tightened its strap. Looking down, I realized that if I fell I would plunge 75 feet before reaching a landing space.

I met a couple who were descending and asked them if they had made it to the top. They were surprised by the question and said, "Of course."

I asked them, "Are we close?"

They smiled and the young woman said, "I'd say you are just beginning the meat of the climb." The man added, "You have many miles to go."

I retrieved my camera and took a photo of them with the newly visible views as a backdrop. Filled with the euphoria of having just begun, David and I were determined to make the summit.

When Karen caught up with David and me, we joked about how we could feel the blazing sun drying up the rain clouds and calming the wind. Karen just smiled and said, "We aren't at the top yet." She was very right.

We climbed over boulders and rocks for what seemed like miles to get to a relatively flat area aptly named "the tabletop." Hostile clouds blew past us, with occasional patches of sunlight shining down like a moving beacon. I was too hot to wear my rain gear and stowed it in my daypack. I also hung my hiking poles on the outside of my pack, transforming it into a giant praying mantis. When I had climbed Springer Mountain in Georgia, the southern terminus of the trail, there was a plaque which stated that the trail was a "footpath for those who seek fellowship with the wilderness." My definition of "footpath" was about to expand. I scrambled over rocks, sometimes on my stomach and all fours, and realized the scabs on my knees were now scrapped off and new scratches were oozing blood. The blood seemed thin and watery and I wiped it off with my bandanna.

I could see a dot of color up ahead that turned out to be a person at the other side of this endless mountain gateway. I gave myself a pep talk to remind myself that I would eventually be a colorful spot for the hiker behind me. What I didn't know at the time was that this same scenario would be reenacted many times over the six weeks to come. The views were spectacular above the tree line and my camera's shutter was in constant motion. Ravens allowed the wind to blow through their feathers as they floated in the air before turning and flying powerfully, against the current, like jets, as if proving who was boss. By the time we reached the tabletop, the rain was just a drizzle.

A mile later, when I climbed onto the coveted wooden sign for a photo at the summit of Baxter Peak (named after the Governor of Maine who used his own wealth to purchase the mountain and surrounding land to make it a protected state park), the sun's rays were fiercely burning through the haze. Glimmering lakes and ponds were scattered before us in all directions. I was seeing what Thoreau had described as a million pieces of broken mirror.[8]

Having reached our destination, we sat down for a well-deserved lunch of peanut butter, honey spread on tortillas, and gorp, which is a mixture of nuts, pretzels, M&Ms, cheerios, and raisins. And we passed around the Merlot to toast a successful summit. When I looked over the edge of the

mountain that was behind the Baxter Peak sign, I saw a dramatic drop-off leading down to a small lake called Chimney Pond. I looked around the lake for the cabin where Game Warden Roy Dudley once lived, told his tall tales to entertain the visitors, and dispatched rescue teams for lost hikers. Some rescue efforts ended in success and happiness, others in tragedy. Someone told me that Katahdin as seen from Chimney Pond was so beautiful it was more sacred than any cathedral they had ever entered. Looking down on what appeared to be a miniature lake in Katahdin's basin, I said to myself, "Another day, maybe I'll be able to hike there and view Katahdin from that sacred spot."

Katahdin was formed over 350 million years ago by the alpine and continental glaciers sculpting its coarse-grained granite. The rocks contain large crystals and are composed of white quartz, white or pink feldspar, and some dark minerals. According to geologist Collins Chew, Katahdin is, for some reason, more resistant to erosion than other mountains around it.[8] Thoreau said that Katahdin was "primeval, untamed and forever untamable Nature…made out of Chaos and Old Night. Here was no man's garden."[9] I wonder if the soulfulness of the mountain has something to do with its resistance to erosion.

The Appalachian Trail Guide to Maine states that the top of Katahdin is an arctic alpine zone. Being from Alabama, I was not sure what this meant, but as I encountered more and more hearty lichen-covered rocks, mosses, and other plants, I realized that the arctic alpine zone, though treeless, supported a range of beautiful vegetation.

I had wanted to walk along the "Knife's Edge," a particular narrow bony arm of trail that extended from the peak and consisted of piles of angular, projected stones with extremely steep drop-offs on either side. A friend told me that walking on this trail as a child had nearly frightened her to death. The hiker we had met that morning, who told me that poles would be useful, had taken his sons up the day before but had them wear safety harnesses tied to him. I began maneuvering the knife's edge until I saw a flash of lightning and decided it was time to get off the mountain. We began retracing a tedious 5.2-mile trail back to the Katahdin Stream Campground.

Knife's Edge

On my way down, I stopped at Thoreau's Spring to have some time alone for my morning prayer. I gathered rocks for each person I wanted to pray for—my family and others—and stacked them on top of one another, making artful statues and prayer cairns. I asked God what the word was for today, and the word that came to my mind was "perseverance." We made it to the summit because we persevered and kept going when others quit. As the Apostle Paul wrote to the Romans, "Not only so, but we also rejoice in our sufferings, because we know suffering produces perseverance; perseverance, character; and character, hope (Romans 5:3-4). Was this hike a trial? Would bloody knees and being disoriented and humiliated produce character? Would hiking with blisters in the rain with smelly packs produce hope? Usually we seek things to entertain us rather than test us, but it dawned on me that, yes, this hike was a test, an exercise in perseverance. I prayed that the same perseverance we found climbing Mount Katahdin would take David as far as Carratunk, would take me 443 miles to the

Vermont border, or farther, and would take Karen down to New York. I suspect the angels smiled at my naïve plans and prayer.

When we reached the tree line, I welcomed the protection from the wind and breathed in the smell of the evergreens. Farther down the trail, I heard the sound of a rushing stream and stopped to refill my canteen. To hike lighter I had left my water filter at home and brought the small "Aquamira" water treatment bottles to purify the water. Not having used them before, I tried to read the directions, but the writing was too small. I knew I was supposed to put seven drops from the Part A bottle of chlorine dioxide into a cap and add drops from the Part B bottle of phosphoric acid and wait for five minutes until the combined drops turned yellow. Then I was supposed to pour the yellow solution into the bottle of water and wait 10 to 30 minutes before drinking. Putting the small drops in the large canteen cap seemed odd. As I waited for the liquid to turn yellow, I wondered why one of the little bottles had a little cup on top and considered throwing it away. Then it dawned on me that instead of using the cap from my water bottle, I was supposed to use the little cup to combine the drops.

"What in the world am I doing here without knowing how to use my equipment?" I asked myself.

When I caught up with David at the bridge where the trail crosses the stream, he was soaking his bare feet in the cold water. He was having a good time nursing them, and I was glad I had an experienced hiker to get me started.

"The water is healing, you know," he said, but I was in too much of a hurry to take my boots off and join him.

We had a snack and waited for Karen, but after a while David said, "Everybody has to hike their own hike," and we headed off toward the campground, without her and in silence.

But then we took another break and soon heard her cheerful voice and saw her bright red shirt. She came up to us, all excited. She had met a deer and, as she looked at it she realized the deer was looking into her eyes. This intense encounter lasted for some time, and Karen wasn't sure who broke the trance, but for a moment she wanted to leap into the woods after the deer.

David said wryly, "Well, we've seen you leap from rock to rock, and so we know you have it in you, or you can climb like a mountain goat, if you'd rather."

By the time we retrieved our backpacks at the office, it was getting dark, and we still needed to set up camp and cook supper. The ranger had written our campsite number in big script on a paper lying on our packs. David and I began to put up our tents, but Karen just sat down staring at the nylon and aluminum poles she had brought. David went over to see what was going on and she confessed that she had never put her tent up and didn't know how. She had decided to go on this hike at the last minute and bought the supplies without testing them. It didn't take David long to pop the tent up, and then we all sat down at the picnic table to cook our dinner. David lit his stove to boil water. I had dehydrated some spaghetti sauce at home and had forgotten to add water to it in the morning when we switched packs. It takes more than an hour to rehydrate, so I was not in a big hurry to start cooking. I found my first aid kit and treated my wounds, and took some Advil for my sore muscles.

Karen kept screwing her "Pocket Rocket" stove on and off its gas cylinder, but had no success lighting it. After I couldn't light it either, we determined her new stove was faulty, and I offered her the use my jet boil. However, this was a temporary solution. With the food Karen had brought, she needed a replacement stove before she entered the 100-mile wilderness. This problem seemed to paralyze her, but I had an idea. Since our shuttle driver from the A.T. lodge would be bringing new hikers the next morning to the ranger's station, I went there and wrote a note that asked the ranger to contact the driver and ask him to bring a working stove. I hoped I hadn't insulted Karen by stepping forward and "fixing" the problem, but she was happy that I had "interfered" and didn't think that I'd acted like a condescending male.

There is a scripture on prayer where Jesus encourages disciples to ask, seek, and knock (Matthew 7:7). It seemed from the beginning that each of us was forced to seek help and trust forces beyond ourselves. I took an evening stroll along the pond near our campsite and listened to the frogs and looked up at the vast sky of stars. In the darkness the stars are much brighter than in the city lights. I stared at the beautiful Milky Way stretching from east to west and thought of wishing on a star or on a cluster of stars. In a scene in *The Lion King*, Mufassa, the father, takes his cub Simba to look at the stars and explains that when the two of them are separated,

Simba can gaze up and know that he is not alone. Although my family and I were many miles apart, looking upon the same moon and stars somehow brought us closer. I imagined my wife and daughter going about their routines in our house, and I missed them, and I felt a good bit of guilt for leaving them. As I gazed up, I did not know what to wish for, or exactly what I hoped to learn. Thoreau went to live at Walden for a few years to see what the wilderness would teach him, expecting that it would be a total surprise. I wondered what surprises the wilderness held in store for me.

After my evening prayers, I tried to get comfortable in my sleeping bag on my sleeping mat. I was tired but kept groaning because my muscles were sore and aching. And, though my skin was dirty, I had turned in without cleaning up. Since the campground and park did not have electricity, the only running water was the stream, and I was freezing. I had opted not to go in. I knew I hardly smelled like roses, but, at this point, I was grateful my stench wasn't as bad as the stench of that anonymous daypack.

DAY
2

Carrying the Past

Katahdin Stream Campground
to Hurd Brook Lean-to

The next morning, little zigzagging log bridges aided our hike through the boggy woods. Later I would name them "Surprise Logs," but on this day I thought these simple structures were the neatest thing since the invention of the touch screen. Under the evergreen canopy, the little walkways allowed me to see the beautifully contrasting colors of gray logs and bright green ferns that covered the forest floor. Light filtered through the canopy and created spot-lit pockets. The air hung thick and smelled of plant decay. Although Karen, David, and I walked in close proximity, we gave one another the gift of silence. I was excited about being on the A.T. and prayed my walking prayer, "Peace with every step," taking four strides with each verse and using my fingers to count how many verses I had uttered before repeating. "Peace, grace, joy, love, hope, forgiveness, and "community" were easy to remember, but knew I was missing one. After perhaps 30 minutes of walking and chanting, I realized that I'd forgotten "Jesus" and gladly began to pray, "Jesus with every step." Unlike the day before, the path was mostly flat, which let me establish a steady rhythm of prayerful walking, and soon I felt an overwhelming sense of joy, happiness, and love. The ferns, trees, large rocks, and moss came alive, and I felt connected to them. I had forgotten that prayer of the heart kindles a desire for more prayer, just as sharing love kindles a desire for more love, and this is what I experienced while enjoying the beautiful sights of Grassy Pond, Elbow Pond, and Daicey Pond.

Shifting my prayer mantra to include others, I imagined each person through the series: "May she have peace with every step, joy with every step, love with every step, hope with every step, grace with every step,

31

forgiveness with every step, community with every step, Jesus with every step." Again, as I prayed for my family and members of my congregation, I felt connected to them in a special way. I pictured them in a warm, softly lit blanket of peace, love, grace, joy, hope, community, and forgiveness, and imagined Jesus descending upon them.

The sound of rushing water became so loud that it penetrated my thoughts, and it was hard to hear the squirrels chattering and the birds singing. I had read about both Big Niagara Falls and Little Niagara Falls in the guidebook and thought one of those places would be perfect for a morning snack and prayer. I could count on the roar of the cascades to drown out my out-of-tune singing of Psalm 63: "In the morning, I will sing glad songs of praise to you. As I lie in bed I remember you O God… Your love is better than life itself," and focus on the intended message.

When I told David that I wanted to have a morning prayer at the falls and invited him to join me, I was surprised when he said, "Thanks, but no. I've got my own business to attend to." He hemmed and hawed and finally admitted that he had been carrying the ashes of his brother Mark and intended to put them in the river at the falls. Mark, a lifetime smoker, was David's older brother and had died of lung cancer on the eve of Thanksgiving prior to our hike.

"You carried them up Katahdin?" I asked, astonished.

"Yes, that's why my pack was so heavy. It just didn't seem like an appropriate place. My brother loved streams and rivers."

In an instant, the mood between us turned somber, serious, and sacred. David's act of carrying the ashes of his brother was an invitation for me to remember and call forth the communion of saints.

Arriving first at our destination, I scouted out a rock below the falls for my morning snack and prayers and gave David space and privacy for his ceremony. While praying for him and his family, I was surprised to be filled with grief. My emotions were closer to the surface than I realized. Drawn to the cuts and carvings in the rock canyon, all created by melting glacial waters over thousands of years, I intentionally let down the protective walls that guard the grief and wounds I carry. I prayed to a God, who was both ancient and present, and who, like the force of the water, had carved and shaped this earth and its many lives. Contemplating the immensity and majesty of God and the power of water, I felt a strange mixture of awe and sadness. The scars beneath the clear stream reminded me that most of the people I loved when I took my first A.T. hike as a Boy Scout were dead. Although their graves were 2,000 miles away, I closed my eyes and felt their presence as I allowed myself to recall their faces.

One by one, I visualized them surrounded by the secure, steady voice of the water. My mom had loving, encouraging eyes. My dad had a quizzical look on his face, as if ready to listen. Deep within I felt a hungry yearning for him. Thirty years had passed since his unexpected death that had left me with his guns and fishing poles, but no mentor. My grandfather Carter, with the dark complexion of his Native American heritage, shook his head as if to say, "You are strong and tough." My grandmother's smile was mischievous and her eyes invited me to play. My scoutmaster, Mr. Tucker, had a contagious grin, as if he knew that he had passed his love of the A.T. on to me. In a way, this trip was one of his unfulfilled dreams.

One by one other faces came until I pictured my four-year-old daughter Hannah poking a stick into holes on the other side of the river. She looked up and smiled, and I felt tears on my face, little bits of moisture from the wounds of blessed memories. The crashing sound of water seemed to merge the past, present, and future and offer a liminal space where the dead could live again. In prayer, it is all one. I imagined my wife, Kelly, and daughters, Laurel and Sarah, with me on the rock surrounded by the

sounds of the cascades. Death does not silence the words of our lives. They can be heard through the echoes of the Spiritual canyon walls.

As I opened my eyes, the prayer meditation dissolved into the present. I glanced up the stream and, although I couldn't see him, I knew David was allowing his broken heart to open to the healing water, too. The day before he had dipped his toes in it, and today he was offering it his tears. A white stone the size of a corn kernel caught my eye, and I picked it up. Upon examination, I imagined it had been worn smooth by water, wind, and ice. Opening a Ziploc bag, I placed it inside with a few angular, flat, grey stones that I had retrieved from the top of Katahdin. I felt silly collecting a few stones to remember meaningful places, but something told me I would be glad.

I wondered how many times I had stood on the edge of an open grave, numbed by grief. When my daughter Hannah's tiny coffin was lowered into the grave, I wanted to cry out, "No!" As much as we'd like to plan and control, there are times when we have to let go and trust. Even the pain of grief has an element of celebration because of the joys and gifts shared with the departed. After a while, I went and offered to take a photo of David next to the waterfall. He reluctantly agreed and we shared a quiet moment.

Later, when we resumed our hike, he told me the story of his brother, and it was a hallowed time. Mark had lived most of his 57 years between work and home in Lawrenceville, near Atlanta, but as teenagers he and his brothers and sister spent their summers helping their grandparents on their farm near Coweta, Oklahoma. The rich, dark brown and sandy farmland was a quarter of a mile from the Arkansas River and part of the Choska Bottoms. It produced quality wheat, barley, and soy beans. Like most small American farms of the past, the land has changed hands and purposes, and it's now owned by someone else and used to grow sod. When Mark died, leaving behind a 19-year-old son, a 33-year-old daughter, and three ex-wives, the family decided to give his remains to David to spread on the farm in Oklahoma, along the A.T., and at other significant spots. Since Mark did not like to travel and had never been north of the Mason Dixon line, and David thought that it was time for Mark to get out and experience the wider world, David had already strewn some of Mark's remains in Georgia and Pennsylvania.

"Human remains are surprisingly heavy," David remarked. Then he told me that it had been a spiritual moment for him when he had poured his brother's ashes into the clear mountain river while whispering, "Earth to Earth, ashes to ashes, and dust to dust" and then had watched Mark make his slow journey to the welcoming sea.

The first two Beatitudes which Jesus teaches are about being vulnerable and empty: "Blessed are they who are poor in spirit, for theirs is the Kingdom of God. Blessed are those who mourn, for they will be comforted" (Matthew 5:3-4). I reflected on how my friend had become vulnerable with me, on how our conversation quickly deepened in ways it never had before. What a blessing it is when we are able to move from the surface of our lives to the deeper things which really matter. Perhaps hiking itself was an invitation to become empty and open and vulnerable, an invitation leading to a venerable time. In the days that followed, strangers told me their deepest fears and hopes, and I shared some of mine with them, as well. Hiking along the Nesowadnehunk Stream as it poured into the West Branch Penobscot River, I was struck by nature offering the parallel of water gaining in depth as it flowed, much as my conversations deepened with each step of the hike.

Soon we were walking in a rut of a trail which had been worn down by years of constant use and erosion that left behind tangled roots and projected rocks. Football players run through a series of tires to practice picking up their feet, and I thought this trail was a good series of obstacle for making us tough. After blundering through mile after mile of roots and rocks, I became irritated and remembered what a friend had told me: in some places, the A.T. in Maine is a sorry excuse for a trail. The more I thought about it, the more exasperated I became. "Why don't they move the trail up 25 yards so it isn't a rut with roots and rocks?" I muttered in frustration.

Sometime later, I met a woman whose boots had lasted 2000 miles; they'd lasted until she got to the 100 Mile Wilderness where, she said, a root jumped up and ripped the sole from the boot's toes. Thinking about roots jumping and rocks rising up to trip hikers made me laugh, and I was happy to give her some duct tape to hold her boots together. While hiking though, the more I had to climb over the roots and rocks, the angrier I became. Negativity and irritation issued from me instead of peace and harmony. My attitude had become oppositional. I was fighting the discipline and work of walking the trail and wanted it to change rather than changing myself.

Suddenly, I became aware of the shell tied to my backpack. The shell symbolized transformation, and it reminded me of how often we get stuck in our thinking and resist allowing ourselves to be changed. It occurred to me that I would never have peace as long as I did not accept life as it is, including detritus, and change myself and my expectations. To have peace as I hiked, I needed to accept what was beyond my control: weather and terrain, and calibrate myself to the journey's demands without wasting energy whining or wishing things were different. When you are tired, hungry, or feel threatened, it takes a conscious effort to let go of judging, condemning, and spreading negative energy. As Richard Rohr, a Franciscan friar and ecumenical teacher, says, "You don't drive out the devil with your own devil energy. The best criticism of the bad is the practice of the better. Oppositional energy only creates more of the same."[10]

So I called the rocks and roots "R&R" and joked they were neither restful nor recreational, but I decided I could make them be so with a change in my attitude. I listened to the singing rhythm of water and began to pray for peace, again, sending the blessings to echo among the lush green ferns, trees, and burbling water.

When we met two young thru-hikers having lunch, we stopped and had a snack with them. As we chatted, one of them said, "I am hiking to find a purpose in this life, but no light bulb has gone off, yet."

I told him, "You still have one more day."

When I asked what he had learned, he shared that when he'd started out he hadn't known much about backpacking and had all the wrong equipment. After the first 100 miles, he changed his stove, tent, and sleeping bag.

His companion, a cute, 20-year-old woman, admitted, "When I began the hike I didn't know anything about backpacking, either."

We told them that they were very courageous to undertake this journey without having any experience.

They laughed at the idea of being courageous and said, "Well, you guys are courageous for hiking south."

It dawned on me that people do courageous things but don't think of themselves as brave because at their moment of courage they are preoccupied

with their task and experiencing both fear and excitement. Emotions can be complex.

Then the young man asked me, "What's the hike about for you?"

I said, "My lofty answers is that I wanted to live like a monk or hermit for 40 days and encounter God in nature, strangers, prayer, animals, and myself, and to allow the experience to shape me. My other answer is that I was restless for an adventure and looking for an excuse for an extended vacation."

Everyone laughed.

I was sad that Karen had decided to stop for the night at Abol Bridge Campground and would be a day behind us. We would miss her witty sense of humor and delightful Australian accent. When we reached the store, Karen borrowed a phone and spoke to the person who was bringing her a stove the next morning. Our last meal together consisted of cheeseburgers and soda. We sat down at a picnic table with some northbound hikers who were drinking beer and telling stories about their journey. Some were very loud and obviously trying to impress. Their posturing and revelry was an incentive to eat quickly and keep moving.

One hiker, though, had a beautiful black lab that greeted us as we had approached the picnic table. Because dogs are not allowed in Baxter State Park, the young man's father arrived by truck to pick up the dog so the son could finish the hike. As soon as the truck rolled into the gravel parking lot, the dog's ears perked up and he took off running, circling the truck. He greeted the father and jumped into the truck bed, wagging his tail. I expected to watch father and son embrace, but their hello was awkward. Minutes before, the young man was laughing and exhibiting bravado, but his mood changed to irritation in his dad's presence. I winced inside as I witnessed an example of the complicated and often painful relationships between fathers and sons. The deepest pain most men carry with them is a father wound.

Research shows sons long to be noticed by their fathers and want a place in their hearts. But they often question whether their absent fathers are secretly doing something demonic. They "deconstruct" and devalue their work, sometimes only seeing them through their mother's critical eyes. When I was this young man's age, I, too, was overly critical of my father, but now I am interested in his life and would like to see him through my own eyes. Sadly, the son and father before me did not have hearts that joined, and I prayed that warming winds of forgiveness, grace, and new beginnings would dance between them.

We said goodbye to Karen and missed her immediately, as though we were not complete without a feminine presence. We stopped along the road South of Abol Bridge and took in the great view across the lake to Mount Katahdin. As I took a photo of the magnificent peak, I found it hard to believe that we had been on its summit just the day before. We crossed the road and hiked on through the woods, walking on worn cedar logs to cross over the bogs. Although tired, I was happy to reach the Hurd Brook Lean-to (elev. 710 feet). As I crawled into my sleeping bag, I gave thanks for the past and for the many people, both living and dead, who enrich my life. As I wrote in my journal, I reminded myself to remember to write during rest stops, when I was not so tired.

DAY

3

Renaming Fear

Hurd Brook
to Crescent Pond

A stubborn, four-foot snake was the reason three female hikers chose a tent site some distance from the Hurd Brook Lean-to. When David and I arrived, we were greeted by comforting cooking smells. The two remaining hikers, a long haired young man taking a break from college and a soldier just returned from Afghanistan, were disappointed as they watched David and me walk through the tent site without panicking about the snake. Later on, sitting around the campfire, we laughed as they told us about the women shrieking and "freaking out." I apologized for not providing entertainment and wondered aloud if the snake had moved into their sleeping shelter to chase the mice.

The warmth of the flickering flames provided a pleasant atmosphere to share other stories of frightening or funny hiking experiences. When my friend Bill and I backpack together, we always bring several stories to share to help us pass the time. My friend Michael creates a limerick about each day and recites it during dinner. Sometimes he had a silly limerick for each person in the group, for example:

There once was a hiker named Dale
who refused to complain when he fell.
Though bloodied and bruised,
he climbed like a mule,
and finished the day looking cool.

As the evening progressed, the common theme became fathers and Boy Scouts. We pondered if young men today had male elders who could initiate them into the worlds of the forest and men. The conversation got around to the soldier and that he was using the hike to help himself

43

re-enter society. The desire to do something noble motivated many young men like him to volunteer to serve in the war, but their participation sometimes turned into something shameful.

A few of the soldiers I've gotten to know have told me that when we civilians say, "Thank you for your service," they think to themselves, "If you only knew." They don't want to talk about what they did because they fear we'll think they're monsters. Only 20 percent of U.S. servicemen in World War II killed someone, according to a psychologist friend; but today, our training and equipment are so good that most soldiers kill and experience the trauma of combat.

When I asked the ex-soldier if re-entry had been difficult for him, he admitted that it was. He added that some people join the military because they want a license to kill someone, which troubled him. He, like many others, had signed up to defend his family and country. He was very interested when I related how people who have experienced sexual abuse or any other trauma, including certain wartime experiences, can lessen the pain they carry and be helped to see a better future for themselves. In my community, the injured can take a rock, ribbon, or photograph of themselves prior to the trauma, and carry it along the winding prayer path of the labyrinth at our church, and leave it in the center of the labyrinth as a way of release, and then walk out envisioning their new life without the burden.

David contributed to the conversation by saying, "One of the deepest wounds we carry is self-hatred. Letting go and forgiving ourselves is a ritual we do over and over until we can really find healing."

"Soldiers," I added, "need to hear from the nation that they don't have to carry alone what they did in war. Instead, all citizens share the weight and responsibility of a soldier's actions. Soldiers don't need to carry the shame, not alone." *

---

* Turning Point Consultants, LLC has helped veterans, their families and others who have experienced traumatic experiences find healing through pilgrimage, labyrinth walks, and rituals. For more information, contact *www.turningpointconsultants.com.*

When I shared that one of my military friends told me that what keeps him awake at night was not the killing he did, following orders and protecting his fellow soldiers, but making the moral jump to be willing to kill, the young soldier changed the subject. He asked me what trauma I was walking off and, without hesitation or thought, my words flowed: "My father died suddenly when I was 23. I have been angry at him for dying. He died before I was able to appreciate his positive qualities and before we could spend time together as men. I still miss him."

We pitched our tents away from the lean-to and near some large 10-foot boulders in an area with very young trees. The saplings were tall but only three to five inches in diameter, and they had no limbs we could use to hang up our food and keep it away from animals. The absence of older trees was a clue that some trauma had occurred in this area of the forest.

After heating a dinner of roast beef and green beans, it was dark when I went to hang up my food bag on the cable system near the lean-to. All the cables were already in use, and I was reluctant to attach my bag to someone else's. I stood there paralyzed for a few moments before lowering a stranger's bag, hooking mine with it, and raising the combined bundle about 10 feet off the ground. It was totally quiet now. The fire at the shelter had died down to embers, and as I walked near the lean-to, I thought I smelled marijuana.

Back in my tent, I listened to the gurgle of Hurd Brook flowing nearby and tried to go to sleep. Questions flooded my mind. Can I really hike 15 miles tomorrow? Will someone steal my food? Where is that snake? What are those sounds coming from the woods? What is my family doing? I was glad I was alone in my two-man tent so I could freely toss and turn from one uncomfortable position to the next.

The next morning, after I forced myself from the sleeping bag, put on the moist clothes from the day before, and unzipped my damp tent, I was surprised to see the world cloaked in fog. Although the air was cool and moist, the birds were singing. I was anxious to get my food bag before my dehydrated spaghetti and beef jerky tempted a stranger. I wanted to trust the hiking community but felt haunted by a pre-dawn dream of finding my bag missing. When I returned to the cable system, I found it hanging just as I had left it. Apparently, I had attached my bag to the hook used by the friendly woman who was getting some water from the stream. She and her female companion were walking north and wished me a good southern hike.

Feeling a little silly, I went to get my toilet paper, which some hikers called "mountain money," and head to the outhouse. Climbing the stairs of the privy, I heard sounds from within. I called out "hello" but received no reply. When I carefully opened the door, I saw that the scraping sounds were coming from a five-gallon plastic bucket which normally held leaves and small sticks. The idea was to toss a few handfuls into the toilet after using it to help in the composting process. How had an animal gotten trapped in the privy bucket? It had claws, so it wasn't the missing snake. I carefully lifted the lid just enough to get a peek—I didn't want an angry squirrel to jump out and attack my face. Inside the mostly empty bucket was a small mouse clawing on the plastic. I took the bucket down

the stairs and turned it on its side so the mouse could escape. It joyfully scurried off to freedom and disappeared in the foliage. I filled the bucket with leaves and sticks and returned to do my business.

Returning to the campsite, I heard talking from David's tent. At first I thought he was on the phone with someone, but then I quickly realized that he was having a conversation with his gear and food, trying to decide what to eat and how to arrange the contents of his pack. While we heated water for oatmeal and coffee on our portable stoves, a northbound hiker arrived. He suggested that we drop the idea of camping at the Rainbow Stream Lean-to and, instead, hike another 3.5 miles to Crescent Pond where, he assured us, there was a tent site and a place to swim.

Packing our gear for the day took over an hour, and I was frustrated. "David, we are slower than molasses!" I exclaimed.

Sitting cross-legged on a rock, David grimaced and scratched his head. "I'm just slow in the morning."

I took a deep breath, and tried to relax. "Patience with every step," I said a few times to myself. As in a marriage, one way to get along with hiking partners and friends is to overlook things. I wondered what I did that David found irritating. I imagined that my hovering and impatience had to be pretty annoying, so I wandered over to the lean-to. The young hikers were not yet stirring, but the three women who had been frightened by the snake were long gone. I sat down, took a deep breath, and watched the leaves shiver in the morning wind. The early sun sent beams of light through pockets of leaves to the forest floor.

When we finally got going, David and I were in high spirits. We talked about how happy we were to hike on this trail as we jumped from log to log and crossed the Hurd Brook. We had not attempted to backpack together before and were discovering that we had different paces. David planned to hike with me for two of my six weeks. Over the years he had covered the A.T. in sections from Georgia up to New Jersey, so he was the veteran backpacker. To pass the time, we tried to remember the stories of some movies we had seen. When we ran out of stories I quickened my pace and walked alone, reaching Rainbow Ledges just after the fog had burned away and the sun had started shining on the bare rock ledges. I had been chanting my walking prayer and was filled with happiness.

The sunshine on the mountain top felt like a celebration. I took off the Green Giant, hung up my damp tent to dry, had a snack of pemmican, drank some water, and said my morning prayers while waiting for David. I hadn't grown up eating pemmican, a dense, heavy bar of dried meat, fruits, and berries. It was invented by Native Americans—the word comes from the Cree language and means "fat" or "grease." My friend Jeanne had suggested I make it because it's a high energy food and doesn't have to be refrigerated.

After David arrived, we enjoyed hiking together down the mountain that was beside Rainbow Lake. Still, the miles seem to creep by slowly, and I felt impatient that we weren't making better time. David asked me if I was in a race, and I wished that I could relax and enjoy the walk rather than worry about conquering the 15 miles. Only later did I realize that it was my fear of not making the distance that robbed me of enjoying the hike.

As we neared Rainbow Stream Lean-to, we met a hiker who was obviously distraught by what he had just witnessed. "Don't go to the lean-to," he said. His voice broke off and he looked away to regain his composure.

I remembered that a young woman, Jennifer Pharr Davis, on her first thru-hike of the A.T., had discovered the dead body of a man hanging from the rafters of a shelter, an apparent suicide.

The young man was shaking and I wasn't sure if his eyes were full of terror, sorrow, or both. "Just don't go to the lean-to, it's nasty," he continued. "I counted seven dead rats, and there's a strange man sitting in the middle of them, eating his food like he didn't notice the smell." The peace and beauty of the hike had certainly been disturbed for this hiker. He walked on, muttering, "It was gross, don't go up there."

As I continued on, I tried to get his startled look out of my mind. The refrain "All things bright and beautiful, all creatures great and small, all things wise and wonderful: the Lord God made them all" floated up into my consciousness. The fact that a human body wasn't hanging in the lean-

to was a relief. Rodents didn't bother me, though mice were one reason I preferred sleeping in my tent. My previous pack still has a hole in it where mice ate through to get at something tasty. Curiosity got the best of me, and I decided I wanted to see for myself rather than let my imagination run wild. I entertained the generous thought of even cleaning the rats out of the lean-to.

Bernard of Montjoux lived from 996-1081 and served for 40 years at the cathedral of Aosta in Italy. One of Bernard's responsibilities was to make the Alpine mountain passes safe from robbers. Permanent rest houses for travelers were built on the top of two passes which bear his name. He also founded an order that has maintained these hostels to this day. That is why St. Bernard is the patron saint of mountaineers and why Saint Bernard dogs, which are used to aid mountain travelers, were named for him. I called on St. Bernard to keep me safe as I cautiously approached the lean-to. It turned out that no creepy person was sitting in the midst of dead rats. I hiked onward, confident that Nature would take care of itself.

When I finally arrived at Crescent Pond, I found a campsite and made my way down to the water. The pond's surface was calm and there were no sounds except for the churring of the wrens playing in the nearby bushes. I sat on the large slanted flat rock, which reached down to the water, and undressed. I wanted to gradually lower my body into the cold water, but but just as I took off my last stitch of clothing, I slipped on the slick, slimy rock and careened down the natural rock slide and plunged beneath the lake's surface. "Whoa!" I cried, shocked at the bracing cold, but I soon became accustomed to the temperature. It was actually rather refreshing, and it soothed my feet and legs, which were sore after hiking 15 miles over Rainbow Ledges (elev. 1,517 feet) and around Rainbow Lake. Relaxing and floating on my back, I thought about the beaver dam and lodges that I had seen as I walked along the stream and reflected on the beauty of the light as the sun began to set. I recalled the terror in the eyes of the hiker who had been disturbed by the dead rats and the creepy man. Scanning the perimeter of the pond, I wondered if the creepy man was now watching me. Should I have cleaned up the carnage and buried the rats? Setting free a living mouse was more appealing to me than cleaning up messes and burying the dead.

Feeling chilled, I climbed out and got dressed. I set up my tent beneath the pines on top of the hill and lit a fire. As the sun dipped below the tree line, soft red light was reflected on the water. A loud splashing sound from behind the curve of the lake startled me, sending my eyes peering toward the source, but I couldn't see what it was. The next day I met a young man who'd been hammock camping on the lake at that same time, and he'd watched a moose and her calf splashing in the water for hours. At some point, the moose walked right by him, as if checking him out, and then disappeared into the forest. Later on, I met another hiker who'd swum in a lake and noticed a hump close by and assumed it was a rock. Imagine his surprise when the hump rose up and a moose looked at him from less than 15 feet away.

It was getting dark, and I hoped David would be along soon so we could eat together. I wondered if he'd met up with the creepy man and then realized that I didn't need ghost stories or horror movies to ignite my fear. Fear seems to breed fear, and my imagination could generate plenty on its own. I worried that David was hurt and began kicking myself for not slowing down to walk with him. Guilt was robbing me of feeling the joy of accomplishment that I'd earned by completing the day's hike. "I am responsible for my friend and I have let him down," I chastised myself. Was it selfishness or fear that had made me move ahead without waiting? Even as I thought this, I could hear David's answer echoing in my head: "No, everyone must hike their own hike at their own pace."

The stars were bright and glistening in the sky, and I lay back watching and saw a satellite pass overhead. I was glad to have left the computer, internet, and T.V. behind. I heard splashes from the pond and imagined a beaver swimming with his head poking above the water, or fish jumping. The quiet night deep in the 100 Mile Wilderness was so different from my noisy city. When I saw the beam of a flashlight, I went to greet David and told him I was glad to see him, and I meant it. He had actually walked through the campsite once already but missed my tent on the hill. How many others may have quietly walked by unnoticed?

We sat around a fire and started telling stories of when we had been frightened. One night, some friends and I hiked to Ice Water Springs shelter just north of Newfound Gap in the Great Smoky Mountains National Park. A pile of tarps sat on the edge of the shelter, but we didn't think much about it. In the morning, as we were getting ready to leave, the pile started moving and we jumped with fear. A sickly man with long, greasy hair and beard emerged from underneath the tarps. After he talked with us, we got the feeling that he may have been homeless and gave him food. Whenever we hike now, someone usually says, "Remember tarp man?" and we shake our heads at the memory of jumping when the tarps began to move.

Another friend, Jeanne, retired early from the University of Alabama in Huntsville and became an A.T. thru-hiker. On the trail she met a man who gave her the creeps. When he began to follow her, a petite woman,

she got scared, left the trail, slipped down the side of a mountain, and hid underneath an overhang for several hours until she felt safe enough to continue her journey.

After David and I went to our tents, I lay in my sleeping bag and prayed for a peaceful night. I was wrestling with my fears and, obviously, they were winning. I recalled how the day had begun with my freeing a trapped mouse at a campsite of new beginnings, and about how it had ended with my taking a dip in cold, healing, baptismal waters of new birth. As I considered my life's purpose, I realized that I don't want to spend my life cleaning up dead messes; instead, I want to help set free the trapped, chained, and enslaved so they can find a place of new beginnings, resurrection, and deliverance from the past. I remembered seeing the crowds lining up in the Church of the Holy Sepulcher in Jerusalem to visit the tomb from which Jesus is believed to have emerged three days after his crucifixion. I joined with the crowds in wanting to touch and see the place of resurrection. Everyone has this holy longing for rebirth and a second chance. I want to be used by God to help others release their chains. I looked over and saw the shell and feather still attached to the Green Giant. Before I got all lofty about helping free others from chains, I needed God's help to release me from the shackles of fears that were keeping me awake.

As always at night, I thought of home. Was Kelly still angry at me for leaving her for such a long time? Her main question had been, "Now, why are you doing this?" I didn't have a good answer for her. To live as a pilgrim or monk for 40 days, to encounter God in nature and in strangers, prayer, and animals had sounded like crazy reasons to her. Any answer I gave made me seem grandiose. Thoreau wanted to experience the whole of nature. He wanted not just to see, wear, or smell a flower and its beauty; he wanted to use all of his senses to experience these things, and to know their effect on human sentiment and how all of it's connected to the universe. This deeper seeing was what I was after, but I didn't understand it well enough to explain it.

Jesus told a story about the young man who had given much as a follower and who had asked him what he needed to do to have eternal life. Jesus told him to sell and give away his possessions and follow him. The young man was sad because he could not (Matthew 19:16-22). Is it possible for us to "give it all" before we totally trust God? Taking slow and deep breaths, I imagined myself floating on the peaceful lake, upheld by an orange raft, reminding myself to trust God as I trusted the raft to keep me above the water. When new questions or thoughts came to mind, I became focused on my breathing and tried to think only about resting in the warm sunlight on the orange raft. Soon I drifted off to sleep.

DAY
4

Spiritual Nourishment

Crescent Pond
to White House Landing

The morning sun warmed the surface of Crescent Pond and mist rose, swirling upward and drifting around the water. We packed and left in record time. Songbirds were warbling across the lake and crows were calling. It was peaceful and reminded me of a line from Psalm 23: "He leads me beside still waters, he restores my soul." The beautiful quiet scene really did restore my soul, I just wished I had slept on a thicker mat and restored my body as well.

The first mile and a half before we began the steep climb up Nesuntabunt Mountain (elev. 1,520 feet) was easy. The name "Nesuntabunt" is a Native American word from the Abenaki tribe and means three heads or three summits, a clue to what waited ahead. My leg muscles did not complain, but my lungs soon did, and so I took a rest to catch my breath and quench my thirst. When my lungs gave my legs permission to continue the climb, I came to a clearing with a spectacular view of the long, rectangular Nahmakanta Lake. Looking back to the north, I could see Mt. Katahdin, some 35 trails miles away (or 16 miles as the crow flies). I carried with me a Morning Prayer sheet that was based on the Book of Common Prayer, a book used by monks and nuns in monasteries and by congregations in churches and cathedrals around the world. Even though I was miles from anyone, just knowing that others were praying the same prayers helped me feel connected. The sound of howling coyotes drifted up the mountain and joined with my song of praise. I couldn't have asked for a more beautiful day! When David joined me, I asked him if he thought the coyotes would like those dead rats at the lean-to a few miles north. He said some forest animal or bird surely would find them tasty.

I mentioned that I had passed a number of logging roads, and David said that if we had been up here 100 years ago we would have seen lots of boats and people on the lake below, moving logs from one end to the other. Soon we were hiking in a beautiful patch of old growth trees, mostly red spruce and white pines, which had to be well over 100 years old and had somehow escaped the logging madness of the last century. Another mile down the trail there were some interesting rock formations—huge 20-foot boulders that looked as if giants had played with building blocks and constructed a little rock house with one massive slab for a roof. It made me think of Stonehenge in southern England, although on a smaller scale.

A mile beyond the giants' playground, the trail passed close to Nahmakanta Lake. I decided it was time for a break and took off the Green Giant, drank some water, breathed deeply and built a prayer cairn on the beach. If giants could play and build with giant stones, I could do the same with small stones and, at the same time, be prayerful and mindful. The wind blew gentle lapping waves onto the sandy shore as I surrounded my family and pets with prayers of love and security. I wondered what it would be like to camp on this beach and watch the stars in the night sky.

The trail soon left the lake and continued in the woods, eventually running alongside the powerful, life-giving Rainbow Stream. The rushing whitewater contrasted with the deep black soil of the forest and trail. The trees and fauna made me feel alive. The clouds were dramatic, as well, and when they let go of the water they were carrying, David and I ducked into the Rainbow Stream Lean-to and put on our rain gear because we were determined to keep walking.

The rain soon made the trail muddy and slippery, and after walking about seven miles, I was getting tired. The oatmeal I had for breakfast did not provide the energy I needed. One hiker I met had observed that the difference between a good and poor hiking day often depended on what she had eaten in the morning. As I thought about her comment regarding the physical demands of the body, I wondered about the inner journey of the soul. Was it also true that the difference between a good and bad spiritual day has to do with what has nourished the soul? We will reap a dreary harvest if we feed the soul with criticism and negative thoughts and doubts about ourselves: I'm not good enough, they don't love me because I'm not worthy of love, I'm powerless, I'm a failure, I don't belong, I'm a fake. Likewise, we will have a garden of weeds and thorns in our soul if we plant it with seeds of cynicism and doubt about others and the world outside the self: I doubt there is a Spiritual World, no one is trustworthy, they are in it for what they can get out of it, this is a dangerous world out to get you.

To the Philippians, Paul wrote, "Whatever is right, whatever is pure, whatever is lovely, whatever is admirable, if anything is excellent or praiseworthy—think about such things" (Philippians 4:8 NIV). The day before, I was enjoying my hike and saw the world as beautiful until I saw the frightened eyes of the hiker who warned us of the creepy man. Then I became suspicious of everyone. Paul's idea of battling the negative with the positive made sense to me. It was an interior battle of thoughts. Maintaining faith and belief keeps us anchored and steady in times of storms. Trusting that we long for love, are lovable and loved, as well as have love to share with others, gives us fortitude. Hope in the future, in rebirth, in the next life also produces perseverance.

These virtues are the offspring of our love of God. It is this longing and love for God from which the walking prayer stems. St. John of the Cross, a Spanish mystic, priest, monk and poet from the 16th century, warned that those who are just beginning a life of prayer and spirituality often desire peace, joy, and contentment—the gifts of the spiritual life—rather than desiring God. As I pray the walking prayer for those gifts, I hear St. John say to me, "Is it God you seek, or the goodies?" If it is God I seek, then I must cultivate the Divine within me. Paul writing to the Colossians insists that the secret many do not understand is that Christ is within them (Colossians 1:27 New Phillips Translation). If I want to be nourished on my spiritual journey, I must remind myself of the secret in my everyday life. If I only think of God as other-worldly and distant, I am missing the secret. I need to feed my soul with uplifting nourishment. If I just watch television, read racy novels, or follow reactionary political blogs, my inner life will not be nourished.

I was glad to encounter two women who were hiking north. They were about my age, and one was wearing a necklace and earrings and looked more like she was taking a stroll at the mall than hiking the A.T. I learned that the ornate hiker and her friend had been thru-hikers last season but that the friend had had to leave the trail before finishing and was back to complete it this year. Last year, they had met on the trail, hit it off, and hiked hundreds of miles together. Now the woman with the necklace had flown in by floatplane and landed on a lake in the 100 Mile Wilderness to meet up with her friend so they could finish the hike together. I really enjoyed talking with them and when they asked if I was hiking alone, I told them to look for David, who was behind me, somewhere. For some reason I mentioned that I felt guilty about hiking ahead of him, and they shook their heads and said, "No, you must find your own pace or it will drive you crazy." According to them, it was very common to meet up with your hiking partner at the end of the day at a designated place. This made me feel better and we wished each other happy trails.

At the end of the lake, there was a public campground, and I took advantage of its privy and decided to wait at a picnic table for David. When he didn't show, I walked on, but somehow I followed the wrong trail and got lost. Backtracking, I discovered the A.T. along the Nahmakanta Stream. As I met hikers, I asked if they had seen the sign for the White House Landing Wilderness Camp. To my surprise, some people had never heard of it. One guy said he'd heard that the owner was tired and grumpy, and he suggested I avoid it. Finally, I met a man who told me that there was a small business card on a tree at the junction of a logging road, a card I wouldn't miss seeing. Going on, I kept wondering if I had missed it, or completely bypassed it when I'd briefly gotten lost. Fortunately, another hiker confirmed that the card was just up ahead. My body was really dragging by the time I saw the long-anticipated business card.

The White House Landing Wilderness Camp had been my friend Jeanne's favorite stop of the entire 2100 mile A.T. hike, so I wasn't going to miss it. She'd told me that the food was wonderful—breads, hamburgers, pizza, Ben and Jerry's Ice Cream, and an all-you-can-eat breakfast. The remarkable thing is that the hosts, Bill and Linda Ware, live there without electricity and get their water from the lake. I was looking forward to a

hot shower, home cooked meal and, above all, a soft bed. After walking a few hundred feet down the logging road, I saw a large sign with arrival instructions and a menu for the White House Landing. Before my hike, I had called Bill Ware and asked about making a reservation, and he assured me that they didn't take reservations but there would be plenty of room. He said, "Hikers don't need to be tied to a schedule." He also suggested that I plan on replenishing my food supply while there so I wouldn't have to carry so much. I took his advice.

I was glad to find the large sign with its list of instructions about the camp, which is located across Lake Pemadumcook. By hiking one more mile south along the shore, I would get to a dock where I could call for a ferry that would deliver me to my next stop. The instructions also said that the evening meal would be served at exactly 5:30, and that hikers needed to at the dock no later than 5:00 if they wanted to arrive in time to be fed. I wasn't going to be late, so I made my way on the winding path and finally found an air horn with instructions to blow it once only and then wait on the dock.

I could see the camp across the lake and hikers hanging up clothes on a clothesline and sun bathing on some chairs. "Should I stand or sit on

the dock?" I asked myself, feeling suddenly awkward. A man—Bill Ware, I assumed—moved from building to building and then finally down to a small aluminum boat.

The sound of the boat motor seemed amplified as it interrupted the quiet of the lake in the middle of the wilderness. The man expertly pulled up beside the dock, wordlessly reached for my pack, and plopped it on the floor of the boat. I climbed down unsteadily and settled on the bench. Eager to connect, I asked about his life at the Whitehouse Landing, but his look let me know he was not interested in making conversation. After a smooth landing on the other side, he unfolded his burly body from the boat, tied it up, and lumbered toward the buildings. I scrambled to hoist up my pack and catch up.

Bill gave me a quick tour, pointing out the outhouse, named "The White House," the shower building, and the bunkhouse where I would stay. He gave me a pillow and pillowcase.

His manner was all business until I asked him, "Have you ever seen a moose?"

He smiled, pointed to a garden plot and said, "We have a moose that our son named. In the fall, it comes to this spot every day."

When I asked him about washing clothes, he pointed to the lake, a bucket, and a clothes line and said, "Use your camp soap and go to it."

I did my best with the leaky bucket, and soon my shirt, shorts, and socks were hanging on the line. With water heated by propane, the shower felt like heaven. It was wonderful to experience such comfort in the middle of the 100 Mile Wilderness.

I worried about David but told myself to relax. Just as the group was gathering at the house for dinner, we heard the fog horn go off. I went to the window and saw several hikers on the dock across the lake. As if programmed, Bill started for the boat without a word, and soon David, Grizzly, and Joe arrived ashore and added their trail scents to mingle with the smells of good food.

Another great thing about White House Landing was that it was pervaded by a sense of camaraderie. It was here that I first encountered the

A.T. community spirit that I had heard so much about. It was a very different atmosphere from the pretense and bragging I'd noticed at the Abol Bridge. Here, the hikers were at peace and had nothing to prove. They sat around telling stories of their experiences, and the northbounders had plenty of advice for us southbounders. At mealtime I had a choice of pizza or the famous one pound hamburger.

When I said I couldn't imagine eating such a big burger, the northbound hikers laughed and said, "You are just getting started. Your appetite will grow the more you hike."

People of all ages were staying together and caring for one another. Debbie and George were from the northeast. Debbie was a thru-hiker, and George had come to join her for the last 100 miles. She was a gentle spirit and greatly encouraged me. We talked about the most difficult mile on the trail in southern Maine, the Mahoosuc Notch.

She told me not to worry, but to just enjoy it and think of it as problem solving. "Take your time and figure out your moves and soon you'll be successful," she said.

A man from Nashville had a big fat notebook full of scribblings and stories he had collected. "I'm going to write a book," he said.

Hikers talked about trail names, challenges with their feet and equipment, and asked for my trail name. I had no immediate answer and asked, "How does 'prayer man' sound, because I came to pray?" They shook their heads, no, and commented that it just didn't feel right but that the right name would come. Linda, our hostess, offered great hospitality and encouragement to everyone. In the bunkhouse, we all stayed up late telling stories and looking at pictures taken by Grizzly, who was a photographer. The whole evening made me more excited about hiking so it took me awhile to settle down and fall asleep.

The next morning I got up early to see the reds, yellows, and oranges of the sunrise reflect on the lake. The mist burned off as the sun heated the air. A family of ducks lined up for a journey across to the shore. I wasn't surprised to see Grizzly snapping some photographs of the early light. I enjoyed the eggs and pancakes of the all-you-can-eat breakfast and was sad to leave. Bill began taking groups across the lake to a spot where we didn't have to retrace the mile-long arrival trail. That was good news to me. David and I said good-bye to our new friends and continued on our way.

DAY

5

Accepting Kindness

Whitehouse Landing
to Cooper Brook Falls Lean-to

David and I were both refreshed and happy as we began our morning hike. We wondered how Karen was doing, confident that she was plugging along. The trail was flat and there was evidence of past flooding and beavers at work. The sun was shining, and when we got to Antlers Camp Ground we decided to have lunch on the shore of the lake because it was such a lovely spot. Beneath the tall red pines were sturdy bushes on which I hung the damp clothes I had washed the day before. I debated about going for a swim, but the water seemed too cold. At one time the site had been a wilderness hunting camp, but the buildings had been torn down, and the place now serves as an A.T. campsite. Soon the trail left the big lakes and followed an old logging road. We had reached the middle of the 100 Mile Wilderness, the longest pure wilderness stretch in New England. The sign at the north entrance had said that each hiker needed to bring food and supplies for 10 days because there would be no towns or major roads until Monson, Maine.

We continued along the flat, easy trail, an unpaved road in the privately owned Jo-Mary forest, accompanied by the sound of Cooper Brook and the sight of intriguing beaver dams and lodges. I kept looking for the beavers until I remembered that they were nocturnal animals. Crossing the brook gave me an opportunity to view the whitewater as it rushed beneath my feet. We had heard another hiker say he'd seen a moose wade through the brook, but the moose was gone by the time we arrived. I went back to the trail and found a rock to sit on while I wrote in my journal and ate a snack.

To my surprise, a car with New York license plates drove over the bridge and pulled in next to the trail. A woman got out and asked, "Would you like a sandwich?"

I was so shocked I just said, "No, I'm fine."

I was not used to trusting strangers who offered me help. She brought me a homemade cookie, saying she knew I couldn't refuse it. Other hikers came by and I saw their excitement as she opened her trunk, made them sandwiches, and treated them to fresh fruit and drinks. Her name was Jan and she was meeting her husband who was "slackpacking." The term refers to a hiker carrying only a day's supply of food and water, being dropped off at one spot on the trail in the morning, and then picked up at the end of the day at another, agreed upon location.

When David arrived we did accept a sandwich and drink and learned that this type of charity was called "trail magic." I had heard that sometimes people performed random acts of kindness for hikers. Encountering trail magic was a pleasant reminder of the genuine goodness in people.

A pastor friend in England told me about a woman in his church who felt called to rely upon God for everything. She lived in a Methodist Church in a spirit of prayer and service, and people would bring her food and things she needed. I thought it was strange to test God's generosity in such a way, but on the trail, I, too, began to trust that any real need I had would be met by the generosity of the universe. Accepting the generosity of strangers was difficult for me because I was so accustomed to taking care of myself, but learning to trust and accept the gifts from strangers is one of the gifts of travel.

There is religious precedent for such faith. Going off to strange countries was a form of asceticism for the Irish monks. These pilgrims were in search of solitude and exile, wandering and entrusting themselves to Providence without a definite aim other than to do the will of God. It was a mortal sacrifice to leave kin and community and endure hardships, abandoning themselves to the Lord of the universe. Ireland being an island meant that some monks should simply float off into the currents of the sea in solitude, trusting God to lead them to their new home. Others, like St. Columba, used their navigation skills and landed in Northern Scotland and founded the Iona community, which today is still a vital place of worship. Still others went to Wales, Scotland, Brittany, and Iceland. Legends tell of St. Brendan finding his way to the paradise island in the West known as America. The monks' outer journey echoed their inner journey of relying upon God to take them to the center of their transformation and place of resurrection. Such openness to God on the sacred journey unlocks doors for revelation, cleansing, and renewal. The task today, according to Thomas Merton, is for pilgrims to leave home and discover the Divine within themselves and also within the stranger. To find the Christ in the stranger occurs when we realize that we are all together on this island known as earth, and that we are all blessed with the Holy Other, Divine presence.[11]

I heard the writer Wendell Berry say that throughout his life he'd been amazed at the generosity of the universe. Every time he needed guidance,

a book or a mentor would appear with what he needed at that time. Trusting the generosity of the universe is counter-intuitive when the ego is in charge. The ego wants to feel self-sufficient and capable. It blocks our ability to receive, as if receiving somehow makes us feel inadequate. On the hike, an unexpected task for me was breaking down my ego and learning to ask for help. To my amazement, when I trusted in the generosity of others—whether it was to hitch a ride, purchase food, or ask for encouragement, if I was patient, someone would come along with exactly what I needed.

That evening David and I set up our tents on the bank of Cooper Brook, not too far from Cascading Falls. After supper I decided to take a scrub bath. Since I was alone, I took off all of my sweaty clothes and rinsed them out. I squirted camp soap in my cooking pot, along with some water, and began to scrub my naked body. Just then a fellow hiker

appeared, looked at me strangely, and kept walking. I was embarrassed and glad he was not a woman. I dried off and put on some dry clothes.

When I met the hiker again the next day at the lean-to, he told me he was glad I was cleaning up. He was a soldier just back from deployment in Afghanistan and Iraq and had chosen to hike the A.T. before he began the next phase of his life. He was enjoying the freedom to make his own choices. Like us, he was just beginning to hike south and was searching to heal his spirit. We talked about how the solitude, quietness, trail magic, authentic honest conversations between hikers, and beauty of nature has its own healing power in the face of a cynical and busy world. The A.T. was a good way to walk off the war. Making the move from warrior to civilian can be tricky, especially if the soldier carries inner wounds in need of healing.

In the ninth and tenth centuries, soldiers who had killed in war under the orders of their officers were required by the church to undergo some sort of penance, which often included a pilgrimage for the good of their souls. These practices helped establish the major pilgrimage sites, including Jerusalem, Rome, Canterbury and Compostela. In Medieval times it was understood that trauma may cause us to separate from our soul.

After doing years of research on how to recover from trauma and Post Traumatic Stress Syndrome, Peter Levine, a researcher with a PhD in psychology, suggests that our bodies and muscles carry the memory of the trauma, and they must be cleansed so healing can begin.[12] The movement of hiking or walking while carrying a symbolic representation of the memory—a photo or piece of writing or even a rock—and doing some sort of cleansing ritual can be the first step of healing. A friend and I took such a cleansing hike. He had named the traumatic event in a letter he carried as we walked. When we reached a natural well, we built a fire and he read it aloud. Then he burned it and we threw the ashes down the well. In his ritual, he named the pain, told the story, and performed physical movement before and after to cleanse his cells of the memory. In order to move from thinking and behaving as a wounded sufferer, my friend had to turn into someone who overcomes suffering. My presence was important because I represented the larger community's responsibility for the trauma. Similarly, if soldiers who are fighting on behalf of our country are going to recover from the trauma of their battle actions, the country needs to claim responsibility for the soldiers' actions; and this doesn't always happen. What interests me in Peter Levine's work is his understanding that the mind is not in charge of the body, but the body is in charge of the mind—it takes the lead. Descartes was not correct when he said, "I think therefore I am." This soldier's body was taking the lead in the same kind of cleansing hike as I had taken with my friend. By walking with the wound and somehow naming it and telling the story, in a community that shares the responsibility, the soldier could enable his own healing.

After I got married, I gave up backpacking because it was not something my wife enjoyed. Finding recreation that both partners like is an important part of a relationship. Our lives were shattered after the death of our daughter Hannah, and, in my grief, I was looking for transformation. Grief is a journey which cannot be shared. I was 36 years old then and my immediate family had become my wife and a two-year-old daughter. As I tried to reconstruct a new life, two things came to mind. I needed to develop a better support system of male friends, and I wanted to get back into the woods and pick up my childhood dream of hiking the Appalachian Trail. Backpacking with friends would meet both of my goals. Kelly kept encouraging me to do it, and so a plan emerged. I was approaching 40, and I made it a goal to hike all of the Appalachian Trail in the Great Smoky Mountains National Park. Using the poetic imagery of St. John of the Cross, it was my "Night" and "I went out."

When we are stuck in a time of darkness, we must move out before our world can expand and take us to a new place. Hiking the A.T. in the Smoky Mountains was a huge undertaking for someone who did not have a regular exercise program. I got out the backpack and equipment I had saved from my Boy Scout days and figured I was ready to go. Some friends and I practiced by completing some short backpacking trips. After that, and because I was comfortable in the woods, I thought I was prepared.

On one trip with my friends, our first leg began at Fontana Dam, North Carolina. From there we would hike north and come out at Cade's Cove.

When I got out of the car and hoisted up my pack, my friend Dale (we have the same first name) watched me swaying under the weight and asked, "Are you okay?"

I shrugged and said, "I'll get used to it."

We began climbing Shuckstack Mountain, and the weight got heavier as my muscles quickly tired. After many stops to catch my breath, and one bear encounter, we made it to the top. When we arrived in Cades Cove a few days later, I was hooked. After that trip I updated my equipment to lighten my load. Several times during the year, I made pilgrimages to the Smokies. On my last trip, I went by myself and realized that I could hike alone and enjoy it.

When I began those trips, I did not know how walking the A.T. would bring healing and other benefits; I was just answering a call. But that hiking did help. I deepened friendships, gained self-confidence, learned to be alone, and saw some wonderful sights. The overall experience did bring

healing to my grief. There was still a painful hole in my heart, but my life experience expanded and these ripples of grace now opened up new possibilities for healing.

Throughout that time, Kelly encouraged me. That's why I was surprised when she said, regarding my current venture, "Six weeks is too long for you to be gone on a hike." In response, I felt hurt and dug in my heels, not understanding that instead of being a giver in the relationship, I was becoming a taker. My desire to make myself happy sent her a signal that I was withdrawing from caring for her. Her reaction made me think she was withdrawing her care and support from me. Fortunately, we had a rainy day's supply of goodwill engendered by years of loving one another, and Kelly rose to the occasion to support my dream. But in doing so, her workload at home increased. As I hiked, my guilt over leaving her on her own lingered like a low-grade fever. Relationships are so complicated and, when it comes to marriage, even the smartest people often become clueless.

The Cooper Brook Falls were so beautiful that I climbed above them and out onto a precarious log over the stream to wash out my pan and simply enjoy being there. Later, I glanced in the shelter and the young former soldier was alone, reading with his headlamp. I thought of talking to him further, but decided I would grant him his space and hoped he did not feel lonely. Instead, I wandered down to my tent to talk to David about the next day, and then wrote in my journal and went to bed.

DAY

6

Seventeen Mile Challenge

Cooper Brook Falls
to Sidney Tappan Campsite

At the Cooper Brook Falls Lean-to (elev. 880 feet), the sound of the water rushing over rocks was inviting, refreshing, and pure delight. Life could not get better than pitching my tent next to the falls. I had thought that listening to the symphony of hissing splashes and gurgles would gently rock me to sleep like a soothing lullaby sung by Mother Nature herself, but I was mistaken. When I closed my eyes, cozy in my sleeping bag, my ears were filled with a furious sound which seemed to get louder, as if someone was cranking up the volume. I began to toss and turn, and tried to put my arms over my ears to stop the overwhelming noise.

The next morning, it was hard to move and get going. Unlike me, David had slept great, but we were both nervous about our decision to hike 17 miles from Cooper Brook Falls to Sidney Tappan Campsite (elev. 2,245 feet). It would be our longest hike to date and would take us over Little Boardman Mountain (elev. 1,980 feet), the White Cap Mountain (elev. 3,650 feet), Hay Mountain, and West Peak. It would also be our first challenging climb since Mount Katahdin.

The sky was blue and the birds were singing and we were proud of our brisk pace. The red squirrels chattered when I approached, and I told them, "Calm down, just passing through." These critters are more territorial than the eastern gray squirrels that live in my backyard. Their territory extends to a 50-meter area, and they don't allow another squirrel to overlap their section. Another interesting thing about these squirrels is that they gather fungi and mushrooms and take them up the trees to dry in the sun. They also have stashes of nuts that they throw down on intruders. At a bench I took a break without my pack, and the noisy squirrel high in the branches began to rain nuts on my head. I couldn't help but laugh as I tried to stare it down. The squirrel, unintimidated, seemed to hurl its eyes at me as if to say, "Now, get out!"

The trail offered beautiful views of ponds and the east branch of the Pleasant River. The views were still and quiet—a pleasant contrast to the noisy waterfall which had kept me awake the night before. At lunch time, I felt on top of the world because I was doing well and my energy was high. I continued the prayer mantra, "Peace with every step, joy with every step, grace with every step, forgiveness with every step, etc.," and it made me want to pray more. My heart seemed to expand with warmth, which spread throughout my body. I was filled with love and respect for the trees, squirrels, rocks, and each person I met. I imagined the warm light of Christ surrounding those for whom I prayed. Climbing Little Boardman Mountain was not so bad and I rejoiced in my success.

Unfortunately, after walking 10 miles that included the run-up to White Cap Mountain, the joy and peace quickly evaporated. My pack seemed to gain weight and cut heavily into my shoulders. Exhausted and out of breath, I managed only a snail's pace for the constant climb. Everything irritated me, especially my own body odor. At the top of a ridge, someone had built a bench and I thought it was a good place to take off my pack and rest. I took out the map and realized I was just beginning the climb to Logan Brook Lean-to (elevation 2500 feet) and had many miles to go before the real ascent of White Camp Mountain (elevation 3600 feet) would begin. I waited for David to catch up, but after 30 minutes, I kept going alone.

The day before a young man, a hockey player from the Ukraine who was northbound, had told me, "White Cap Mountain is going to kick your ass." The map showed what seemed to be 2.4 vertical miles to the summit. I struggled to find a place to step amid so many rocks and wondered if the trail builders, as they were choosing the route of the trail, became exhausted and said, "Ah, here is a rock slide, just paint the blazes and we'll be finished with this section." My breathing was short and shallow, and my muscles ached. I tried to pray for peace in every step, but I

couldn't. My exhaustion put negative thoughts in my mind. "Why must it be so difficult?" Again I took off my pack to rest. I looked at the shell and feather still hanging on the Green Giant, symbolizing transformation and the spiritual world. The angels could not help me up the mountain.

When I resumed, the climbing got a little easier because the trail maintenance crews had built thousands of steps into the rocks. I climbed and climbed, staggering like a drunk man. After an hour, when I thought I must be nearing the top, I asked a hiker coming down how far it was and he figured I had about another mile to go. My throat felt parched and my heart sank. The mosquitoes added to the misery. Bug spray kept them from landing, but sweat washed away the repellent, giving them an invitation to bite. Buzz, buzz, swat. Buzz swat! Negativity overcame my peace mantra and became a heavy weight on my spirit. I was so irritated that I wanted to cuss. While I refrained from shouting out cusswords, I remembered "Grizzly" at the White House Landing had not. He reported

that when he got tired and frustrated, he shouted all the cusswords he could think of, and it made him feel better. I had laughed about his habit, but now I perfectly understood his motivation.

The higher I climbed, the more there was to climb. The Ukrainian man was right. A 25-foot level section curved to open up to another set of steps. By now the trees were short, stubby bushes that gave me a chance to see the distance I had come. There was a great view of the valleys, ponds, lakes, and mountain ranges. "Without the pain, you would never get the reward of the view," I said to myself.

I met a man coming down, and when we talked we discovered that we were both in the "50s Club."

He said, "You know what I tell people about you and me?"

"What?" I asked.

"I say we are two old men trying to prove we aren't old." We laughed and he added, "This isn't a hike, it's a challenge."

I agreed, "The word 'footpath' doesn't really fit the trail."

A little higher up the mountain I saw an animal poke his head out of a hole under some rocks, then disappear. It was larger than a squirrel and I thought it was the elusive pine marten. I noticed a good bit of its scat along the trail. The pine marten looked like a weasel to me, and I recalled stories about how weasels become so focused and determined that they will die rather than quit. A man once reported that when he reached around a log, he surprised a weasel and it bit his hand and held on. When he shook his hand, the weasel still would not let go. He spun his body around, but the weasel continued to hang on. He beat the head of the weasel, but the weasel remain attached. He tried to use a knife to pry the locked jaw open, but the weasel just looked at him with determined eyes. The man considered cutting the weasel's head off, but he didn't want to kill it. Instead, he walked a half mile to a pond and he plunged his hand and the weasel under the water. Even unable to breathe, the weasel kept its grip for a long time before finally releasing it to come up for air. I needed some weasel mentality. "Stay focused like the weasel and keep walking," I told myself, but my negative thoughts kept distracting me.

Loose boulders shifted and rolled under my feet, and one caused me to fall. I almost smashed my face on the rocks. Unable to lift both the Green Giant and myself up, I just sat. Finally, I rolled onto all fours in the rocks and managed to stand up. At this point, I began to consider what objects to purge from the pack to lighten the load. The stove was great, but heavy. The tent was comfortable, but heavy and bulky. A razor, a small book, and some straps would have to go. At this elevation, the trees and shrubs were only 12 inches high. The rockslide I was climbing still had roots extending from the small trees. Somehow, after two hours, I made it to the top and the view was stunning.

Mount Katahdin was there, 73 miles away to the north. The sun was bright and air crisp. It was glorious. Suddenly I felt shame for allowing my negative thoughts to ruin my climb. I felt childish, like the kid who doesn't want to memorize spelling words or multiplication tables, mow the yard or do chores, because it is work. The child complains, "Why must life be so difficult?" Real transformation involves discipline and work. "What I am doing is real," I thought. The fantastic view was a reward for the difficult climb. The trail led around the top of the mountain and I built a prayer cairn with rocks representing my family and church. I sat to rest, pray, and absorb the view. The rolling mountains reminded me of waves on the sea where one follows the next. "This footpath continues up and down along these waves, all the way to my home in Alabama," I thought. Crows were noisily calling to one another, riding the wind currents. I watched them rise and fall. I gave thanks to God for this wild mountain and the many unknown hands of volunteers who worked on the trail building steps so we wouldn't have to hike only on rockslides. I contemplated about how the hands of many who remain unknown save us from deeper toil every single day. The hands of ancestors, family, spirits, and angels help us and we are unaware. The feather on the Green Giant fluttered in the wind and I wondered which of my unseen angels had helped me up the mountain.

Most worthwhile things in life require effort, and what we get out of life depends on the effort we put into it. I continued to relish the beautiful scenery and waited for my hiking buddy. Thru-hikers going north marched by, ignoring the view. Were they stuck in their weasel focused state, stridently marching toward a goal and missing the majesty of the view? A few hikers mentioned they were supposed to see Katahdin and I pointed them to the right mountain.

One girl smiled and said, "Seeing that puts a spring in my step."

There were four miles and two peaks to go before I arrived at the campsite, so I decided not to wait for David and pushed on.

Hiking down White Cap Mountain gave me renewed energy. As I climbed the mile over Hay Mountain I heard, then spotted, several grouse that were making sounds to distract me from their young. I was fascinated by these large birds and later learned that in their mating season they drum on their chests. Coming down West Peak was a steep descent, but I enjoyed it because I knew I was within a mile of the campsite.

When I pitched my tent, it was the only one at the campsite, which was located on a saddle between two mountains. From there a steep trail descended to a spring where I observed lots of animal prints in the mud. I climbed back up and cooked dinner. As I was eating, sitting on a log

under the stars, a pack of coyotes ran through the campsite, giving me a start and thrill.

Afterwards, I sat on the log for a long time and savored the stillness and silence. My thoughts wandered back to when my family and I camped and sat around the fire in silence. My dad was a quiet man, but thinking about him made me tense, I realized. He had very firm ideas and rules about what he expected of me, and the memory of me sitting on my bed, crying and saying, "I'll never make him happy," brought tears to my eyes. After all these years, I was still seeking his blessing and approval. Perhaps he would have wished to have my approval, as well. In my mind, I began listing his attributes. He was consistent, a hard worker, a faithful son who took care of his mother. He was faithful in attending church and volunteered to serve on the finance committee. He provided for our family, enjoyed working in the garden, and when my sister and I wanted a horse, he went out and found one and taught us how to ride. He even moved out of his comfort zone when he bought a boat and trailer and took us fishing. I smiled, remembering the time when he first tried to back the boat down a boat ramp. Other dads backed down straight, but my father zigzagged.

My sister and I were embarrassed, and it probably made him ashamed. He said, "Well, the boat is in the water isn't it?" Years of resentments also came to mind. I was not good at baseball or basketball and blamed it on him because he was always working and did not take time to pitch and shoot. When he died of a heart problem in the midst of my mother's first cancer chemotherapy, I thought of him as weak.

After gathering a pile of small sticks and leaves, I started a small fire. With each twig I placed in the flames, I forgave my dad for my perceived failings. I asked for his forgiveness of my youthful indignation toward him. My tears dropped into the fire, making a sizzling sound. The wind picked up and I heard rustling in the night. The biblical story of Jacob wrestling with an angel came to mind, and I named what I had been doing "wrestling with my father," hoping for a blessing.

Taking a deep breath, I tried to imagine my dad giving me a hug and saying, "I'm proud of you, son."

I responded, "I'm proud of you, Dad. Thank you."

Since David had not arrived yet, I set my flashlight on the trail so he could see the camp. I didn't know what else to do but go to sleep. After the day's hard climb, and the release I felt from having made an attempt to be at peace with my dad, sleep came easily. Before drifting off, though, I thought about how different my climb would have been had I given thanks for each step instead of allowing the negative thoughts to captivate my mind, and how different my climb would have been if I had eaten some food and recharged my energy. Recognizing the need for spiritual and physical sustenance would prove helpful to me in the weeks to come.

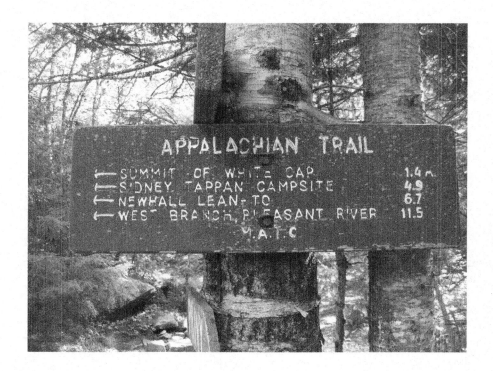

DAY

7

Releasing the Grip of Fear

**Sidney Tappan Campsite
to Ledge on Chairback Mountain**

The next morning when I ventured from my tent, the flashlight was still burning on the tree where I had left it. David never showed up. I figured he would be along shortly and decided to walk back up the trail to meet him. By the time I got to the top of West Peak Mountain, my legs were sore and aching. I checked my phone and had one bar of service. Backtracking north to find David was what I wanted to do, but it was not a life or death situation, so I decided to preserve my energy. I called his cell phone and left a message that I would wait for him at the campsite. My heart was racing and my breathing was shallow from the climb. Although I knew he was an experienced hiker, I was getting worried. Dangerous scenarios started to pulse through my mind like lightning flashes. He could have broken his back, or a leg or foot, in a fall on the unstable rocks and cliffs. I visualized him lying down in a ravine with his bulky pack pinning his face to the ground and a bone from a compound fracture protruding from his body. He might be delirious from a concussion. He could have been attacked by a bear—I had read about the increased number of black bear attacks. According to scientists, the bears were actually stalking and hunting hikers as if they were prey. David also could have gotten dehydrated. I'd seen a hiker rolling on the ground in pain from dehydration and cramps, so sick he had trouble breathing. "St. Bernard, protect him," I prayed.

My heart was beating faster now and the "what if" fears felt like fast growing vines and weeds rising from the ground and encircling my arms, legs, and body, entangling me with paralyzing fear. "Stop" I said out loud.

"No more!" I stood up, taking deep breaths to calm my fear. "We have enough troubles without inventing more," I said to myself. Suddenly I wanted to talk to Kelly, but I knew the conversation could make her feel helpless and fearful for both David and me. As I punched the numbers into my cell phone, I practiced talking in a chipper voice, "Hi, how are you? I'm a little sore from overdoing it yesterday, but I'm fine. Today I'm taking it easy, waiting on David, who will be along soon." After a number of rings, the answering machine kicked in and I left my upbeat message. I called another hiker friend from the church, hoping I could be honest with him and seek his advice, but he didn't answer. I felt alone and helpless inside the 100 Mile Wilderness. Then I started getting paranoid about animals ransacking my tent and pack, back at the campsite. Bears have been known to drag packs into the woods, and porcupines enjoy eating the salt on clothes and packs. I suddenly felt vulnerable and hungry and returned to the campsite. It was just as I had left it. I took my time taking down my tent and packing up, hoping that David would show up.

The campsite had a composting toilet, and while using it I read the trail journal that I found in a wooden rack on the inside wall of the outhouse. A girl had written that she had a standoff with a moose at the spring. The moose drank and stayed there for over 30 minutes while she impatiently waited for her turn. I learned that Sidney Tappan, after whom the campsite was named, was one of the two volunteers who oversaw the entire A.T. in Maine for nearly two decades, from 1952 to 1971. He, the guidebook editor, and the Appalachia Trail Conference Chairman developed a plan in 1963 to establish a protective corridor for the A.T. in Maine. They decided that it would require considerable funds and that the Federal Government was the candidate to provide them. Through the efforts of many volunteers and politicians, the National Trails System Act was passed by Congress in 1968. The story made me feel good—I was glad to be in a place named for a visionary like Sidney Tappan.

An hour later, the sun was blazing and I decided to pretend I was happily resting at the beach. I took off my shirt and stretched out on my ground cloth, surrounded by my packed tent and the clothing I had hung

to dry on bushes and low-lying branches. I kept telling myself that everything was fine. I was close to the trail and think my appearance shocked a number of northbound hikers, but they all stopped to chat. I helped one couple purify their water because their system had failed. A guy wearing a kilt and carrying Tibetan peace flags was remarkably chipper, and a woman, her hair tied in a bun on top of her head with a red scrunchy, sang beautifully to herself: "Why is everybody in such a bad mood today?" I told them all to look for David.

It was around lunch time when David finally arrived, limping badly. I jumped up and greeted him, not sure if I should give him a hug, or not. He was in pain, and I showed him to a log in the shade. It turned out that he had not been bothered by any four-legged or two-legged creatures. His knee had given out.

Exasperated and disappointed he complained, "Why now? I've walked from Georgia to New Jersey and my knees have been fine, but here in Maine, after just seven days, they give me trouble."

I tried to comfort him, "Well, you've had a pretty rough year emotionally with your brother's death and a divorce, so your body may be responding to the inner journey in your life."

He had stayed at the Logan Brook Lean-to the night before, halfway up White Cap Mountain. I suggested we stay at this campsite for the night. That way we could both rest and then continue. But he had resolved to call it quits and wanted me to go on and keep up with my schedule. I felt torn. I wanted to go on, but didn't want to abandon my friend. He assured me that he would be fine—he would slowly find his way to a place where he could consult the guide book and call one of the people who shuttled hikers.

As we ate lunch together, I made my decision. It was 1:00 p.m. when, with a hug and handshake, we agreed to meet in Monson in a few days. My having rested for the morning made the Green Giant seem lighter, but leaving my friend made my heart heavy. My goal was to ford the west branch of the Pleasant River and climb to the shelter on Chairback Mountain (elev. 2,180 feet). Twelve miles at two miles an hour would put me there at 7 that night, which would mean hiking the last hour in the dark. Perhaps I could hike faster, I told myself.

The first seven miles were downhill and I made good time. The trail plunged down the mountainside, following the Gulf Hagas Brook, and I crossed several side trails that traversed around the side of the canyon named Gulf Hagas. Living near the Gulf of Mexico, I wasn't used to the term "gulf" referring to an abyss in the wilderness. The grey stones, green leaves, and dark rich forest floor felt ancient. Occasionally, I saw a red or yellow leaf and knew that the color changes here in autumn would be breathtaking. A brisk breeze whipped the clouds above and the waving trees with noisy shaking leaves below. The waters of the brook were

gently falling and the pace of my walking prayer joined what Thoreau called "the circulation of God."[13] Hornets buzzed around a large, low-hanging nest near the trail, and at another spot I saw where an animal had torn a nest apart. The destruction looked recent and I began to look for a bear. I imagined its skin was tough enough not to be bothered by stings and was reminded of Winnie the Pooh and the honey bees, and home.

After following an old tote road for a while, I came to a river with a crudely made sign that pointed the way to a waterfall. By the stream was a wonderful, smooth, five-foot tall rock, and I couldn't resist building a prayer cairn. The smooth lines seem to lift the circulating spirit to God. After taking photos of the cairn, I decided to cross the river and follow the trail to see the waterfall, but the farther I went, the more I doubted my decision. Did I really have time to be fooling around looking at waterfalls when I had many more miles to hike? I chuckled about thinking of "fooling around" in reference to seeing a waterfall and not applying the same

term to much of what we consider productive activities in our everyday lives—fixing our hair so we look good, watching sports on television, or going shopping and purchasing things we don't really need. One of my least favorite jobs as a pastor is having to do "paperwork" to evaluate and report the progress of our church toward various goals; and a favorite is simply visiting with families in their homes, talking about life. The latter is an investment in deepening relationships, and is by far more life enriching than pushing around numbers on a page; yet it would still be considered "fooling around" by some, while paperwork would not.

When I finally rounded the curve of the mountain, I was stunned by the power and strange beauty of the waterfall. I was not sure if the water had carved the shoot into a corkscrew shape or if humans had done that, but it was impressive. There was a contrast between the lustrous white foam of the cascading water and the black wall of rock. This turned out to be my favorite waterfall in Maine. By building another prayer cairn, I gave thanks for the waterfall's natural beauty. Soon I was back on the trail and walking through 130-foot tall pines in a no-camping area called the Hermitage. I had to take my shoes off to ford the west branch of the Pleasant River (elev. 600 feet), which was about 50 yards wide, and I was glad to have my Chaco sandals to navigate over sharp rocks as I walked through the water. Although the stream was cold, my feet really seemed to enjoy the gentle current. Once across, I hiked in the open-toe sandals until they dried, which was about the time I had had enough of stubbing my toes on roots and rocks. It was getting to be late afternoon and I still had five more miles of hiking to do, and most of it was uphill.

It was dark when I began the steep ascent of Chairback Mountain. The wind started to blow harder and seemed to match my frantic pace to get to the shelter. To my surprise, it began to rain. In my soldier-like determination, I hadn't noticed the smell that announced its coming. I put on my rain jacket and pants and kept going as fast as I could. The trail was hard to follow over the slick granite slopes between the low-lying, bushy trees. Above the tree line, on what I thought was the summit, I wanted to take out my map, but in the rain this didn't seem like a good idea. Besides, because I had left my headlamp burning all night, it now only provided a dim and useless light. I put a tiny flashlight between my teeth and plunged ahead. The pouring rain and fog reduced visibility to three or four feet. As I prayed, "More light," Psalm 199:105 came to mind, "Your word is a lamp to my feet and a light to my path." I laughed to myself, thinking "Well, I needed a light to my path, but the only way the Word would be helpful in this situation would be if I used it to build a fire."

Suddenly, there was a flash of lightning, and I realized how close I was to the edge of what appeared to be a steep drop-off. If I wasn't careful, I would find myself tumbling off the side of mountain to where only the coyotes would find me. Determined to get to the shelter, I slowly felt my way with each footstep as the trail descended half a mile. Bill Irwin, the blind hiker who, with his dog, Orient, hiked the entire trail in 1990, tripped and fell frequently every day, but he kept going. He wore knee pads, but still his knees became bloody from the many tumbles. When I stumbled in the dark, I thought of him and knew I could keep going.

Then to my surprise, the trail began to climb again. Slowly, taking a step at a time, feeling my way in the dark as I went, I began the half mile climb to what I imagined was the peak of Chairback Mountain. The storm was getting stronger, but I kept going. The occasional lightning flashes helped me get a better view of what I was facing. I scaled hand-over-hand up the side of a cliff, as if climbing a ladder, and came to a rockslide of large boulders. As I began crawling over them I realized they were heading off the mountain. My gut told me that I was going in the wrong direction, and I didn't see any white blazes—my visibility was limited by the downpour, darkness, and fog. Fear suddenly sent a shiver through my body as I realized that I was in serious danger. I was irritated that those who kept up the trail didn't provide more white blazes, and this caused me to laugh because one response to trouble is blaming someone else. Frustrated, wet, and miserable, I climbed back down the cliff while looking for a cave or overhang to spend the night.

In my desperation, I found a small overhang with some dry spots, but realized my bed would be a bunch of different sized rocks with one as a pillow. This would not be acceptable for the delicate princess who couldn't sleep on the mattress with a pea underneath, but I was grateful. I unpacked my ground cloth, sleeping pad, and sleeping bag, and changed from wet clothes to dry. The feather and shell still dangling from the Green Giant epitomized to me the protection and care of the Spirit world. I covered the pack to protect it from the rain. I knew it was important for me to send a "SPOT" satellite message that would indicate my location and let my family know not to worry, so I called Kelly and left a message that I was in survival mode, but okay. Then the signal faded and disappeared altogether. This sleeping arrangement was far from ideal. The air was damp and smelled musty, and the storm raged around me while the thunder shook the whole mountain, sending vibrations to my bones. I put a large plastic garbage bag over the bottom of my sleeping bag. I knew it was not a good idea, but I was desperate to give my aching legs a stretch and could only stretch them into a wet area. When I woke up after a brief sleep, the portion of my sleeping bag wrapped in plastic was moist from condensation.

I used a combination of the ground cloth and the large garbage bag to cover myself up from my knees down. To give myself more room to stretch out, I moved my shoulders and head deeper into the wedge of the overhang. If I raised up my head 10 inches, it would hit the overhead rock. I muttered to myself, "If Elijah could sleep in a cave and watch the storm, so can I." But I wondered if Elijah had had a flat surface where he could stretch out, rather than an uneven, rocky, cramped space with rain blowing and whistling through the trees.

Elijah was waiting to hear the voice of God, but didn't hear it speaking in the storm; however, he did hear God speak to him in a quiet, still voice. I came to the same conclusion: God speaks to us in whispers, not in thunder. Even though the furious wind shook the trees, I felt secure and safe in the cliff's shelter. Even though it was impossible to get comfortable, and it was noisy and I was occasionally splattered with water, at times I did nod off. I wondered why I hadn't stopped earlier and pitched my tent before

dark. Then I remembered that I wanted to reach the town of Monson in time for my daughter Laurel's 16th birthday so I could call her. This thought renewed me. Having a clear purpose associated with love made the difficulties seem small.

Not surprisingly, I was awake at first light. The storm had passed and left the forest soaked. A squirrel came down a tree and looked at me. I laughed out loud when I saw its eyes widen, and I grinned as it pitched a noisy fit. It scrambled up the tree, and then came back down to look again as if it did not believe what it was seeing. This was my cue to pack up and move out. I scaled the cliff to the rockslide for the second time and saw in the light of dawn the white blaze farther up ahead. Scrambling up the wet boulders was easier in the light, and 30 minutes later I arrived at the shelter, where I bid some hikers good morning, got water, and cooked breakfast. Unfortunately, soon afterwards I experienced cold-like symptoms that turned into an infectious sinus irritation that lingered for the remainder of my journey.

The next time I saw David, he told me he had limped down the seven miles to the Hagas Wilderness Park, where no camping was allowed, and had slept under a small kiosk sign. To stay dry he had to lie on his back and extend his legs up the side of the post. Coming down the mountain, he kept checking for a phone signal. When he finally got one, he called a shuttle driver, an older woman, and asked her to pick him up and take him to Monson. She agreed, but when she came the next morning he learned that it would have been much cheaper to have traveled back to Millinocket, and also easier to catch a ride to the airport from there. But he had agreed to meet me in Monson, and his paying more to be taken to this "out of the way" place to wait for me was worth it to him. His loyalty as a friend was touching.

DAY

8

Seduction vs. Commitment

Chairback Mountain
to Long Pond Stream Lean-to

I met "Tortoise," a thru-hiker from Maine, in the Chairback Lean-to after my night under the cliff's ledge. He said, "That is like your worst nightmare. I couldn't do it." I assured him he could and would. In life, occasions arise when we must "man up" or "woman up" and do what we have to do. Tortoise was a sensitive soul and after hearing about my adventure was concerned I would hurt myself on the trail ahead. My new friend had hiked from Georgia to West Virginia and then "flip-flopped" to hike from Maine to West Virginia. I felt like a novice in his presence. He was hiking about 25 yards in front of me and yelled out "porcupine." When I caught up to him, he showed me where the animal had scampered into the woods. Sometimes to see the wildlife, you need to be first, and this time he got the reward. He noticed that my left ring finger was purple and swollen, and my walking pole, bent. I confessed that I had taken a tumble on a slick granite slope and landed on my hand and walking stick. He asked me if my finger was broken. I said, "It hurts like the dickens and might be." He looked closer at the swollen finger and said, "You've got to get that ring off."

I was not against it, but didn't know how it would be possible without cutting the wedding band, and damaging it was the last thing I wanted to do. It was a reminder to me and the world of my commitments, and I assured him and myself that the swelling would go down after a few days. I was grateful to spend time with someone who cared. My hips and knee were sore and bruised from the fall, too. Each day brought different aches and pains. The trail and rocks were slick and dangerous after the rain and I moved gingerly with each step, afraid of another tumble.

When I asked Tortoise if he had any stories to help pass the time, he told me about his barefooted hiking sister and her friends. They had managed to hike a good bit of the trail and were going to thru-hike it one day. They were inspired by Susan and Lucy Letcher, two legendary hikers whose trail names were "Isis" and "Jackrabbit." To everyone's amazement, they hiked barefoot, and the soles of their feet became so tough they were able to walk on gravel and even glass and not feel it. They wore boots only to keep from slipping on ice. After completing the A.T. from Maine to Georgia, they "yo-yoed" all the way back to Maine. Tortoise told me that there are whole communities of hikers who think that walking barefoot helps us to connect with Mother Earth. The feet and toes are sensory organs and feel the grass, moss, pine needles, and mud. This natural way to hike also makes less of an impact on the earth than a shoe or boot. Tortoise laughed at my surprise and shock. I like the idea of walking gently on the earth, but I wouldn't go to such extremes.

"Don't knock it till you've tried it," he said.

My throbbing finger reminded me of the story of "Iron John," a pre-Christian fairy tale. As I remembered it, a young prince lived in a palace with his mother and father, the king and queen. One day the prince played with a golden ball on the grounds where a wild, hairy man was locked up in a cage. When the golden ball rolled into the cage, the boy wanted it back, and the hairy man said, "Unlock the cage and I will give it to you." When the boy asked how, the wild man told him that he needed the key from under his mother's pillow. The boy got up the courage to steal the key, but as he was using it to unlock the cage, he hurt his finger. I tried to remember the interpretation of Robert Bly, an American poet who wrote a whole book about this story,[14] and shared that I thought it meant that for us to grow up, we always have to "cut the cord" with our mother, for mothers have great power over us.

We started to talk about our own mothers. Tortoise's mom was a master manipulator, but when he had declared how he would live his life, she had let him go. We agreed that his standing up to her was the moment he took the key. Letting the wild, hairy man out of the cage symbolizes the

male befriending his inner wild man, a step in the process of growing up to become a man. When the boy did this, he hurt his finger. My ring finger pulsed with pain, turned blue, and swelled up from a fall on a slippery rock—my real and symbolic badge of exploring the wilderness. When we let the wild man out of the cage, there is always a wound. Tortoise and I talked about the innocence we lost when we ventured into the darker areas of life. I had idealized a family friend early on, but leaving home and attending college helped me realize that he was very racist. It was hard to forgive him for his hatred. Growing up and moving away from parents always brings wounds. We fell into silence and began to hike our separate ways.

As we were descending Fourth Mountain (elev. 2380 feet), I was ahead of my companion and noticed that he had taken a path parallel to the trail. I started to yell, "Hey, Tortoise, where are you going?" but decided he was on his own journey. Soon he disappeared and I kept going, eager

to see the famous Pitcher Plants. These plants seduce insects with a sweet smell, and then trap them inside and eat them. The plant's crimson red leaves, with their white and yellow intertwining veins, were striking. The plant itself was smaller than I expected, and I wished I could find a place to sit and cheer as one of the biting gnats would land on a leaf, crawl inside, and become the plant's victim.

Insects are not the only living creatures drawn to the rich color red. It somehow moves the senses to sexual arousal. The "red light districts" in cities throughout the world have deliberately led people astray in sexual pursuits, sometimes resulting in diseases and death. The intentional enticement of seduction is part of creation and is reflected in the Biblical stories of the snake seducing Eve to eat the apple of knowledge; or Satan tempting Jesus with power, prestige, and food; or the Sirens of Greek mythology tempting sailors with their sensual, beautiful songs. These stories warn us of the dangers of following the senses without thinking about the consequences. Dating itself is a dance of attracting potential mates. It seems the dance of seduction is also part of the circulation of God. As is the example of the pitcher plant and its prey.

What a gift it was to see these interesting plants and animals. Later in the day, when Tortoise and I met up again, he told me that he had gotten lost. If it hadn't been for a northbound hiker's help, he still would have been looking for the trail. As I was looking for the seductive pitcher plants, I'd failed my new friend, and I promised myself that I would do better. In our quest to live independent lives, our culture has created an environment where advice is not always welcomed. We don't want to interfere with people even though they are wandering around lost and need some direction. If we suggest a path, is it really interfering with their independent search? Do we have a responsibility to warn others when they're taking a destructive path? Even the best of us have blind spots. Nuns traveled in pairs for accountability. I've never been a fan of the puritanical advice to beware of anything that tastes too sweet, but can appreciate the wisdom behind it. To live well, we need to have the courage to seek advice from those who have experienced the pitfalls and temptations along the journey. I thought about the young men I know and those whom I met on the trail who seemed lost. Many have absent fathers. Many do not have good job prospects. My hunch is that the advice problem will not be addressed as long as we think it's not our place to step in and offer a new direction.

Being from Alabama, I was painfully aware that one of the greatest seductions is the idea that it is acceptable to dehumanize others because of their race, class, or nationality. While I was taking my wilderness walk, my state's government officials were proposing a bill that, if passed, would be the nation's strictest anti-illegal immigration law. Despite the pleas from Alabama farmers, who claimed they couldn't find citizens to work the fields, our Hispanic neighbors were feeling the full force of resentment and anger for supposedly stealing jobs from Americans. My fellow Alabamians claim to want a society based on Christian values but resist having their tax dollars used to support the poor or to show hospitality to illegal immigrants. Is it my job to point out that we can't have one without the other? Why do persons of privilege and power yield to the temptation to keep the underdog down? In our history, the sweet allure of profits has led many to think that if the poor are kept undereducated they can then serve as a steady supply of routine labor for businesses and factories. The pitcher plant reminded me of the complexity of seduction in situations where others are harmed.

Two birch trees grew on opposite sides of the trail and each tree sent out above-ground roots toward the other, and the roots overlapped and intertwined, as if they were working together to support both trees. The Proverb, "Two is better than One" (Ecclesiastes 4:9) came to mind. The trees would provide a perfect setting for a wedding. The steadfast, clutching roots might present an ideal for those who feel isolated, lonely, and long for companionship or for those who feel their relationships are claustrophobic and are overwhelmed. Nature reflects not only seduction, but also our longing and security. The connected birch trees reminded me that we do need one another's help to stay on the path and one another's help to get up when we fall. In a way it was good that my wedding band was stuck on my purple swollen finger because I desired to remain a faithful husband to Kelly. And if a ring symbolized that, what did an appreciated stuck ring symbolize? I missed having a friend with me to hold me accountable. I also longed to be near my father. It was strange that 30 years after his death, while on a hike, I would long for his presence and touch.

When I limped into the Long Pond Stream Lean-to (elevation 940 feet) area, after climbing Columbus Mountain (elev. 2325 feet), Third Mountain (elev. 1920 feet), Fourth Mountain, and Barren Mountain (elev. 2660 feet), I had traveled only 11 miles, but I was worn out. So many hikers were gathered there, the atmosphere was like a festival. Most of them knew one another well and made no efforts to welcome me to their campfires. The only place I found to set up my tent was a piece of slanted ground, so I tried to spread some clothes under my sleeping mat to keep it level. The spaghetti and snickers bar were wonderful, but with all the groups gathered around fires, eating alone just made me feel more isolated. I wondered if David had gotten out of the woods.

As I said my night prayers, I acknowledged that I was feeling low. Another hiker had asked me how my hike was going and I didn't know how to answer. My finger and hip were throbbing, I had slept very little under a ledge the night before, and my hiking partner had gotten injured. I just told them since Katahdin there had been wonderful days, but today was not one of them. They understood.

DAY

9

Conquering Fear Leads to Thanks

Long Pond Stream
to Monson

It was early when I left the Long Pond Stream Lean-to, and I noticed that some hikers had set up their tents in the middle of the trail. It was a level spot and I wished I had had the nerve to do it. As I got closer, I saw Grizzly's head poke out of a tent. He shook his head and said that the day before had nearly killed him. He quoted the guidebook: "Although the five major peaks in this section are all under 3000 feet in elevation, this section of trail involves significant gain and loss of elevation over a rough footway."[15] I asked him if it gave him an opportunity to cuss and he smiled.

He looked at my swollen, purple finger and bent pole and said, "It got you, too, eh? You need to get that ring off your finger, man."

I nodded in agreement.

As I was walking away, he added, "And you know what the guidebook says about today?" I turned back to listen and he continued, "Two difficult streams which are dangerous to cross in high water."

I said, "It's a good thing that we didn't try to hike it yesterday after the rain."

We were both trying to get to Monson, 15 miles away, and planned to meet at the Lakeshore hiker hostel. Today was my daughter's 16th birthday, and I wanted to find a telephone signal so I could wish her a happy birthday.

The forest was beautiful in the morning light and the trail followed the Long Pond stream. At the stream's edge was a large rock, with water noisily pouring around it. A hiker had pitched a tent right on top of the rock, and I hoped that he enjoyed the sound of the rushing waters more

107

than I had. Farther downstream, Tortoise sat outside his solitary tent and was cooking breakfast and tending to his feet. He'd punctured the blisters and put a gel pad underneath but needed duct tape to hold it in place. I was happy to share mine.

Caring for feet was a constant topic for hikers. As Tortoise said with a smile, "Sometimes you need a hand in working on your feet."

When the time came to cross the stream, I replaced my boots and socks with Chaco sandals and slowly picked my way through the chilly, rushing water. Climbing up on the other side, I interrupted some lovers who thought they'd found a quiet, secluded spot by the flowing stream. It was an awkward moment, but I just kept going, looking straight ahead with a smile on my face and wondering if "Surprise with every step" would be the appropriate walking prayer this morning. The picture of the seducative red pitcher plant was still fresh in my mind. By then I had worked the soreness out of my legs and was feeling loosened up.

The geological formations of this area include a good bit of black slate, and this rock supports many of the interesting and powerful waterfalls along the Long Pond Stream and the Big Wilson Stream. Over 100 years ago there were a number of quarries in the area, and the extracted slate made excellent grave stones. President John Kennedy's marker in Arlington cemetery is made from Monson Black Slate.

The trail proceeded with some winding turns and, at some point, it took me a moment to comprehend what I was seeing. There was a pond, and the trail that went across the pond was a pile of sticks and logs. I was delighted when I realized that I was seeing a beaver dam. Then it dawned on me that I would have to walk across it. Fearful, I looked for an alternate route. Would these sticks and logs sealed with mud support my weight? Had the government bridge and dam inspectors given their okay? The wind was blowing the water in waves over what I assumed were waterlogged sticks. I was about to trust my life to the strength of small twigs and the workmanship of North America's largest rodent! For 53 years I had not given beaver dams a second thought, but now I wondered about every detail.

Beavers were once thought to be very intelligent because of their work ethic and ability to build dams and plug up any leaks. Their creations reduce soil erosion, help control flooding, and result in ponds that provide nesting grounds for birds and habitats for fish and plants. Beavers build their lodges with an underwater entrance by using their teeth, front claws, rear webbed feet, and flat tails as tools. A double coat of fur and a layer of fat keep them warm underwater. Their ears and nostrils seal, and they can stay beneath the surface for as long as 15 minutes. They work all night to cut the trees and build, and then sleep during the day. The beaver is the national symbol of Canada and of several schools, including MIT in Boston and City College of New York. When studying beavers, one scientist put a tape recorder on a dry section of the forest floor and played a recording of the sound of running water. Attracted by the sound, the beavers covered the tape recorder with mud and sticks. They were plugging what they thought was a leak. After this experiment, scientists doubted the intelligence of the beaver.

It is funny how, when you're afraid to do something, you can just stand looking ahead for a long time, trying to somehow get up the courage to proceed. I once stood paralyzed on a diving platform, but I went ahead and dove off because there were lifeguards there to rescue me if something went wrong. If I fell into the water here, with my clothes and pack fastened to my body, who would rescue me? To gain the courage to cross the beaver dam, it was helpful to acknowledge that I was afraid of doing a new thing. My friend Zara Renander, who leads spiritual pilgrimages and has written a nifty little book on the power of labyrinths, advises, "Examine your resistance and you may discover what is blocking your growth."[16] The first step in overcoming the fear is simply acknowledging that the resistance is fear. As President Franklin D. Roosevelt famously said, "Our greatest fear is fear itself." The shell and feather attached to the Green Giant also gave me assurance, and I told myself it was only perceived risk because if I fell in the water, I could swim. It would be cold and would get everything wet, but falling in was not a life and death situation. Surely those who built the trail could be trusted. My first step was tentative, and the second as well. Balancing myself with my hiking poles, I gained confidence as I moved forward. The dam was surprisingly sturdy and only sunk a few inches under my weight. Success and triumph sent my soul soaring.

I gave thanks for the beavers and began a new walking prayer, "Fearless in every step." After repeating it in my rhythmic walking, I wonder if it should be "Trust in every step," as a reminder to put our trust in God, and in our abilities, rather than in being fearless. As I continued, I thought about how beavers had been hunted and trapped for centuries as part of the fur trade, which provided both profit and warmth for many people during the winter. With the additional loss of habitat, by 1988 the North American beaver population had shrunk from 16 million to 10 million. Considering these numbers, I felt even more privileged to have walked across the beaver dam, and it made me think of other animals that have benefited humans. Certainly before the age of machines, humans depended on animals for travel, working the land, and for food. Wars were fought with cavalry. My father and grandparents plowed mules to raise vegetables and cotton on the farm. It was the wool of sheep that kept my feet dry and warm as I walked. I thought of how we eat a hamburger or chicken dinner and prefer not to think about the cow with the big brown eyes, or the hen looking after her chicks. I did eat beaver meat once, in a restaurant in Lithuania, and heard the meat was a specialty in Sweden. When I asked a Swedish friend about it, she said her diet was not that special!

Despite my upbeat spirits, the last five miles of the hike had many ups and downs and left me exhausted. At one point I took off my shoes and boots and massaged my aching feet, they hurt so badly. I was completely out of food, which was deliberate, so my pack was lighter than ever. I told my feet and legs that they could go a few more miles, and when they continued to ache I assured them that rest was coming soon. My toenails were sore and a few were turning purple, but I had to keep going to meet David in Monson and to call my daughter on her birthday. Love can cause us to be reckless and do unreasonable things. Love is the flame which drove Jesus to give and give. It throws everything to the wind.

A family passed by with a young daughter. We had passed one another during the day a few times, and I was impressed by the energy of the young girl. When I was dragging up a hill, I said to myself, "If that 12 year old girl can do this, so can I."

The mom asked, "Are you all right?"

"I'm just tired, that's all," I replied.

She looked at my swollen, purple finger and said, "You hurt your finger. You need to get that ring off."

I nodded in agreement, and said, "Yes, I know."

She looked at my swollen, purple toes and said, "You need to give your feet a break."

I later passed them at Leeman Brook Lean-to. They were making hot tea and offered me a cup. I didn't take up their hospitality because I was determined to finish the last three miles as quickly as possible.

When I emerged from the 100 Mile Wilderness at the parking area on Highway 15, I was too exhausted to be excited. It had been a long, difficult 15-mile day, my feet were aching, and I was hobbling more than walking. For 40 minutes I tried without success to hitchhike into Monson. Then the family I had met on the trail emerged from the woods and offered me a ride. Gratitude filled my heart. In the car they spoke a foreign language that I recognized as Russian, and I learned they had immigrated to New York. I mentioned that I had lived in Lithuania, and in the course of our conversation I realized that I had visited the father's hometown in Belarus. The radiation effects in the aftermath of the Chernobyl nuclear reactor explosion had made them decide to come to the United States with their oldest daughter. We had breakfast together the next morning and I learned that the father was a mountain climber who had scaled most of the highest peaks of Europe. They were now hiking the A.T. in sections with their younger daughter.

In Monson, at the Lakeshore House, the friendly staff told me to make myself at home. I met David and noted that even with his hurt knee, he was walking better than I was. A strong phone signal allowed me to wish my daughter "Happy Birthday." As a cheerleader, she was busy preparing for the football season's opening game and pep rally. Kelly told me of her busy days of work and taking care of our home and pets, alone. I hung up and felt guilt for leaving her with so much responsibility, but then it occurred to me that it was good for her to discover that she too could do more on her own than she imagined. In a way we were both being tested to live outside our comfort zone.

I took a hot shower in a bathroom with fluffy towels and all the toiletries you don't carry on the trail. Wearing the clean "town clothes" the Lakeshore provided, I joined David for dinner. The pot roast and vegetables were mouth-watering and delicious. Grizzly was hunched over with exhaustion as he entered the restaurant, but he came back to life after a half hour rest and a beer.

Upstairs in the small living room, I spoke with a group of young women who were northbound hikers. They were proud of their high mileage and warned me that climbing the Mahoosuc Arm would be difficult because it was so slick. Still haunted by the experience, one of them ventured that she could not even imagine hiking south on the slippery granite. Several of them went to the gas station and purchased a half gallon of ice cream each and then sat on a sofa and ate it all while watching a movie. I couldn't imagine having such a ravenous appetite. When talking about lightening my load, Jonah, a fellow hiker, offered me his denatured alcohol stove to experiment with as I hiked the next leg to Caratunk. He had carried it hundreds of miles and was ready for a change. I sent David home with the dim flashlight, book, straps, and razor. I hobbled up the stairs and was grateful my bunk bed was on the bottom. The mattress was the softest one I'd slept on in weeks.

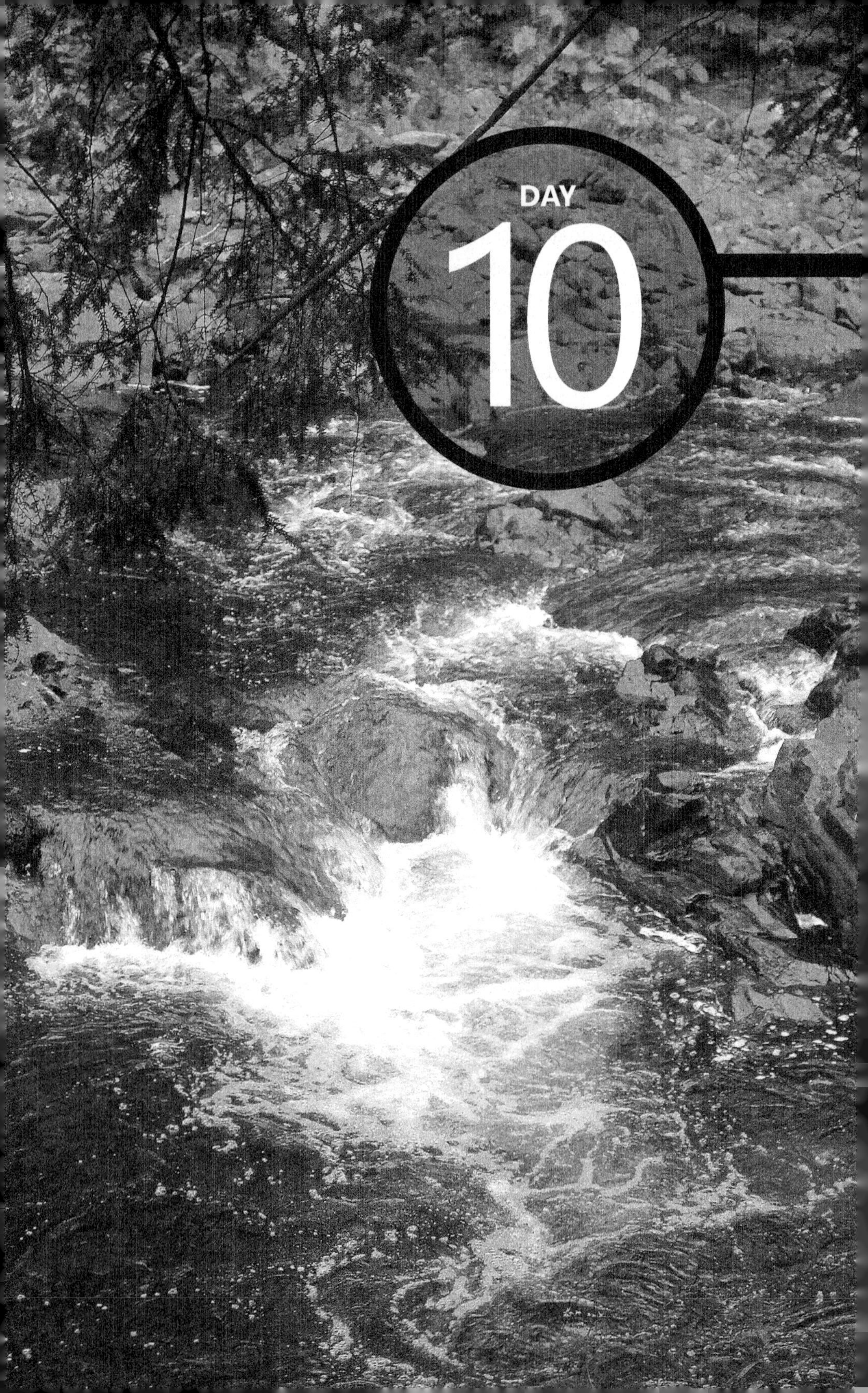
DAY
10

The Power of Mentorship

Monson
to the East Branch of the Piscataqua River

With a population of only 660 people, Monson, Maine was a surprisingly small town. As much as we had heard hikers talk about it as a destination, I expected it to be bigger. David and I walked to Shaw's lodging, the other hiker hostel, which served the only breakfast in town. Unlike the Lakeshore, which provided evening meals at individual tables, at Shaw's you ate family style, gathering around large tables with people you might not know. Ordering consisted of holding up your fingers, two thru five. Each plate had the same food, but the quantity was determined by the number. I held up three fingers, which meant I would receive three blueberry pancakes, three sausages, three hash browns servings, three slices of bacon, three eggs, and coffee with half and half and as much sugar as I wanted. My appetite had expanded, but the thru-hikers going north ordered fives and then placed another order.

One young woman said, "I just think about food all the time."

Her friend added, "I'm a salivating machine."

I enjoyed meeting the hikers and hearing their stories. At Shaw's, like at the White House Landing, I felt at home around the large table.

When David and I walked back to Lakeshore, we noted the number of houses and storefronts boarded up or for sale. Monson has seen better times economically, but the simple way of life was attractive. The coin operated laundry machines were a welcome sight, but I examined the coin operated showers dubiously and imagined trying to scrub my shampoo-soaked hair when the water supply ended, and imagined fumbling to find the coins to restart the flow. When the post office opened, I walked over and received the first of the food supply boxes I had mailed ahead.

Lakeshore had a small room for resupplying what was needed on the trail, and I looked at what other hikers were buying. A popular item was water flavor packets and I decided to give some a try. From the hiker box, where people put unwanted items to share with others, I retrieved some denatured alcohol for my stove. David quietly put a load of food items into the box and enjoyed watching hikers discover them and add them to their food bags. The swelling in my finger had gone down a little and I could wiggle it, so I determined that it was sprained rather than broken. However, my ring was still stuck. Swollen flesh surrounded it on both sides like a knot with a bow.

I dried out my tent and sleeping bag on the clothesline, collected my laundry, and put on clean hiking clothes. After returning the clothes Lakeshore had provided, I felt the urge to hit the trail. We bought some lunch at the one gas station in town and ate it while sitting on the sidewalk. The Lakeshore had a free shuttle service to the trail, but the staff was busy, so the driver handed David the car keys and said, "Honey, would you mind running him up to the trail?" "Wow," I thought. "That is trust." When David dropped me off at the parking lot by Highway 15, I wished him well on getting a ride back to Portland for his flight home. It was sad to leave him, but knowing I would see my family in Caratunk took away some of the loneliness I felt heading out on my own.

Some hikers skip the few miles from Highway 15 to where the trail comes close to Monson, but I didn't want to do that. After studying the guidebook, I had decided to hike seven miles to a campsite at the East Branch of the Piscataqua River. Along the way, some movement in the woods caught my attention and I came face to face with three deer. Frozen, we looked into one another's eyes. The young doe's stare was so intense that I wondered if she was trying to enter my brain. While we were locked and deeply engaged, I wondered about her concerns and fears. It was as if we were communicating at a level beyond language. Suddenly she turned, breaking our intimacy, and casually scampered into the thick woods. A geneticist friend who has worked on the human genome has told me

on several occasions that humans share a huge chunk of DNA with the animal world. He suggested that we are more related than we think.

Later I saw a brown snake. It was not interested in making eye contact, only in slithering away under some leaves. It reminded me of several encounters I'd had with rattlesnakes on the trail in the South. One six-footer stretched across the trail, rose up, and politely rattled to scare me away. I was frightened but determined to pass. The snake looked into my eyes and watched my every move. I waited, thinking it would tire of rattling and move out of the way, but it seemed to gain more determination with every minute. When I got a long limb and tried to shoo it off the trail, the snake just got angrier. Finally, I lifted it up and threw it into the woods so I could keep going. I didn't like the idea that humans and snakes share so many DNA sequences. I was glad to have read that no poisonous snakes live in the wild in Maine.

I met a number of northbound hikers who were anxious to get to Monson. We shared stories about Shaw's and Lakeshore. They were eager to eat the supper and breakfast and enjoy a soft mattress. It amazed me that some of them had gone 20 to 30 miles that day. One lively and energetic hiker with the trail name of "Fish Man" was a retired fisheries professor and Dean of the Department of Agriculture from Auburn University in my home state of Alabama. He was finishing the entire Appalachian Trail, having hiked large sections over the course of several years. While working at the University, he served as an advisor to hundreds of students, guiding them to explore their vocations. He was doing the same on the trail when he encountered young men and women searching and in need of direction. He asked questions, offered suggestions, and helped steer many of them toward life choices and their future careers. In the past he had brought a number of hikers to Auburn. They were artists who excelled in landscape design and loved the outdoors. He asked me my trail name, and I told him I didn't have one. When I mentioned "prayer man" to other hikers, they hadn't thought it fitting.

Fish Man asked, "Just out of curiosity, how do you define prayer?"

I replied, "The bottom line about prayer is simply being with God."

"Are you using your skills on the trail?" he asked.

No, I'm hiking incognito and not telling people that I'm a pastor."

He gave me a strange look, and I got defensive, saying, "You know, people treat me differently when they find out I'm a pastor, and they act

differently, as well." I could tell he was disappointed, so I changed the subject by asking him, "What do you tell the young people?"

His face lit up and he said, "I tell them to dream big, make a plan, and go after it."

He was an inspiration to me, and my chance encounter with him changed the way I thought about hiking. While people are away from the distractions of modern culture, they can relax and actually contemplate who they are and want to be, and listen to a mentor. As I thought about our conversation, I remembered how Thomas Merton disliked prayer as withdrawal or "quietism" because he said it was a complete contradiction of true Christian contemplation. Christian contemplation seeks perfection in love and ultimately leads to action.[17]

As I walked, I reflected upon the positive encouragement "Fish Man" gave to others, including me, and considered it in contrast to what I had observed a few days earlier. I had walked off the trail to see a Lean-to by a lake and met a young man who had recently graduated from high school and was hiking with his grandfather, a tough, wiry old man. They were hanging a rope and stretching their tents out so they would dry out before they set them up, and when they'd finished the young man went to see the shelter.

Soon the grandfather was barking orders: "If you plan to camp here, you better get down here and set up your tent. Do you expect someone to do it for you?"

When the embarrassed young man returned, I overheard him apologize sheepishly, "I was just reading the trail log."

The grandfather barked more orders.

When I talked with them, the grandfather didn't let the young man answer for himself. I told them about the barren Chairback range and White Cap, and said, "I thought it was a hard climb."

The man discounted my comment with, "It was hard for you because you don't have your climbing legs yet. After you hike 500 miles, you'll get there. Those mountains will be nothin' for me because I have my climbing legs."

He was probably right, but I felt put down rather than encouraged. I felt sorry for the young man and his grandfather, who was stuck in the ego energy of comparison, superiority, control, and judgment. Reflecting on that encounter, I hoped that at some point the grandson could forgive his grandfather. I am sure the man thought he was doing a great thing to take his grandson on this adventure. And perhaps he was.

In contrast, I remembered the exhilaration on the faces of the junior high school boys from our church, who stepped in the cold water and forced their bodies under the powerful Long Creek Falls on a "boy to man" backpacking trip. We hiked south to Springer Mountain, the southern terminus of the A. T. About five miles north of Springer, Long Creek Falls sends a cascade of water from three mountain streams to form Noontootla Creek. We had learned to trust our night vision and intuition by hiking in the dark. We shared stories about the knives we carried and the men who had given them to us. We became good at working together and looking out for one another. The boys were on their first backpacking trip, and over several days they learned to follow the white blazes of the trail, cook their own food, carry their own packs, and sleep in both tents and shelters. We drummed and told stories around a campfire. The program built to the moment when, after painting a symbol of their choosing on their bare chests, they waded into the water and crossed through the falls, signifying their moving from boyhood to manhood. The next day when we arrived in the Amicalola Falls State Park, they beamed with pride about their accomplishment.

Some scholars have begun a debate about "the end of men" in America. Unable to find work, some boys end up living at home, drinking heavily and playing video games. Some find more success as heroes in a virtual world than they do in school, relationships, or work. That is not surprising. In the book, *Boys Adrift*, Dr. Leonard Sax identifies five factors driving the epidemic of unmotivated boys and underachieving young men. He cites changes at school, video games, medications for ADHD, endocrine discrepancy, and what he calls "the revenge of the forsaken gods, as contributing factors to their failure to launch into adulthood.[18]

If Sax is correct, the elders of our culture certainly cannot remain silent and retreat into comfortable cocoons. Young men between the ages of 17 and 24 commit most of the violent crimes. Finding order, purpose, and meaningful work will help to channel their uncontrolled energy. Scouting, church, and marching band provided this for me when I was young, but after high school and college, what else besides the military can supply the necessary structure and order? Churches and organizations such as the Rotary Club and Lions Club can serve this role, but increasingly young men don't find them attractive. Movies and T.V. often portray young people as figuring things out on their own, without mature role models, but this is not a good prescription for entering adulthood in a mature way. As someone once told me, "All men are males, but not all males are men."

During my teenage years my emotions were on a roller coaster, running from high to low, from hot to cold, from laughter to anger. One crisp, chilly morning in winter, my father and I went hunting. As we walked around a soy bean field along the frozen mud ridges of deep ruts, he gave me some advice that went something like this, "During your life there will be times when you need to be tough and hard like this frozen mud. There is a fighter in you who can defend you, like the time in the eighth grade when that kid was picking on you and you took it for a while and hated yourself for being weak. Then one day, you stood up and fought back like a storm sending lighting all over the place. That mean kid left you alone after that. It's not a bad thing to be hard." Walking over to a long, slender briar coated with ice, he easily broke it in half, and then he continued, "But when you're hard, sometimes your inflexibility will make you vulnerable and you can be hurt. You know how hard it is to break a green briar in two pieces when it isn't frozen? You can fold it, but the fibers will remain connected. They are flexible. Sometimes we need to be flexible and not rock the boat. Like your insistence on not registering for the draft. You have high ideals of not wanting to kill people, and that's good. But if you are too rigid in a culture which has different ideals, you may find yourself easily broken, like this frozen briar."

I had righteously announced that, unlike my dad, I would not serve in the military. I think this hurt him worse than anything else I could have said. Vietnam was still fresh on our minds, and American society did not accept the responsibility for the violence that the soldiers carried out on our behalf. As someone influenced by the anti-war movement, I said I would live in Canada to avoid the draft. Luckily, I didn't have to follow through on my announcement. The government did away with the draft just before I turned 18. What I didn't understand at the time, and I doubt my father did either, was that I was inclined to refuse to acknowledge the darker side of humanity.

In Jungian psychology, the *puer aeternaus* (Latin for "eternal boy") archetype probably fits me well. The positive aspects of this archetype, which Jung also calls the Divine Child or god-child, symbolize newness, potential for growth and hope for the future. The negative side is that the child refuses to grow up and meet the challenges of life, waiting for someone else to solve their problems, instead. People living with god-child energy love their independence and freedom, and push back at limits or boundaries. I think in my youth and young adult years I wanted to live in purity above the mundane world. To say that I was naïve is an understatement, as I've learned numerous times as I've gotten older. I decided that the next time I built a fire, I would place a stick on it that represented my father and his hurt when I did not honor his military service. I silently asked his forgiveness and prayed that I could be fierce and strong like frozen mud, yet flexible when called upon. I gave thanks that Fish Man stepped up to offer guidance and that he saw it as his role to mentor along the A.T. With his encouragement, I found I wanted to leave the world of self and reach out to others. He helped me realize that a chance encounter with a hiker could be a divinely arranged appointment. I wanted to be more like him and decided I would no longer hide from others the fact that I was a pastor.

When I reached my destination for the day, a nice quiet campsite next to the river, I came upon an instance of trail magic, a cooler of drinks.

As I washed my dishes in the river, a family of ducks came in for a closer visit. In the last light of day, they appeared as silhouettes. I sat a while on the bank of the river, savoring the gentle energy of the wilderness. When I slid into my sleeping bag, I listened to the gentle gurgle of the water and heard the call of a barred owl, "Who cooks for you?" At first it occurred at some distance, then there was an answer from somewhere down the river, and the owl came closer with its song. I couldn't help but smile at being in such a lovely place. In Monson I had bought some Nyquil for my cold and constant cough, and now I looked forward to a quiet night's rest in my tent without the snoring of friends. The owl moved right into my campsite and I fell asleep.

At some point I awoke thinking about Jacob from the Old Testament, who had a vision while sleeping outside. He was so excited about God being present that he poured oil on the rock he used as a pillow and named it "Bethel—House of God." On another occasion, when coming to meet his brother Esau after years of estrangement, he camped by the river Jabbok and wrestled with God all night long. He named the place Penuel, meaning "I have seen God face to face" (Genesis 32:22-31; Genesis 28:11-17). Then it hit me: God and the spiritual world would not leave us on our own but would send teachers to those who search. The spiritual world is ready to offer guidance, if we ask. Perhaps the job of a pastor or mentor is to remind and teach people to watch and listen, and ask.

DAY

11

Thresholds

East Branch of Piscataqua River
to Bald Mountain Lean-to

At daylight I put on my Chaco sandals and forded the river. Although my pack was full and heavy with a resupply of food, I had a reason to move forward with renewed energy. Today my wife, Kelly, and daughter Laurel would fly to Maine, spend the night at a friend's home, and then drive up to meet me in Caratunk. I made good time and, later in the day, forded the west branch of the Piscatqua River. When we cross waterways by driving a car over a bridge, we think nothing of it, but when do it on foot, we know the waterway deserves respect. When the blind hiker Bill Irwin crossed the Piscatqua at this spot, he lost his footing and almost drowned as the current swept him downstream. He struggled towards the calls of his friend on the bank, who helped him out.[19]

I crossed five rivers before reaching Bald Mountain Lean-to. Several had a rope stretched across the water between two trees and a life jacket hanging on a tree, and I said a prayer of thanks for the volunteers who were looking out for hikers. Fords and other river crossings are often associated with rites of passage, thresholds that indicate great change. When Joshua ceremoniously led the Hebrews across the Jordan River after they had been wandering in the desert for 40 years, they set up 40 stones to remember the significance of finally entering the Promised Land. In human development, traditional rites of passage include first steps, baptism, first day of school, first date, getting a driver's license, first car, graduating from school, first job, marriage, children, grandchildren, and retirement. But there are also personal thresholds, and at each crossing I tried to focus on a momentous threshold in my life.

One that came to mind was the time in high school when I became comfortable enough with my dad's boat to go fishing without him. When I got back, he was eager to hear how it went and laughed as I described how my friend David had accidentally cast his pole into the Tennessee River, and how he had stripped down to his underwear, jumped in and retrieved it. My dad was interested in the fish we caught and the fish that got away. The fact that I could go with my friend on my own and fish signified to him that he had taught me well. Another threshold that shaped my self-image was my achieving the rank of Eagle Scout, and, of course, my marriage to Kelly and the birth of our three daughters. When I saw the life jacket hanging on a tree at one of the water crossings, I wondered what life-saving threshold the jacket could represent. The time I first gave my life to God felt like the right one, a good fit, because that step has shaped my life more than all of the others. God's grace and love, like the life jacket, has kept me going through the joys and fires of life.

I wondered how my sense of accomplishment for work that would outlive me signaled that a threshold event might have happened. Each undertaking of life, whether successful or not, made the next undertaking possible and deserved to be celebrated. As a campus minister, offering leadership to build a Wesley Foundation program and a facility at Jacksonville State University were deeds that I was proud of. Facilitating the start of spiritual retreats for young adults, called Chrysalis, in North Alabama and in Eastern Europe was gratifying too. Leading the First United Methodist Church in Rainbow City and Monte Sano United Methodist Church to expand their membership and build a new building also gave me a sense of accomplishment. Just recalling these "success" stories made me beam with pride, even made think that I had become an accomplished man. But my recollection also brought a shadow of shame because naming them to myself made me feel guilty for being a show-off. Did I have a need to prove I was worthy to myself, others, or God?

Thresholds are also openings. They offer opportunities for changes in perception. I recalled several experiences where I personally observed systemic oppression and political manipulation. As a student at Birmingham-Southern College, I was awarded a Bible Lands Travel Award and visited Israel. In addition to enjoying the beauty and spirituality of holy sites, I also witnessed the horrors of a Palestinian refugee camp and watched American news cameras show up for a staged rock-throwing demonstration by Palestinian boys. When the cameras were turned off, the boys stopped tossing their rocks in the road. "Trouble is brewing in the West Bank" was the leading story that evening on the news. My naiveté was shattered just a bit as I realized how news organizations can manipulate situations to curry political favor or boost their ratings. While in seminary at Duke, I went on a trip to Mexico and visited the barrios of the poorest inhabitants. Experiencing their hospitality and hearing their stories made me realize that decisions made in Washington, D.C. had direct consequences on other countries around the world. A pastor friend, who faithfully served Methodist Churches until he retired, learned that the FBI had kept a file on him for years because he had attended an anti-war protest in college and was considered an unpatriotic agitator.

Another series of threshold moments began for me while sitting with my parents and hearing the doctor tell my mom, "Usually patients with similar cancer die within two years." Within three months my father died suddenly, followed by my mom's death almost two years to the day after that prognosis. I never would have guessed that both my parents would die before they were 52 years old. My parents had loved and supported me, and suddenly, at the age of 23, I had to help my mom pick out my dad's casket, and two years later, we were planning her funeral. Questions about life and death weighed heavily on my mind. It had been one thing to sit in a classroom and discuss the role of God in the midst of suffering, but now it was very personal. My sister and her husband bought our family's home and moved into it with their three children. A few months later, at Christmas, there was a fire in the house. They safely made it to the street, but had had to move so fast that they wore only their pajamas. Neighbors wrapped them in blankets to keep them warm. In the midst of pain and grief, I was surprised that I kept functioning. It felt as though I had entered the adult world through an initiation of fire. Perhaps the most powerful threshold moments, which hit me like an earthquake and its aftershocks, occurred in the days and months following a tornado destroying the Goshen United Methodist Church where my wife Kelly was pastor. This disaster killed 20 people, including our four-year-old daughter Hannah. The story is chronicled in my book *Winds of Fury, Circles of Grace* (Abingdon Press, 197, Bardolf & Company, 2010).

Thinking about thresholds reminded me that there are stages we go through in our lives as we mature. As I walked I thought about the young hikers I had met and how they were struggling to get their lives together. I applauded the 18-year-old girl who was driven enough to leave her mother, who wept because she thought her daughter was too young to hike the A.T.

"You're going to make it," I told her.

She asked, "Do you mean on the trail?"

"Yes, but I was referring to your life."

With many of the young men, I witnessed the chaotic, restless energies of puberty, which made the struggle for meaning and dealing with forceful sexual impulses, loneliness, and self-worth so difficult. The Parable of the

Prodigal applies to these young people who must leave home, driven by their powerful urges to discover who they are.

I told one couple, "An identity isn't given to you on a silver platter; you, yourself, must figure it out."

We laughed about how they hadn't found personal profiles of themselves hidden under rocks with their names on them.

At one point I was with a group of hikers who were enjoying the "trail magic" of a fifth of whiskey and a case of beer. These young people didn't know that I was a pastor, and while they drank they talked about their longing to find a home in a church. They had cut their families off, severing contact in an effort to mature, but this had left them longing for the structure of belief, acceptance, and guidance.

I met an older man on the trail who said it took him 30 years to be at home with himself. He had retired from his career but had been restless for more experiences, like Ulysses in Greek mythology, who sets out for further adventures in old age. During those 30 years, he had learned to be responsible for others, to do his duty at work and home. I could tell he was

proud of his accomplishments, and I imagined he was well respected in his business, community, and church. He said that he had been addicted to staying busy because he had equated being busy with success and importance. He laughed derisively when he supposed that his diligence and industriousness would be a good role model for his kids. Throughout the hike, he second-guessed his decisions, and it was clear to me that he was in the process of crossing yet another threshold, one that that Rolheiser and Richard Rohr call "the second half of life."[20]

Hearing this man's stories caused me to wonder what hidden wounds I carried. Hiking alone, I was able to make multiple lists of my resentments. Knowing that doing something symbolic to let them go could be healing, I imagined collecting small sticks to represent my unresolved wounds and resentments. And I imagined that when I was ready, I would toss the sticks into a flowing stream and pray that God would help me heal my wounds as the sticks floated away. The thought of carrying a backpack full of finger-sized sticks labeled with my grievances and, occasionally, when in a threshold moment, letting them go to lighten my load, actually made me laugh out loud.

But it was the humiliations of backpacking and living with simplicity that finally pushed me to let go of my need to control. Backpacking makes it clear that there are many things that are out of our control. Crossing the threshold of the rivers reminded me of the distinct phases of our lives, each with its passion, gifts, and struggles. I prayed I would find my identity in God, would face my struggles gracefully, and would keep moving toward being grateful and at peace and away from being a judgmental, bitter man.

DAY

12

Surprises below the Surface

Bald Mountain Brook Lean-to
to Caratunk

At first light I forced myself out of my sleeping bag and put on my clothes, which were damp from the day before. I was eager to get going. Today I would be meeting my wife and daughter in the town of Caratunk. I quickly stuffed my clothes, sleeping bag, and cooking bag into my pack. Bald Mountain Brook Lean to (elev. 1300) was a good place to sleep on level camp sites, but when I unzipped the front tent flap, the cold air rushed in, causing me to shiver. I walked to where I had hung my food bag. It was on the high limb of a tree, where it was protected for the night from bears and chipmunks. It's not a simple task to throw a rope over a limb 15 to 20 feet up, and having to find a limb that will work to hang a feed bag adds to the challenge. Many trees are not big enough to do the job, and few have branches at the appropriate height. I untied the rope and began lowering the bag. Somehow, a knot had formed halfway up, and I wondered whether I should take the time to untangle it now, or wait. Cold and impatient, I unhooked the carabiner from the food bag and pulled the rope over the limb. I jerked at the rope and worried that the carabiner would hit me on the head, but it flew through the air and landed on the ground at my feet. Morning light spread through the forest, and I was about to roll up the rope when I decided to get the knot out after all, before it got too constricted. Maybe the knots are like conflicts in life—it's better to deal with them before they grow tight and become more difficult to resolve.

From the food bag I took what I would eat for that day. Normally, my main repast would be one of the dehydrated meals I had made at home from leftovers. I'd open the package, pour the contents into a quart-sized

Ziplock bag, put that into another Ziploc bag, and then cover the dehydrated food with water before sealing up both bags. But today I anticipated taking a shower, washing my clothes, and eating at a restaurant with my family. So I retrieved a Ziploc bag filled with granola and powdered milk, poured in the water, and began eating. This was my favorite breakfast. For lunch, I placed peanut butter, honey, and a burrito into the blue trail bag and next to a small bottle of merlot and a flour burrito, which had special significance as the Blood and Body of Christ. As a pastor, I had consecrated bread and wine as the Body and Blood of Christ many times, and this led me to my decision to carry these elements of Holy Communion up and down the mountains, over the streams, and through the woods of Maine and New Hampshire as a sign of God's presence. Now I considered making an altar in my tent to sleep in their holy presence, but I decided not to because I did not trust the chipmunks to treat them with respect!

I got the idea for carrying the Body and Blood of Christ from reading Carlo Carretto's book *Letter's from the Desert*.[21] Carlo heard God call him to leave his active church duties for a season and live instead in the desert of Northern Africa. He placed the elements of Holy Communion on a rock altar in the cave where he was staying so he would be continuously exposed to them in the silence that surrounded him. It takes faith to believe that the bread and wine are the body and blood of Christ, and I wavered a number of times. To say, "Here is Christ, in my blue lunch bag" felt sacrilegious. But I kept reminding myself of what St. Francis of Assisi said: "In this world, I cannot see the most high Son of God with my own eyes, except for his most holy body and blood." Walking through the woods, sometimes I would say to myself, "Make way for the body of Christ! Make way for the blood of Christ!" I kept wondering if it would make any difference to the mountains or me that Christ's presence was passing through—the unseen spirit in the elements connecting with unseen spirit in the rocks, trees, flowers, and animals. The writer of John's gospel quotes Jesus as saying, "Whoever eats my flesh and drinks my blood has everlasting life" (John 6:55). Perhaps this scripture was the motive behind Francis and others feeding the bread and wine to pets, and wild animals and birds. I wanted to have the faith of Francis to believe that the bread and wine was not just a sign pointing us to God, but a bridge allowing us to participate in God's presence on earth. Many people who have doubts have told me that they wished they could believe. I advised them to pray like the father who pleaded with Jesus to heal his son, "Lord, I believe, help my unbelief." Jesus healed the boy (Mark 9:24).

The trail through the woods came to a small, 50-foot square meadow, and I wasn't sure which way to go. It looked like the trail went straight across, and I could see a white blaze on a tree on the other side. In a hurry, I walked about 15 feet into the clearing and stepped into watery mud, sinking up to my knees. I saw a rock the size of a basketball and lunged for it, catching it with my hands. It held secure and I began to pull myself out of the mud until I managed to crawl on all fours onto this single-rock island. Panting heavily, I looked ahead and noticed tufts of grass. After a while, I stood up and precariously balanced on the rock. Then I leapt to a grassy spot, and from there to another and another until I made it to the other side. At that point, I noticed that the trail went around the bog. The next hiker I met looked at my muddy legs and asked, grinning, "Did you have a bog bath?" I learned that bogs look like swamps but are really a wetland on a layer of rock that has little drainage. Swamps are nutrient rich, but bogs are highly acidic, which preserves the organic matter accumulating on their surface. What you see is really a floating mat of debris and vegetation that keeps the water out of sight.[22] The people who maintain the trail build log bridges through the bogs to protect this fragile environment. Sometimes a bridge is just two logs secured side-by-side at either end by a shorter perpendicular log. Usually the topsides of the logs have been flattened to make for easier walking, but, after years of winter weather, some logs no longer function as they're supposed to. I called them "surprise logs" because you never knew what would happen when you stepped on them.

Slick logs could send you slipping into the bog. Logs that leaned to the left or right when you stepped on them made your crossing slanted and hazardous. Some logs were not connected to the perpendicular pieces, so when you stepped on them, one end went down while the other end popped up. Others were broken in the middle and became a slide into the water. Still, others were not connected at all and just floated around. When you stepped on one of those, you took a bath.

Muddy bogs are known to suck the boots off hikers who happen to fall into them. I talked to one hiker who fell into a bog about five feet deep and got his boot stuck in a tangle of roots. The water was cold and he had trouble freeing his booted foot. After about 20 minutes of struggling, he was about ready to give up. He had a dog that kept smiling at him, watching and waiting. The hiker finally dove down, got his boot untangled, pulled himself out, and continued on his way, covered with black slime. It's pretty easy to tell when a person had taken a fall in a bog. Several times I met muddy hikers and asked, "Found a bog?" and they sadly shook their heads and told their stories.

I like the predictability of a life unhampered by bogs. There is security in knowing that the bridge won't fall, that the car will start, that a relationship is solid. Living with uncertainly adds stress, but it is foolish to take security for granted.

Hiking down to Moxie Pond (elevation 970 feet) and up Pleasant Pond Mountain (elev. 2470 feet) was challenging, but knowing I would see my family gave me extra energy. I had trouble following the trail above the tree line and got lost, but getting back on course gave me a nice excursion around the mountaintop. The top of Pleasant Pond Mountain offered a panoramic view of all the mountain ranges to the north that I had scaled. I could also see the mountain ranges to the south that I would traverse in the weeks ahead. Soon, on another peak, I stopped to visit with a group of day hikers who were having a picnic. They shared some gorp and an apple and tried to give me more food. For them, this excursion was an annual event. They'd stay in a cabin on a lake and hike to this peak. It sounded simple and wonderful. They were very encouraging and confident that I would reach my goal.

The hike down the mountain provided beautiful views of Pleasant Pond. I had heard tales about the wonderful breakfast served at a hostel there. After the steepest section, I stopped for morning prayers and lunch. I was then joined by a man I had met at the lean-to the night before. As we hiked together I realized he was competing to see who could go faster. I tried to keep up the pace for a while, and then slowed down and let him go.

I was excited to arrive at the highway in Caratunk (elev. 490 feet). When I'd spoken to the owner of the Sterling Inn, he told me of a public phone in the village that I could use to call for a ride to the inn. I looked, but didn't find it because I didn't walk far enough down the street. Since there was no cell coverage available, hitchhiking remained the only option. Fortunately, a river raft guide picked me up and dropped me where I wanted to go. After a glorious hot shower, I collapsed on the soft bed and fell asleep. When I woke I washed my clothes and gave my cooking pot a good scrubbing with hot water.

Later that afternoon I was giddy with excitement, anticipating Kelly's and Laurel's arrival. I sat in one of the rocking chairs on the front porch and watched and waited for them to pull into the gravel lot. Finally, they arrived! As I bounded to the car I was joined by a dog that lived at the Inn. We humans greeted each another with hugs and a kiss. The dog was as thrilled to see them as I was and jumped on them with enthusiasm.

Fending him off, Laurel asked, "What happened to your finger? It's swollen!"

Kelly immediately looked concerned, and she urged, "You should probably take your ring off."

I smiled and said, "I would if I could."

On the way to our room, I showed them my bent hiking pole, which I'd tossed into the garbage bin, and explained about my fall. In no time, their luggage was unpacked and Kelly presented me with the long sleeve hiking shirt that she'd just bought at the LL Bean store. She and Laurel also showed me the purchases they'd made for themselves. Although I had only been gone two weeks, it seemed much longer.

Kelly thought I'd lost weight, and was concerned about my cough. In a motherly tone she said, "You need some medicine, mister."

At the Sterling Inn, I introduced them to a number of hikers. One young man told us how he and his dog had hiked all the way from Georgia. The dog's feet were bruised, cut and sore, and had been healing for a month while his owner worked at the Inn. I was delighted that my family was getting to know some hikers and learning about the challenges and joys of the A. T. When you're hiking, what you're doing seems normal, but to others it seems strange. We went out to dinner, and I was surprised that the big hamburger was too much to eat. When we got back to the Inn, we settled down to watch *October Sky*, a movie about West Virginia coal mining kids who were determined to build rockets. Being from Huntsville, Alabama, where space rockets are still designed and tested, it made me feel close to home. Other hikers arrived and joined us. After a while we went to bed, and the next morning, when I entered the common room, the hikers were still stretched out on the sofas, sound asleep.

DAY
13

A Day at Rest

Caratunk

Caratunk, on the banks of the Kennebec River, has a place in American history. In 1775, at the beginning of the Revolutionary War, George Washington assigned Benedict Arnold, then a colonel, to lead a detachment of over 1,000 men from Cambridge, Massachusetts to British controlled Quebec for a surprise attack. The journey through the wilderness of swamps, bogs, and mountains of Maine didn't go well. The soldiers, maneuvering heavy wooden boats up the Kennebec River, lost control of their vessels in the whitewater and rammed into rocks and trees, resulting in leaks that ruined food and gun powder. Forced to leave the river, Arnold's troops then portaged their boats through the rough wilderness between a series of ponds. The A.T. follows part of Arnold's trail, and the ponds still bear the names they received then—East Carry Pond, Middle Carry Pond, and West Carry Pond. By the time the war party reached the French speaking settlements above the Saint Lawrence River, only 600 starving men remained; the rest had turned back because of the difficulties. The 600 soldiers pushed on and laid siege to Quebec City before attacking it on December 31, 1775. The British repelled them, but the audacity of the Americans signaled to the British that they faced a more determined force than they had imagined. For his efforts, Arnold was eventually promoted to general. The march also resulted in naming the Bigelow range after Timothy Bigelow, one of Arnold's division leaders, who climbed the peak in 1775 for observation purposes.

Today, Caratunk has a population of 108 and little to offer hikers besides the Sterling Inn and a camping resort. Whitewater rafting can also be found a little down the road. The Sterling Inn is in an old farm house that was turned into a bed and breakfast. We had a room with several beds and, down the hall, a bathroom that we shared with other guests. We enjoyed sitting on the porch and playing games and watching hikers light their stoves and prepare their meals. Kelly had brought my next food supplies and took provisions I no longer wanted. During breakfast we met many Canadians who were vacationing in the area. Surprisingly, some spoke very little English, only French.

Just for fun, Kelly, Laurel and I drove to see Moxie Falls, one of Maine's highest single drop waterfalls. Along with other families, we enjoyed a leisurely walk on the well-maintained trail that wound up and down wooden stairs and walkways. I wore my Chaco sandals rather than boots because I was nursing a blister and wanted to give it time to heal. As we strolled along, the subject of our conversation once again turned to "Now, why are you doing this?"

I tried to make a case that walking in nature is good for one's health. When we lived in Lithuania, it was common for a doctor to prescribe a month's stay at a sanitarium in a forest setting. Many people believed that simply being in the fresh air among the trees would make you healthier. The Finnish psychology professor Kalevi Korpela and his research team have concluded that walking in nature can reduce stress and enhance happiness, and they have created health walks in what they call "Power Forests."

Mark Ellison earned his doctorate researching the effects of hiking and concluded that the brain functions better in a nature environment.[23] Being away from cell phones, computers, television, and other noise frees the brain to hear the soft soothing sounds of nature—breezes, running water, birds chirping. When you're hiking, you don't multi-task, so your brain can focus with greater intensity and your memory improves. Nature can also elevate your mood and help you be more productive.

Unfortunately, I didn't achieve much with my family by touting the health benefits of hiking. Kelly and Laurel pointed out that I had bruises, blisters, a swollen finger, a terrible cough, and soreness everywhere. Falling into bogs, spending the night under a rock ledge during a storm, and feeling lonely didn't sound like a good time to them.

"Okay," I conceded, "I'll have to come up with another reason to hike than for my physical health."

We all laughed and proceeded to have a good time together. We took a lot of photos and played around the stream. We stopped at one of the few general stores in the area and were amazed at its wide selection of goods. The store had a deli, and sold hunting and fishing supplies, food for the trail, and clothes. Later, we bought our food for supper from the Inn: frozen pizzas and Ben and Jerry's ice cream.

Home is an anchor. With Kelly and Laurel, I felt at home even in the wilderness. With them I was able to relax and let go of anxieties. I had carried around guilt for leaving them, and spending time together helped me realize that they were behind me all the way. In absence, our imaginations can and will invent scenarios that promote distrust, uncertainty, and worry, but being together reassured me that our relationships were solid. Even though we had talked on the phone, it was only by being with them that I was able to realize the full extent of their support. My soul was nourished by their presence, and a calming sense of being at home allowed me to rest and cherish my last night in that soft, comfortable bed.

DAY

14

Loyalty

Caratunk
to West Carry Pond Lean-to

It was hard to take leave of Kelly and Laurel in Caratunk. After we hugged, kissed, and said our good-byes, they waved as I climbed into the canoe that would ferry me across the Kennebec River to pick up the trail south along Pierce Pond Stream. When people asked me later about my best experiences on the hike, I told them it was spending time with my family. After a day and a half of rest, I was physically ready to hike again, but now I felt completely on my own.

Around 10 a.m. I stopped for a break and watched a bright green inchworm make its way across a moss covered boulder. Unlike other caterpillars, which have legs in the middle of their bodies, the inchworm only has front and hind legs, so it moves when the front legs reach out and attach to something and the rear legs catch up. This movement makes the worm look like it's measuring its path an "inch" at a time. Having no one else to talk to, I asked the inchworm where it was heading and imagined it would say, if it could speak, "Nowhere in particular." When the worm began to fall off the edge of a boulder, it produced a tiny stream of silk. Impressed, I commented, "God has created you with your own rappelling system," and wondered, "When you spin yourself a cocoon and become a moth, what color will you be?"

My walking prayer, "Peace with every step" filled me with contentment, but I felt homesick and needed a boost to continue. I decided to treat myself to listening to country music on my fully charged phone. The music was a distraction and dulled the sadness of being separated from my family. I wished Kelly and Laurel would come back and meet me in a few weeks. It would give me something definite to look forward to.

The 10 miles trail I walked to East Carry Pond was the same route Benedict Arnold and his men took on their way to attack Quebec City. The soldiers' discomfort was worse than mine because they were marching in the late fall when the temperature was much cooler. Carrying the large boats and gear through the wilderness swamp must have been difficult, especially since the soldiers had to make multiple trips between ponds in order to get everything moved. From the map I could tell that West Carry Pond is long and would offer the biggest break from carrying all the gear. Later in the Revolutionary War, Benedict Arnold became bitter when he felt other officers were unjustly promoted over him. He was accused of money mismanagement but acquitted by Congress. Eventually he was given the rank of general, but in 1779 he decided to change sides and surrendered his army to the British. The Americans learned of his plot, and Arnold barely escaped capture as he fled down the Hudson River. As a Brigadier General for the British Army, he led soldiers to fight the Americans in Virginia and elsewhere. In addition to his pay, Arnold received

6,000 pounds from the British for joining them, and his name, like Judas Iscariot's, has been linked with betrayal and treason ever since.

I wondered if I would change allegiance if I found myself in a similar position. Jesus exhorted followers to enlarge their loyalties beyond tribe, nation, and any group, and to include everyone. This all-inclusive vision is a challenge for those of us who are proud to belong to our group. Richard Rohr reminds us that the Bible itself is inclusive, blending Hebrew, pagan, and other cultures' wisdom.[24]

I decided to build a prayer cairn near the shore of the East Carry Pond. One stone was for all the men who sacrificed and suffered and slogged through these swamps and bogs to win American independence. Another stone was for Benedict Arnold, Judas, and all the enemies inside and outside our social and national groups. Jesus asked us to love and pray for our enemies, and, for some reason, we usually have no difficulty finding candidates to fit the bill, giving us plenty of opportunity for prayer. Another stone represented mercy for all of us who get stuck in caring only for our culture, tribe, denomination, and nation. I found a beautiful, smooth, white stone and placed it on top to represent the vision that we move beyond small thinking to include all. This is the vision of the Kingdom of God.

By the time I reached West Carry Pond (elev. 1340 feet), I had walked 14 miles and was ready for a break. I set my pack down and collapsed on a big, warm, sunny rock beside the beautiful lake. Then I had a snack, consulted the map, and was overcome with tiredness. In the quietness of that peaceful space I rested my head on the pack, hugging it like a pillow, and fell asleep. Awakened by the approach of a northbound hiker, I was embarrassed to be caught sleeping.

When I apologized, the older hiker said, "No need. It looks like you were taking care of yourself."

When I got to the West Pond Lean-to, I met a delightful young thru-hiker from Georgia who had walked 30 miles that day and shared his excitement about the awesome sights from Avery Peak. He was looking forward to meeting up with his father, who was going to hike the remainder of the trail with him. The two had started out together, been separated, and now would be together again at the end. I was glad to hear they had a healthy relationship and that, in some ways, his father had taught him to feel comfortable in the woods and develop a love of hiking.

Setting up my tent didn't take long, and I brought my stove and food to the shelter to cook. For that night's dinner I wanted to try a new recipe. I had written the instructions on the plastic Ziploc bag with a permanent marker, but the words had smeared off so I just dumped the ingredients into the pot to cook. Soon the smell of burned food filled the shelter. I was a bit embarrassed, but ate what I could of the half-cooked pasta. Later I used a rock to scrape the layer of burned food from the pan. It was my second time that day to feel humiliated and inadequate. Self-doubt resurfaced. "Am I really a backpacker when I mess up a meal?" I asked myself. The young hiker was polite enough to treat me as though I was. I told myself that without trial and error, I would never learn anything. I was being pretty hard on myself and wondered if I was equally hard on others.

As I tried to go to sleep in my tent, I heard a foul-mouthed man from New York talking loudly at the lean-to. I had met him earlier in the day when he had bragged about walking this trail many times, but he had seemed more interested in talking than hiking. After learning I was from Alabama, he asked if we were still beating up black people. Although I tried to respond, he didn't bother to listen. When he found out I was a pastor, he asked if we were still beating up gay people. It's true that white males as a group have felt superior over Native Americans, blacks, browns, Asians and women.

As a member of that group of white men, I'm aware that through subtle ways and through violence we have wounded our brothers and sisters. We are slow to even discuss, much less admit that we treat women or people of color differently than our white male cohorts. We speak of freedom, but none of us is free from prejudice. Hatred toward gay and lesbian people in the name of God has torn apart families and inflicted deep wounds. I've been told that if we individually, or as culture, wound another person, a likeness of that wound is branded upon ourselves. I've always known that I carried the shame and guilt of this wound, but haven't known how to describe it and bring it to the healing waters so that I won't pass it on to my children. The complex wound remains as hidden as my spleen. The loud man's comments were like fresh paper cuts on my soul. Although he was angry and obnoxious, he did rightly identify the wounds of every American, and especially Southern Christian white Americans. Naming and exposing the wounds can lead to compassion, repentance, and, perhaps, to reconciliation. I couldn't help but overhear him cursing his stove, which he was unable to light. He concluded that it didn't have the correct denatured alcohol in it. The young backpacker, who'd earlier treated me with kindness, built a small fire for him so he could cook his dinner. Even this insufferable, angry man was welcome on the A.T.

In my prayers before I slept, I asked God for help. Here I was in the woods, seeing people I would never see again, and I was still trying to appear strong and competent. I found myself in a defensive posture when I really wanted healing from the wounds of being part of a system of oppression. When I prayed for others, I included a prayer for the safe travels of Kelly and Laurel as they flew home, and for a good reunion of the young backpacker and his father. For the loud hiker from New York, I prayed for sleep to come soon.

DAY

15

Seeing God in Nature

West Carry Pond
to Stafford Notch Campsite

I had a big day ahead of me and wanted an early start, so I broke camp in the cool darkness before dawn. A rainstorm front from Hurricane Irene, which had hit the Gulf Coast, would be arriving in the afternoon and I intended to be settled before it came. During the night I'd been awakened by the nearby tromping of a large animal. Figuring that it was a moose, I thought it best not to unzip my tent and pop out and say, "Surprise." A damp coolness rushed into my tent as I swung open the flap and headed into the day.

The West Carry Pond Lean-to was empty as I went by. The young thru-hiker going to meet his dad was already gone, but the loudmouthed backpacker from New York was still in his tent, snoring. The trail over the round top mountain was pleasant. Later I hiked along Flagstaff Lake and went to the beach to look at the little Bigelow Mountain Range that I soon would be climbing. It was a special time. The calm lake was a mirror for the mountain in the golden morning sun. It was beautiful and I sat by the lake and looked up at the Bigelow Mountains, said my morning prayers, and sang Psalm 63. As I meditated on the spectacular panorama, the thought came to me that I was looking at the face of God, which I identified as true, beautiful, real, and wild. A loon called from across the water that extended 15 miles to Stratton. It was only later that I read that beneath the waters of Flagstaff Lake lie the remains of the farming towns that had been flooded when the Long Falls Dam had been built on the Dead River, which was the West Branch of the Kennebec River. There is no place where God is absent, so God's face would not just be reflected on the surface of the water but in the graves beneath it as well.

I like to watch the light of the early sun, the way the slanting rays send a glow on the rocks, trees, or water. The white paper birch trees seem to radiate. Often they have a section of bark that sticks out from the trunk like an empty sign waiting for a message, and there were several times when I expected to see one

The climb up the little Bigelow Mountain (elev. 3010 feet) was very humbling. Some call it Maine's second mountain, after Katahdin. There are many steep ups and downs. When I stumbled and ended up on my knees, I laughed and reminded myself, "You are on holy ground, so being on your knees is probably the appropriate posture." The wilderness can be gentle or harsh, but it often puts you in your place. I met two hikers who asked me, "When will the ups and downs ever end?" I chuckled and told them that I was going to ask them the same question. With bleeding and swollen knees and aching muscles, I was in need of some encouragement.

Because I felt I needed some extra afternoon energy, I listened on my iPhone to a worship album by Michael W. Smith. At one point Michael asks the audience if they want to see God's glory, and their clapping and roar gets louder, ending in a mighty crescendo. It's a moving moment and often brings tears to my eyes because I, too, want to see God's glory. As I listened to the song, I heard the artist pleading for God to come into the lives of the worshippers, who were sitting in what I imagined was a dark concert hall, and I said to myself, "You want to see God's glory? Go outside and look around! Everything is amazing!"

Henry David Thoreau encouraged people to enlarge their capacity to see. He wrote, "God reveals Himself in a frosted bush today as much as in a burning one to Moses of old."[25] My friend Brenda always reminds me, "You do not know what you do not know." I realized that when it came to nature, I didn't have even the slightest clue. The plants, trees, and rocks were all telling stories which I could understand only if I had background knowledge in the science of nature. I noticed where an animal had dug near the trail, and through investigating further saw torn pieces of paper in the octagonal shape of beehives. This nest could have belonged to yellow jackets or bumblebees and been dug up and shredded by a skunk.

Without expert knowledge, I couldn't read much of the story. The same, I suspect, is true for the spiritual life. There are many signs and stories around us, but how do we read them properly?

In the morning light, I counted 21 spider webs. At noontime, with the sun in a different position, I would have missed them all. Mary Oliver, in her poem "Messenger," beautifully articulates her work of loving the world, of keeping her mind open, standing still, and being astonished. When we learn and practice being astonished, we also develop a spirit of gratitude. While hiking, I continually contemplated the beauty of the earth and was amazed! Tracing the path of a raindrop reminded me of our souls' journeys in, thru, and downward until, finally, we are transformed and rise like a mist. "Knowing" the forest at a deeper level is not just an intellectual exercise of reciting the lifecycles and proper Latin names of plants, but a matter of the heart. When we love the leaf, root, rock, nut so much that it becomes part of us, then we "know" it at a deeper level. In the novel *Hannah Coulter*, Wendell Berry has a character say, "The brook doesn't care if you love it or not. But you had better love it. For your own sake, you had better love it."[26] As the Anglican mystic Thomas Traherne reminds us, "You never enjoy the world aright till the sea itself floweth in your veins, till you are clothed with the heavens and crowned with the stars."[27] To experience the sweetness, light, and glory of God is to see our oneness to all creation.

God's spirit within the trees, ferns, and flowers gives them their beauty. Jesus challenged us to "consider the lilies of the field." When we meditate on the natural world, we need not do it as if the flower or bird were an object; instead, we can view it as a member in our own extended family. The Apostle Paul understood that it is the Holy Spirit that works within us when we pray. The peace and recognition of the holy comes when we are able to unblock the Spirit as it flickers into a flame of spiritual recognition. According to researcher Jane Goodall, even chimpanzees experience awe when in the presence of beauty. She describes a troop of chimps visiting a beautiful waterfall in the jungle. When they come upon it, they get excited and dance for 10 minutes. Goodall suggests that they, too, experience the spiritual mystery of water, alive, flowing and always present.[28]

For me, the trees that find purchase on even the most barren out-croppings are miracles. I consider it remarkable that a seed can land on a rock covered only with moss and lichen, and start to grow roots. The lichen and moss, which amazingly do not need roots to exist, provide a stable environment. Lichen, which can be found in the harshest places, including under the icecap in Antarctica, is made up of two parts: fungi and algae. The fungi provides protection and the algae provide the food, so they do not need to absorb moisture through roots. This way they can live on rocks. It is a symbiotic relationship—neither partner is harmed, and both benefit from the other's presence. Over years, the trees send roots that extend around the rock to the ground. Eventually it becomes secure, with its roots encircling the rock. Seeing the trees on the rocks made me want to shout, "Behold the glory of God."

I also observed a variety of small and giant mushrooms that had shot up everywhere. Their colors were purple, deep cherry, brown, yellow, and red, all reflecting the glory of God. I was amazed at the abundance and diversity of flowers and ferns. The hundreds of varieties of moss that survived in this spongy, fragile ecosystem were incredibly beautiful.

In the ninth century, John Scotus Eriugenea, whose names means "John the Irishman from Ireland," taught that Christ moves among us in two shoes—one being the creation, and the other being the Scriptures.

Eriugenea stressed the need to be as alert and attentive to the Christ moving among us in both these incarnations.[29] The Psalmist understood this in Psalm 104 and in Psalm 148 which basically say, "Go outside and be astonished at God's glory." For me, the changing colors of the leaves, the air, the sun, the clouds, the stars, and the spectacular views were all declaring God's glory.

At some point in the afternoon, I came upon a blue balloon resting on the ground by the trail. Someone had tied it to a branch, and it looked out of place in the natural surroundings, a simple, man-made object among the manifold and complex array of God's creation. I considered picking it up and taking it with me to the next campsite, but decided not to. Perhaps someone had left it there for a reason, as a signal to a fellow hiker.

I was surprised at how quickly I reached the Stafford Notch Campsite (elev. 2230 feet) I hadn't realized how close it was. I could have hiked farther but decided to get my tent tied down on one of the raised wooden platforms before Hurricane Irene arrived. I didn't want to spend another stormy night in the open. The air smelled of rain and the wind was picking up as I cooked dinner. Just as I finished washing my pot, the rain began to fall. A fellow hiker warned me that three inches of rain were expected during the night. I hunkered down and said my evening prayers. As I lay in the shaking tent, buffeted by fierce gusts of wind, I tried to recall all the blessings of the day where I had experienced the glory of God. I listened to the groaning of the trees and the drumming of the rain on my tent and wondered how the storm expressed God's glory and power. I could also hear the water rushing beneath the platform, but I felt safe and tired and slept for a while.

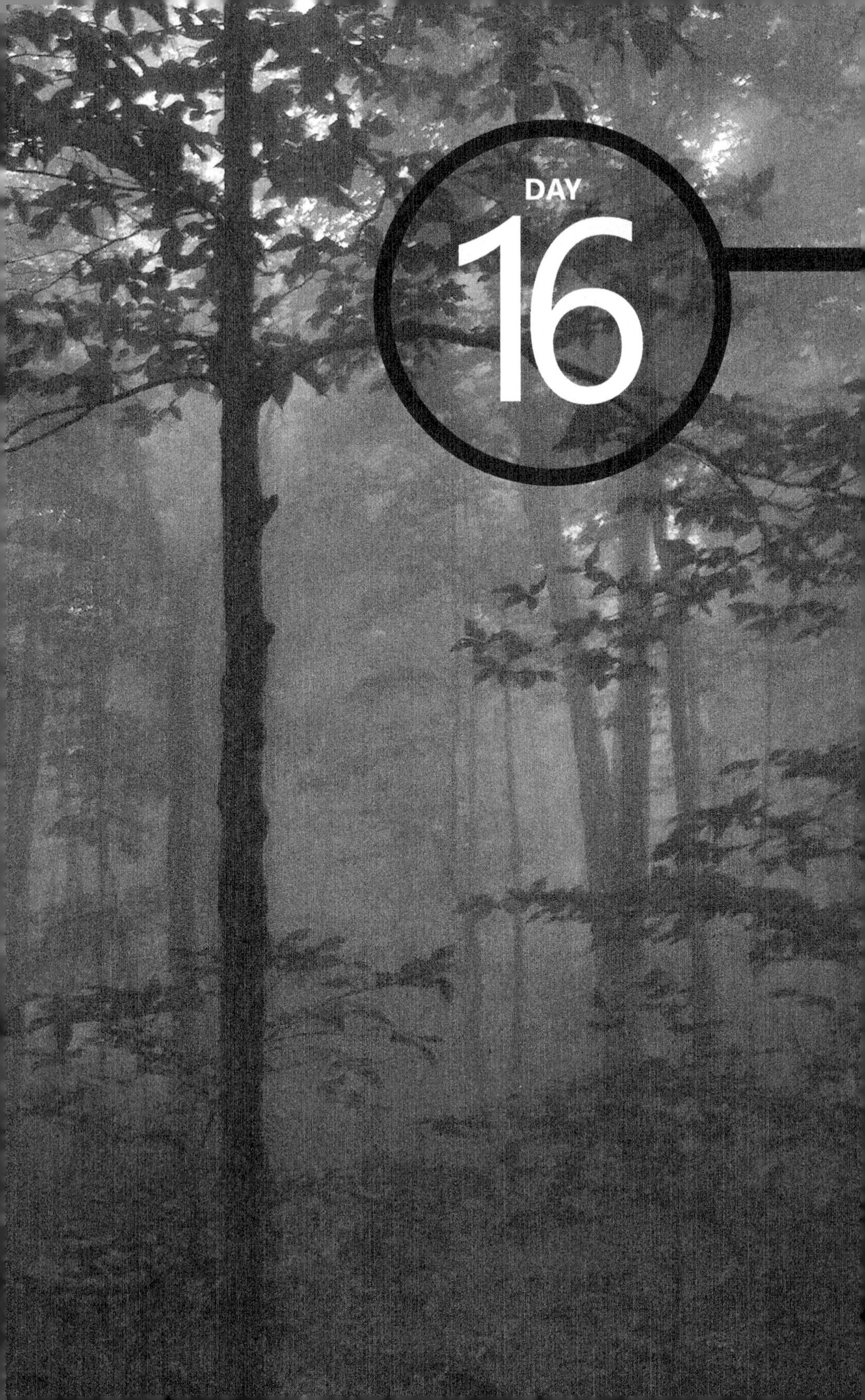
DAY
16

Mother Sue

Safford Notch Campsite
to Stratton

While Hurricane Irene raged, I huddled inside the tent and watched a spider patiently waiting out the storm. It moved only occasionally, and I marveled at its ability to be content. I watched the patterns the rain made on the tent fly and counted myself lucky—for a good eight hours my tent had not sprung a leak. But then the water rose too high, and for the next six hours my sleeping pad became a flotation device. I had to use my cooking pot to bail the water out of my sleeping space. By morning the rain lightened, but I wasn't sure whether it was safe to go outside, whether another storm front was coming.

At some point I decided it was time to move out, and I began packing the wet gear, which had become waterlogged and grown in weight and size. The trail from the Stafford Notch Campsite was a small stream, and I sloshed through it, jumping over the most deeply flooded areas. When I met up with the actual A.T., I kept going, without thinking. After about 30 minutes I came upon a blue balloon, which looked just like the blue balloon that I had passed the day before. Surprisingly, it had weathered the storm no worse for wear. I stopped and considered in which direction I was hiking. After consulting the map, I realized that I'd gone north rather than south. Who would've thought that colorful trash left on the trail would show me the way?

Backtracking, I had to decide whether to be angry that I had wasted an hour or to look for interesting things in the forest that I now had the opportunity to see for the third time. I asked myself, "What am I missing here? What am I meant to notice?"

As I began to climb Avery Peak (elev. 4090 feet), there were roaring streams, mini waterfalls, and flooded trails everywhere. I saw a huge hawk or eagle with white tail feathers fly across the trail and ride the thermal currents in the fog. Purple, red, and green mushrooms had popped up overnight. Small animal spoors in the mud looked like they belonged to a raccoon or maybe a skunk. The tracks only showed that an animal had been there, not what it was or where it had gone. I thought how often, if you looked, you could see traces of where God has been. Considering how foggy it was, I determined the prayer of the day was "Sometimes God is hidden in the fog." and sang my morning prayers to the misty forest around me. I was wet and cold, so when I got to the Avery Memorial Campsite Cabin (elev. 3800 feet) I cooked a warm lunch and made some hot tea and ate and drank while sitting on the cabin's front stoop.

Descending the steep slopes of Avery Peak, I resorted at times to sitting on my bottom and sliding down the polished granite, hoping I could stop when I needed to. I now understood why I'd seen other hikers wearing pants without back pockets. In the early afternoon, I climbed West Peak (elev. 4195 feet) and welcomed the sun as it came out and began to dry the land. One plant with a geometric formation of red berries stopped me in my tracks. The shape reminded me of the pattern of a DNA string or of genes—pictures that I'd seen in a biology book. My face turned to a smile as I studied the short stalks connecting the red berries. Nature is full of surprises, if we only take time to watch and notice. This plant reminded of the "hearts a burstin'" plant, which blooms in the fall for a short time, but provides a quick, important meal for the birds that are migrating south. Being surprised by beauty has to be one of the richest feelings in life.

The first hiker I encountered all day wore a blue parka and blue pack cover. I was slowly picking my way down a steep, rocky trail filled with unstable rocks the size of volleyballs and basketballs, and trying not to fall.

When we met I said, "This is slow going isn't it?"

He looked at me, lifting his head, and said, "Not for me; it's not that steep."

His comment irritated me, but I refrained from hitting him with my walking stick, though in my imagination, I did. My goal had been to get to Highway 27 and then to hitch a ride to Stratton. I kept thinking I was almost there, but when I finally made it, it was 6:30 p.m. It was a typical waiting place, except for the six wild turkeys walking down the side of the road. My phone had no signal to call for a ride to the motel, and I asked a tourist from Quebec for a lift, but she said she didn't speak English. Hitchhiking was useless because no cars passed. I took off my pack and sat on a rock and tried my phone again. Miraculously, I got a weak signal and quickly called the Stratton Motel. The proprietor, Sue, answered and said she was picking up other hikers and would be there soon. After I hung up I tried to call home but, once again, had no signal. I looked over at my pack and saw that the feather and the shell were still there. I thanked God for getting me safely across the wet, slippery mountains and for the miracle of getting a signal for a ride.

Sue, a stocky, middle-aged woman with short cropped hair, arrived in her minivan with two drenched southbound hikers who had left the trail because the Carrabasset River was so high it was impassible. Sue assured us there would be room for all; although the Stratton Motel's five private rooms were booked, there was a bunk house available. The caretaker's quarters had been converted into a hostel with bunk beds, a bathroom, and a kitchen, and a picnic table outside. The drenched couple wanted to stay together, so they found a room at the hotel next door. My accommodations were not fancy, but for someone only looking for a bed, a shower, and a roof overhead, it was great. Perhaps the real miracle was that there are people like Sue. She spends her life shuttling and helping hikers. She was like a kind mother who invited hikers to make themselves at home in the motel. She was also ready with information about the trail and gave plenty of encouragement. In the ancient stories about journeys, there are usually helpers and guides who show up at the right moment to offer advice. When Theseus agreed to fight the Minotaur, the princess Ariadne gave him a ball of string to find his way out of the labyrinth. When Demeter is looking for her missing daughter Persephone, it is Hecate, the goddess of witchcraft, who tells Demeter that Persephone is trapped in the underworld and helps to search for her. The importance of guides at just the right moment is crucial, and Sue was one of those special people, especially after a cold wet day on the trail.

Oddly, the restaurant had scripture sayings posted on the walls. I ate alone. There were other hikers eating at separate tables but no camaraderie between anyone. Without community, the scriptures felt empty. I missed the large tables of the White House Landing and Shaw's, which provided table fellowship. A few hikers cooked their own meal at the picnic table at the motel. At the bunkhouse, I talked with other hikers and learned how they'd managed the terrible storm, but the mood was somber.

The Stratton Motel gave me an opportunity to shower and to wash clothes. I stayed up late, taking advantage of the small library that fit on a single bookshelf. There was a devotional booklet that a hiker had written about his experiences on the A.T., and it planted the seed in my mind that I might want to do the same. The washer stopped working in mid-cycle, without draining or spinning. I played with it for a while and ended up starting the wash cycle over. The second time it worked, but I still had to wait to start the dryer. By the time I finally climbed the stairs to the bunk room, I could hear the other hikers snoring. Covering one ear with my arm helped muffle the noise, and I soon fell asleep.

The next morning when I was making my breakfast in the kitchen, I talked to a young man I had seen the night before when he'd been lying on the couch with a computer in his lap and earphone in his ears. He was the caretaker for the Avery Memorial Campsite, and he'd come down for supplies and seemed desperate to plug back into the world, though hiking and living in the woods was his life. He'd hiked the Pacific Crest Trail, the A.T., and the mountains of Patagonia in South America. I'd seen his empty camp between the Avery Peaks and wondered where he'd disappeared to. During the season his job was to help hikers, protect the environment, and collect camping fees from those staying in the camp-sites. He told me that since the season was over camping was now free. Across the street from the motel was a real grocery store where I bought denatured alcohol, fresh fruit, and a snickers bar. With a group of quiet hikers I waited at the motel for Sue, who would shuttle us to different locations. A young couple who would be slackpacking that day rode with me back to the parking lot. They were enjoying a mixture of slackpacking and backpacking on their A.T. adventure. Sue's motherly presence was a bright spot, and as I said good-bye I wanted to give her a hug; but I refrained, thinking that it might not be appropriate since, realistically, we were strangers.

DAY

17

Being Present

Stratton
to South Branch Carrabassett River

The Appalachian Trail Guide to Maine describes the section between Highway 27 near Stratton and Highway 4 at Rangley as the most difficult section in the state. The gain in elevation is over 10,000 feet and it occurs by crossing six 4,000 foot and three 3,000 foot mountains. It features high peaks, deep valleys, and open vistas. Then comes the warning, "Do not underestimate the time and effort needed to traverse this section."[30]

From the low elevation of Highway 27, I began to climb Crocker Mountain, first through a hardwood and then a hemlock forest. At times the rocks were the size of double refrigerators and seemed to have been randomly tossed around the mountainside. I couldn't imagine how the glaciers moved these big boulders, but also couldn't imagine a one-mile thick ice sheet. The ground was covered with a blanket of ferns, mosses, and small blooming white hemlock flowers six-inches tall. Being there made me feel like I was walking in a giant terrarium. A few miles farther ahead, the trail led into another hardwood forest. Suddenly, I heard a sound to my right and turned my head quickly enough to see a bear dropping out of a tree and fleeing down the side of the mountain. When hungry or feeling threatened, black bears can become dangerous. They can run, climb, and swim faster than humans and have been known to maul people. There are a dozen or so bear attacks each year in the United States. To prepare myself for a possible encounter, I had read some case histories in the book, *Bear Attacks of the Century*.[31] The thought of becoming prey got my adrenalin going. I looked around carefully to make sure there weren't any cubs or momma bears nearby, since I was now in this bear's territory.

Spiders had built webs across the trail and my face and glasses kept finding them. I met a northbound hiker, the first I'd seen all day, and he looked at me curiously. Then he said, "Excuse me," and reached to my face and picked a worm off the edge of my glasses. We both watched as he held the thin silk string and the worm slowly descended to the ground.

I climbed Crocker Mountain (elev. 4228 feet). The sun was fully up and shining down on the north end of the peak, so I took my tent from my pack and stretched it out to dry. When I got going again, a "rat-a-tat-tat" sound announced the presence of a pileated woodpecker. When I stopped and turned to try to locate it, I saw on the ground the moving shadow of a bird's wings and looked up to see if I could find its source, but couldn't. I doubt the bird was conscious of causing a shadow. I admired the mushrooms, which had pushed their way through decaying leaves. The large number of frogs that crawled and jumped along the path was amazing. Step by step, I realized that not trying to control or predict what is coming gave me freedom to live in the moment. In *Star Wars*, when Yoda is trying to teach Luke Skywalker, he complains, "You are always in the future and not in the present."

I'm often unable to enjoy the present moment because I'm worried about something in the past or have some anxiety about something in the future. A prayerful state of mind helps me live in the moment that is present. As I walked I listened and acknowledged the sound of my footsteps and the scrape of my hiking sticks on the rocks. Sometimes I get into an endless, repetitive loop of thoughts where I beat myself up for some decision I made. It's as if my mind has trapped me and I forget to savor the moment. Breathing in and out deliberately sometimes helps me to disengage from the cycle of ruminating and returns me to the present. What a gift it is to relish the amazing beauty and wonder of the moment and not fall into the trap of worrying about foolish troubles. It's clear that we sometimes worry about the wrong things. Annie Dillard reminds us of how invigorating self-forgetfulness is when we are able to simply be in the wilderness without self-awareness. She quotes a Hasid master as saying that when we walk across the fields with a pure and holy mind "then from all the stones, and all growing things, and all animals, the sparks of their soul come out and cling to you, and then they are purified and become a holy fire in you."[32]

I was delighted to meet an older couple from California whose trail names were "Goodness" and "Mercy." I assumed they took them from the 23rd Psalm: "Surely goodness and mercy will follow me…" I wondered if other hikers joked when asking about this couple: "Have you seen goodness?" "Yes, Goodness and Mercy have followed us for all these 2000 miles." Most hikers find their own pace, and with this couple the husband was a faster walker than his wife. All along the trail he would sketch their symbol in the dirt, or make a sign with sticks or rocks to encourage his wife and other hikers, and then the couple would meet at a designated place for the night. I thought this simple act of caring was endearing.

I enjoyed building prayer cairns, and sometimes the shapes of the rocks I found would call forth certain people. When I left Alabama, Thomas was on a ventilator in ICU, and the cairn I build for him was shaped like a "T."

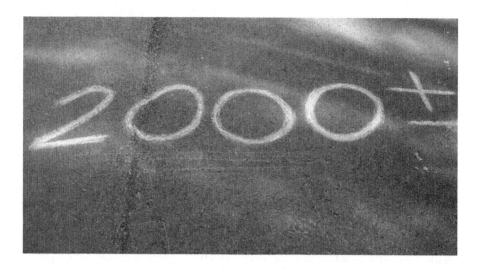

When I found a rock shaped like the space shuttle, I prayed for all those working to support space exploration and, specifically, the astronauts living on the International Space Station. The prayer cairns also remind me to be respectful of the sacred yearnings of the thousands of hikers who have walked the same paths.

Around 4:30, I arrived at a campsite on the south branch of the Carrabassett River. Although I wanted to go farther, and had the energy to do it, the next shelter was another five miles and I'd have to cross both the steep Sugarloaf and Spaulding Mountains to reach it. At the mile-an-hour pace I was hiking, it would be 9:30 and very dark before I arrived, so I decided to stop after a day's hike of only eight miles. After I had pitched my tent, I jumped to a rock in the middle of the river and said my night prayers while water rushed all around me. I then sat on a rock at the river bank where the water was calm, and was surprised to see long-legged water striders glide across the surface to check me out. Dozens of them came close, stayed awhile, and then turned around and zipped back to their resting place. Birds gathered in the trees and sang loudly. When I finally spotted them I was surprised at their small size. Unlike the night before, when I ate alone in the restaurant, I was overcome with the feeling of belonging. I savored the time in God's wild sanctuary.

Having time on my hands, I decided to engage in more prayer, and to move from a contemplation to a centering prayer, which is a prayer that is used to empty the mind of all thoughts. I got comfortable on the rock and focused on my breathing and on relaxing my body. Then I focused on relaxing my tongue. When thoughts and questions came to mind, I let them pass as if they were a boat floating down the river. Soon I was just breathing and existing. After about 20 minutes, I opened my eyes and began to take note of the river and birds. I felt refreshed and content. For supper that night I enjoyed spaghetti. The sounds of the rushing water filled my body as I went to sleep.

DAY

18

Not in Control

South Branch Carrabassett River
to Poplar Ridge Lean-to

The sun was out and the birds were singing as I climbed Spaulding Mountain. At the summit I met a disappointed weekend hiker who had scaled the mountain because he thought he could add it to his list of 4000-foot peaks he had climbed. When he got to the top, the sign said the elevation was only 3988 feet rather than what the *Thru-Hikers' Companion* had promised.

"Somehow the mountain lost 12 feet," he said, shaking his head.

He was the first of several people I met who were working on joining the "4000 foot club" by climbing all the peaks in New England.

An unusual phenomenon I noticed on Spaulding's peak was the survivor trees. Their trunks had been brought close to the ground and then had turned to grow up toward the sky. With their trunks bent low at first and then extending straight to the sky, they looked like a group of ostriches. Seeing the bent trees reminded me of the pine forest next to my grandparent's farm in Georgia. When I was small boy, my grandfather took my sister and me inside the woods and pulled down tall thin pines and tethered them to the ground for us to ride as "tree horses." In those days we would visit our grandparents monthly, and if we ever acted bored, they would suggest we go ride our tree horses. These pines stayed in this position and would match our growth year after year to carry us.

I built a prayer cairn near the survivor trees to give thanks for the spirit of surviving trauma and loss. After the 1994 tornado, a counselor spoke to those of us who remained in our church. He took a wheelchair and put it on one side of a room, opposite the stage at the other end. He said that the wheelchair represented not much healing and that the stage represented healing. He invited us to stand at the point between them that marked where we thought we were in the healing process. Most people stood in the middle, but I stood behind the wheelchair and said, "My healing has yet to begin." One of the things that helped us was to claim that we were tornado survivors rather than tornado victims. This change of words was empowering.

Forests are always changing, with trees in various stages of life and birth. Trees and limbs will fall and sometimes obstruct the trail. In some cases, such as when one tree falls into another, a trunk is left hanging across the trail. In a dense forest there are not many healthy limbs near the ground because not enough light gets through to support that growth. The part of the tree at the top where the branches shoot out is called the crown. If the crown falls across the trail, it usually creates an obstacle that hikers have to walk around, but often it's only the tree trunk that has fallen across, and hikers then face its challenge.

A friend of mine attends a large, formal Episcopal church where the older African American pastor commands the congregation to "Bow to the Lord." When he says it, the presidents of companies, janitors, doctors, and the homeless all pull out the pads in their pews and kneel down in respect and adoration of God. On my hike, I began the practice of saying "Bow to the Lord" and nodding and lowering my eyes in reverence whenever I encountered a tree leaning across the trail. It was a fun and good practice. Occasionally, when the trail required extra attention and I was looking down, I ended up smacking my forehead on the tree or limb that stretched across my path. When I initiated bowing before the Lord, there was no pain, but when I did not, I was left with a tender reminder.

The act of physically bowing mirrors an inward humbling, and it is a good reminder that we are not in charge or in control. Communities are not in control of tornados, weather, or the behavior of others. I need times in my life to bow. When we lived in Vilnius, Lithuania, we often saw pilgrims moving on their knees to the chapel of the Black Madonna in the old town. It was a way they could offer themselves before the grace they wanted to receive.

On an unconscious level, all changes in life require a willingness to leave the comfort of our former lives. Henry David Thoreau spoke of the sacrifice needed if we are truly ready for a walk. He wrote, "If you are ready to leave father and mother, and brother and sister, and wife and child and friends, and never see them again; if you have paid your debts, and made your will, and settled all your affairs, and are a free man; then you are ready for a walk."[33] Jesus called the disciples to leave their mother and father if they were to follow him (Matthew 19:29). God wants all of our lives, not 90 percent of them. This is clear from the story of the rich young ruler. He had given most of his life to God, but Jesus wanted 100 percent. The young man went away, very sad. He was still a good, faithful person, but not a saint. Thoreau also spoke of walking as "sauntering," which has to do with being a pilgrim. For us to be pilgrims who seek rebirth and new life, we must be ready to make a sacrifice. A question I might ask is, "If I want to grow spiritually, am I willing to humble myself and endure the difficulty to offer myself to new learning?"

The hike down Lone Mountain (elev. 3260 feet) was pleasant, and the crisp smell around the Orbeton Stream was refreshing. I forded it at 1550 feet and began a steep 2.7 mile climb up to the Poplar Ridge Lean-to at an elevation of 2920 feet. It seemed to take forever, and I kept thinking, "Surely I should be there by now." However, it was after lunch and afternoon miles are always longer than morning miles. At one point in the climb, I was looking down at the trail and banged my forehead so hard into a log crossing the trail that I landed on my bottom, a little dazed. "I didn't bow to the Lord," I said to myself as I rubbed my forehead.

The lean-to was an older structure with a floor that looked like it was made from baseball bats. They weren't real bats, of course, just round slat-shaped pieces of wood and not the flat planks used in more recent construction. In the shelter was a booklet of facts and trivia written by Dave Field, who, along with his sister, built the lean-to in 1958 and still maintains a section of trail. He mentions that the ridge now has mostly firs and birches because a fire destroyed all the poplars. Before campers carried well-padded sleeping bags, they would collect fir boughs to make the baseball-bat floor softer to sleep on. The "deacon's bench," a long bench at the opening of the lean-to, was a trap to keep porcupines off the hikers.

I pitched my tent on a ridge not far away. As usual, I had forgotten my morning job of hydrating my dinner, so my supper was crunchy and chewy. As I tried to eat, a chipmunk ran under my legs and tried to steal some food. Reflecting on the fact that there were no poplar trees on Poplar Ridge, I began to think about our responsibility to protect the Earth and if we could learn something from the past. In the 1800s, the governor of Maine faced an economic slowdown, so to boost the economy he pushed to sell public lands to the logging industry. The loggers clear-cut the old growth forests and piled up the small treetops and limbs, which later became dry tinder for the great fire of 1823. I don't know if this fire or a similar one caused the extinction of the poplars in this area, but for those who love the Earth, the absence of poplars is a sobering example of how political decisions can adversely affect the natural environment. It would seem to me that caring for our home has something to do with bowing before the Lord. Treating the Earth as holy and with respect is an important part of being a good citizen.

Our children grew up playing on the beach in Gulf Shores, Alabama. They learned to swim in the tidal pools and in the ocean. It was there beside the crashing surf that we watched dolphins and stingrays jump and play, and pelicans and seagulls dive for fish. When I surf fished, large blue herons would stand nearby waiting for their share of whatever I caught. This beach was our family's "happy place." But in the spring and summer of 2010, when I walked on the beach I saw no dolphins. There were no seagulls, sandpipers, or pelicans. The sea air smelled like a gas station. The beach had a six-foot strip of oil that had washed ashore as a result of British Petroleum's Deepwater Horizon oil well explosion, where eleven men were killed and oil freely spewed for three months from the floor of the Gulf of Mexico. Using shells from the beach, I scooped up thick oil and put it into a plastic orange juice bottle that I keep it in my office as a sober reminder of a season when humanity did not "bow to the Lord." After this strip was cleaned up, tiny droplets of oil appeared in the sand. They too were removed, but I fear that more oil will wash ashore in the future.

I tried to imagine the mountains without trees. What would moose eat during the winter if there were no fir needles? Where would the birds make their nests and raise their young? What would happen to the red squirrels, the pine martens, the insects, and all other animals that made their homes among the trees? Was the boost to the economy worth the destruction of a whole forest by fire? It made me contemplate how short-sighted decisions are made in times of desperation. Human nature is such that we're pretty good at destroying ourselves, so regulations and standards seem to be necessary for protecting all of the Earth's species. As the only hiker in this campsite, I both enjoyed the solitude and missed the company. I prayed for wisdom in others and in myself.

DAY

19

Look Up

Poplar Ridge Lean-to
to Highway 4—Rangley

Sooner or later while walking the A.T., hikers will summit a mountain in the clouds and walk in a misty wet fog. From the valley you can see the shrouded top of the mountains, but when you get there, all you can see around you is whiteness. When I left Poplar Lean-to, everything I had was dry—boots, tent, and clothing. But as I climbed up Saddleback, the bushes, trees, and ground were all saturated with moisture. Before I realized it, my clothes, tent, and backpack were soaked.

Saddleback has a very long, rocky ridge above tree line at an elevation of 4120 feet. When I first crawled on all fours across the cliff above the stubby trees, the wind almost sent me back down. It was so strong that I had to tighten the string on my hat to keep it from blowing away. A northbound hiker and I laughed about how others had described the beautiful views from the summit of Saddleback. On a clear day you can see Mount Katahdin, over 214 miles away to the east, and Mount Washington, some 113 miles away to the west, as well as the ocean; but, we were surrounded by misty clouds that were racing east. As a substitute for the view and reward for our fortitude, we both proudly boasted that we had the privilege of walking, slipping, and sliding for 3.6 miles on an ascending trail of solid, smooth granite while clouds and dynamic weather roiled around us.

When we finally reached the Saddleback summit, the wind was so strong that it took me four attempts before I was able to take a photo of the sign, with my bandana flapping beside it to show the power and direction of the wind. I later learned that the wind had caused power outages in the valley below. Tempted to complain or be disappointed by the weather, I stopped myself and said, "Enjoy it! Make the best of it." When I followed cairns down a side trail off Saddleback and found myself at the Sugarloaf Ski lift area, I laughingly opined, "What a treat to see the cool ski area and get to summit Saddleback twice." I retraced my steps and might have entirely missed a beautiful sight if another hiker hadn't told me to look up from the ground.

A hawk was playing in the roaring airstream. It climbed higher and higher and then flew against the wind, testing its power and strength. Among Native Americans, hawks evoke different stories, depending on the tribe. Many see hawks as the guardians and protectors of the Earth. When a hawk flies alone and near a person, it signifies that the person is being called on to play a similar role. My glasses were wet and I could not tell if I was seeing a Red-Tailed Hawk, nor could I hear an eerie and powerful call, which is the call of the hawk but often used when a Bald Eagle is shown on television. The red feathers emerge after several years of maturity, as if the hawk has to earn them. Being so close to the majestic, soaring bird lifted my spirit. Just as the hawk was playing in the wind, and seemed to make the best of it, I, too, had tried to make the best of sliding on the slanted trail and enjoying the dynamic weather situation. I wasn't sure, though, what would qualify me as a hiker and earn me my red feathers.

After I traversed the exposed ridge, dropping below the tree line again came as a welcome relief that offered protection from the bitter wind. I sat on a rock and had a snack while gazing upward at the trees. Taking deep breaths in and out I meditated on the air entering my lungs and the oxygen moving into my lungs, blood supply, and body; I thought about nature slowly cleaning what I exhaled and returning it fresh and renewed to the world around me. What is the appropriate prayer and attitude toward plants and trees which filter and cleanse the air we breathe? A warm feeling of love flooded my heart, and the words "thank you" issued from my mouth. I was grateful not only to the trees that surrounded me, but to the wisdom of the people who fought to protect and manage the forests.

A high school teacher in her forties from Rangeley had brought some students on a hike up Saddleback. I learned that they had lived at the foot of the mountain for years but had never climbed it. Today, through her encouragement and guidance, they were getting to know the mountain from another perspective. The students enjoyed the challenging hike, and I could tell this would not be their last time on the trail. "We want to come back in nice weather," volunteered a bright-eyed 16-year-old boy. When I asked why he had not come before he said, "I never had anyone to show me the way."

By the time the trail dropped down to the Piazza Rock area (elev. 2065 feet), the air smelled of rain. The teacher had told me to spend time exploring the forest's many rocks and cave formations, but as interesting as that might have been, I was eager to get to Rangeley before the downpour started and continued hiking downward.

Along the way, I met several men who were going on an overnight spiritual retreat at Eddy Pond. They toted large cotton sleeping bags, clumsily rolled and without any rain cover. One man carried his snack and sleeping bag in a grocery bag. Their plan was to camp out in the elements and commune with nature and God. Their leader had asked that they gather together by the pond to talk before heading off alone to spend the night in silence. I affirmed the value of their goal and told them that I had received many gifts from nature, but I couldn't help thinking that they would fare better on a calmer night.

"You know, there's supposed to be a big storm tonight. Do you have a plan to stay dry and warm?"

One of the men replied, "I'm up for an adventure."

Wishing them an insightful night, I walked on, worried for their safety. They looked a bit naïve to me, and without tents or ground cloths they could have an especially difficult time. I was still coughing after my adventure of sleeping tentless under a ledge in the pelting rain.

The common phrase among northbound hikers "No rain, no Maine" came to my mind as I was hiking to Rangeley to seek shelter from the storm. Because it was Saturday, it would be two days before I was able to get my next food package from the post office, which meant I would be staying for two nights in a hotel on Rangeley Lake. I was looking forward to nursing my cough with hot tea and sleeping in a bed.

When I got to the parking area at Highway 4, the driver of a utility van loaded with hikers was about to head to Rangeley. He saw me coming and kindly waited, and then lifted my pack onto the roof while a fellow hiker grabbed my arm and pulled me into the van. I sat on the floor, squeezing in with everyone else, grateful for getting a lift, and trying not to breathe the awful smells emanating from the group.

When we got to the hotel, there were float-equipped bi-planes docked on a nearby lake that had signs next it that boasted of some tours that guaranteed its patrons would see a moose. Most hikers had buddies and shared a room, but I was happy to have a private room where I could dry my tent over the shower curtain and spread my things out. The doorstep made a good place to cook my evening meal. Although I was disappointed that the ice-cream shop and bakery were closed, the hot tea I made in my room hit the spot. After charging my phone, I was able to call home and catch up on family activities. Just hearing Kelly's voice was like seeing a sunflower in a foggy field—it brought me joy and hope. I was feeling more homesick than I'd ever imagined I'd be when I set out. When I told her about the difficult climb across the slick, foggy mountains and about the wind, she was glad I hadn't hurt myself. "Now why are you doing this?" she asked for the umpteenth time. She was worried about my safety and confessed that she had shared this concern with Michael, one of my friends and a fellow hiker from home. He had assured her that I knew what I was doing and could take care of myself, and this relieved some of her anxiety. I told her about the men heading out tonight on a spiritual adventure, and how they seemed unprepared for the situation. I was glad she didn't ask, "Now, how are you different from them?" She said she hoped I had better sense than they did, and we shared a nervous laugh because we both knew that there are never any guarantees in life.

After we said good night, I fell asleep dreaming of seeing a moose from the protection and vantage point of a rainproof airplane. Booming thunder woke me up and rain beat on the window. I thought about those men on their overnight adventure.

DAY 20

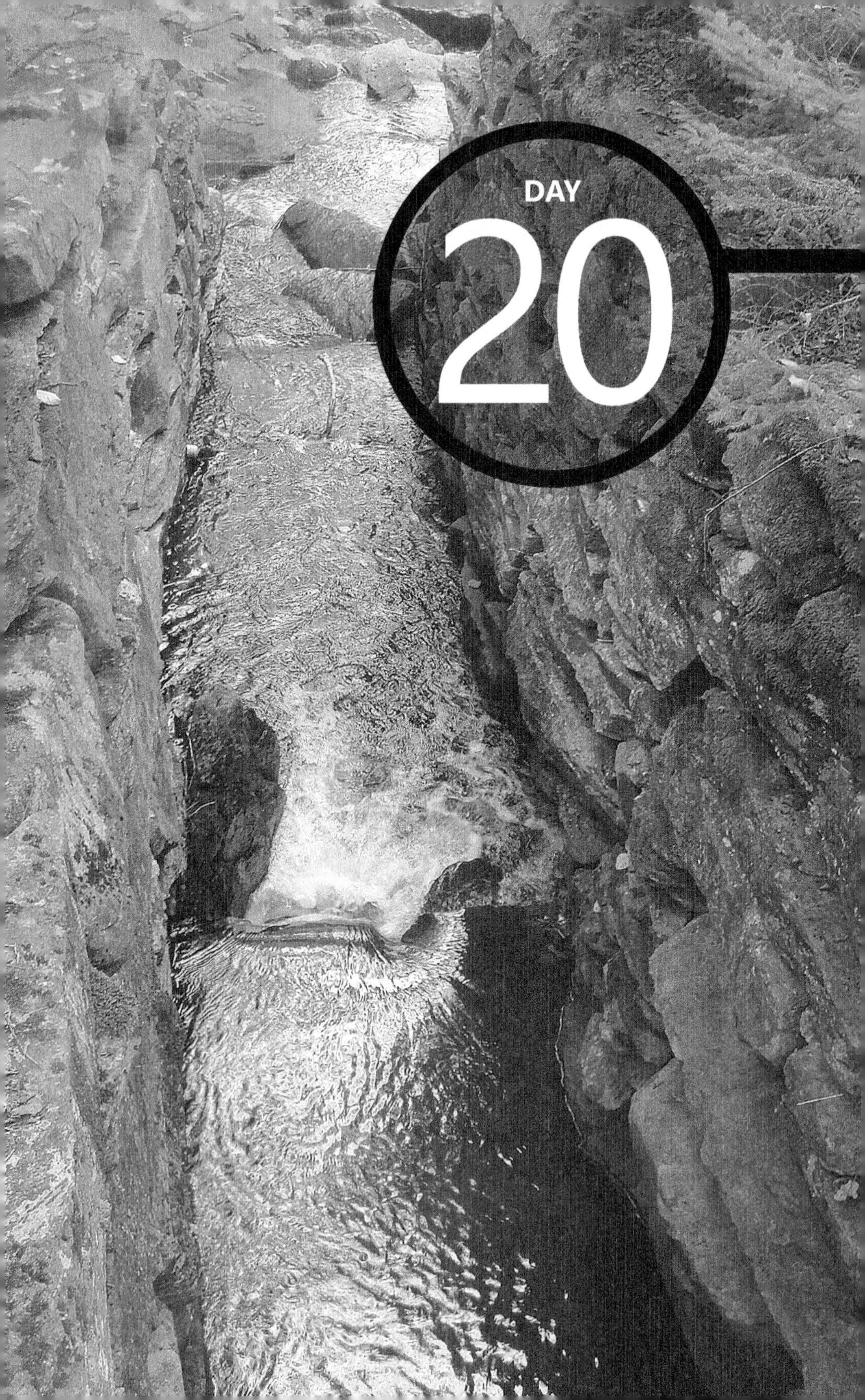

Sabbath

Rangley

The next morning, the storm had passed and sunlight poured into my room. I walked outside on the moist bright green grass that glistened in the light. The air smelled clean and crisp. "What happens in a thunderstorm to make the air smell so different," I wondered. My eyes were drawn to the calm lake. Even the birds seemed asleep, huddled together on a tree near the water. I was surprised at how quiet it was. At home, like so many busy people nowadays, when I wake up in the morning I usually kick into overdrive and rush from one activity to the next, barely pausing to eat, and then I fall into bed, exhausted. If the Rangeley Post Office hadn't been closed on Sundays, I would probably would've hit the trail, would've given in to continuing in haste. St. Benedict said, "Nothing is so inconsistent with the life of any Christian as overindulgence," and advised us to create a balance between work, prayer, rest, and community.[34]

If you are looking for a place for renewal, recreation, restoration and rest, there are many places worse than the beautiful shores of Rangeley Lake. On this Sunday, it was so quiet it was as if the town, at least near my hotel, had successfully resisted our American addiction of always being busy and over-consuming. Every store and restaurant I saw was closed.

Without an agenda, I was free to schedule my hours in a fashion that might please Benedict. I began the morning by worshipping at the Church of the Good Shepherd Episcopal church. It was beautifully nestled next to the lake and just down the street from my hotel. I estimated that the church was built in the 1970s. It had a modern interior, with light-colored wooden pews. It was simple and unadorned, except for a colorful stained glass window that featured Jesus as the Good Shepherd, with crook. The 50 or so older townspeople only filled half the sanctuary. One family with children and another of a father with a teenage son were doted on by the elders. Surely Rangley has more families with children, but they were not at this service. The church had opened its doors to some hikers who were looking for refuge from the storm, and they had slept in the basement. Two came to the service and were easy to spot because of their clothes and unkempt hair.

The sermon was given by an older lay woman who shared how she had experienced God's grace through the loyal companionship of her pet dog. It was sincere and lovely, but the scripture I would have loved to hear her discuss was from Matthew 11:28: "Come to me, all you that are weary and are carrying heavy burdens, and I will give you rest." Pondering the literal heavy burdens that I'd carried for 20 days had been easy. The hard part was meditating on "rest."

Afterward I visited with Father Jud in the coffee and refreshment time, and we discovered that we had a mutual friend. It was indeed a small world. He asked me if there was anything I needed and I suggested a ride back to the trail the next morning. I planned to be at the post office around 8:30 and figured I would be ready to head out around 9:00.

He winced because he was planning to be fishing with a church member in the morning. He made no promises, but he did say, "We will see."

I began walking back to the hotel, hoping to find a doctor or pharmacy that could give me some medicine for my cough. So far, none of the drugs I had taken seemed to help. This included a round of antibiotics prescribed by my doctor at home that Kelly had brought me on her visit, and I was still miserable. A gas station was my only option, and without much hope I bought something over the counter.

As I was leaving the station, a car drove up. Inside was one of the men I'd met the day before, the one who'd wanted an adventure and been heading out for a night in the woods. His red eyes and frizzled hair told part of the story. The rest came when I greeted him and he recognized me. He had stretched out under a large cedar to watch the rain and lightning, and the tree had kept him dry for a while. Then he decided that he needed to sit up if he was going to watch the raw power of the thunderstorm, and he got comfortable leaning back against the trunk of the tree. However, unable to sleep this way, and wet, he eventually left his sleeping bag and made his way in the dark to the rest of the group. Since he was already wet, and couldn't get any wetter, he had decided that being in rain didn't matter. His main problem was being cold. Fortunately for him and his friends, their leader had a large dry tent, warm coffee, and enough dry blankets to prevent hypothermia.

Glad they had survived without mishap, I asked him, "Would you do it again?"

"No need," he replied.

Because no diners or restaurants were open, I went to my room, wrote in my journal, and took a nap. When I woke up, I was very hungry and walked down the highway to a bowling alley that served food. It also had Wi-Fi, so I turned on my phone and began to read emails. Before I left home, I set up an automatic email return with a message that said I would be on Sabbatical and not answering emails for 40 days. Somehow, this automatic return had met the automatic return of another email and created some kind of loop, and now there were hundreds of messages that had bounced back and forth, which made checking email on my phone frustrating and overwhelming. I wanted to rest so I went back to the hotel.

In the room I experienced Sabbath restlessness like an itch that I couldn't scratch. Sometimes spiritual restlessness can be a call from God toward a home beyond this world. In this sense, agitation can be considered a gift from God. "What is the source of my restlessness?" I asked. Was this restlessness a red flag that was signaling me to examine my priorities?

The balance, Benedict advised us, included community, and this was something I lacked. A good deep conversation or connection with someone would have been nice. The occasional camaraderie I had had with northbound hikers was missing in the hotel. The stimulation of hiking and meeting a daily goal gave me something to do, and simply relaxing alone did not restore my spirit.

There is a meditation we sometimes do at our church in which we use the phrase, "Be still and know that I am God" from Psalm 46:10. With each breath, we repeat the phrase and drop off a word until at last the prayer is simply "Be." As I prayed "Be," memories of the hike flowed into my consciousness. The "Be" I had been living was a watchfulness in motion.

When I was on the trail, I always rose early and began hiking, fully expecting to see a porcupine, moose, or hawk. I wanted to be awake to the mysteries of death, life, and rebirth. I asked, "What did the spider catch in its web during the night?" Each day she weaves a new web across the trail. When I walked into spider webs, I apologized and tried to get the spider back home, but I knew it could usually take care of itself. The more I was in the forest, the better acquainted I became with the stories of the trees. I had learned, for example, that a shelf-like fungus called a polypore on a trunk indicates that the tree is dying. The polypore is a maze of fine hairs that eventually bore through the bark and into the tree. As the polypore grows, the hole it creates opens the possibility for insects, such as beetles, to enter the tree, further adding to its decline.

The ostrich-shaped trees, which had obviously survived a major trauma, were a testament of the spark of a life, which endures. The shell that dangled from the Green Giant reminded me of the longing for transformation. When Jesus explained to his disciples that he was leaving them, he said, "You may weep, but it will turn to joy like a woman in childbirth. There is pain but it turns into joy." Even the dying tree will support life by a process of giving itself away. Once it has died, many types of new life will benefit.

That evening in my room I remembered that I had downloaded some books into my phone, and I thought, "Yes. That's it. I long to read." So I began Annie Dillard's *Pilgrim at Tinker Creek* and fell asleep with a smile on my face.

DAY

21

Ordinary Days

**Rangley
to Bemis Stream**

The bakery was open for breakfast, and I was the only pack-laden hiker enjoying the food. I wanted to get a haircut, but the barbershop was still closed. I walked to the clinic, but it wasn't open yet, either. The post office was open, however, and I got the box from my family. Kelly and Laurel had packed some special chocolate treats and a warm long sleeve shirt. I walked across the street and stuck out my thumb. I'd been waiting about 10 minutes, watching each car or truck pass, when a car slowed down and I saw the familiar face of Father Jud. He had gone fishing with his friend, changed clothes, and was ready for the day.

"Thank you. You are an answer to prayer," I told him as I placed the Green Giant in the trunk of his vehicle.

At the trail parking lot, I ran into a couple I'd met at the Stafford Notch camp, where we had weathered the big storm from Hurricane Irene together. They were slackpacking to the next road and invited me to join them. I didn't have a daypack to carry my necessary gear, so I declined. Keeping up with them was also a concern since they were a lot younger than I was. I was impressed that the young woman could perform a loon call that would prompt the loons to cross the lake and settle near her. She and her friend had hiked from Georgia, but they had flip flopped at some point and were now hiking south.

It was 10:30 a.m., and frost was still on the ground as I began climbing toward South Pond (elev. 2174 feet). I felt stronger after two nights' rest. The air still felt clean and fresh from the big rain. After hiking about 10 miles I finally arrived at Sabbath Day Pond. I had wanted to stay here because I liked its name, which made me want to relax and meditate.

I took off the Green Giant for a break and noted that the shell and feather still dangled from it, intact. The chorus "Holy Ground" came to my mind and I began singing, "You are standing, on holy ground, and I see that there are angels, all around..." Surrounding me were trees and ferns. The sun's slanted light was shining on the trees and rocks and illuminating them with a special radiance. I looked out at the beauty and said, "You are the light of the world—you are holy." I had noticed that when I began treating the trees and Earth as holy that I also began to view them with a new respect and reverence. If we believe God is hidden in the physical world, it changes our relationship to it.

One of my most moving and meaningful worship experiences was on a retreat with young college students. We were in a darkened room with music playing. One by one, the students were escorted to a large cross where they stretched out their arms as if they had been crucified. Another person blessed them by sending a beam of light from a flashlight across their legs, feet, arms, and head to suggest that they were holy and bathed in the light of Christ. Jesus said both that He was the light and that we are the light of the world. Scripture challenges followers to be as holy as Christ.

An A. T. hiker said the hike brought healing and peace to him after his wife died. Why? He claimed he felt close to God on the trail. Could it be that the Spirit of God was within the hiker and that he recognized the God within nature—that he was immersed in the holiness of God? George MacLeod, the Presbyterian minister and founder of the modern Iona community (1895-1991) liked to say, "Matter matters. Whether that be the matter of our physical bodies, the matter of creation or the matter of bodies politic, because the spiritual is to be found at the heart of the material."[35] The pain of the loss was still very present with the hiker, but his world enlarged on the trail, and the pain did not take up as much of his life as it did before. Healing comes more readily for grieving persons when their lives are enlarged around the painful hole of loss. This is one of the gifts of time and pilgrimage that I experienced, too, after the devastating loss of my daughter. (For more on this see my book *Winds of Fury, Circles of Grace.*)

Also relaxing at the pond in the warm sun was a former Peace Corps volunteer who was hiking after her service in Africa. She had closed her eyes, and her backpack sat a good way off. For two years she had lived in constant fear of having her belongings stolen, and after a month of hiking the A.T. she was finally trusting that she could leave her belongings without having to worry that they would be stolen.

It was too soon to stop for the day at Sabbath Pond, so I kept hiking. Four miles later, as it was getting close to sunset, I crossed Highway 17. There I enjoyed an unbelievable view of the impressive Lake Mooselookmeguntic, whose name is an Abenaki Native American word that roughly means "place where moose eat." I was looking around for a moose when I heard an odd noise. I looked towards it and saw a man wearing a ski mask, coat, and gloves. I was sweating in my shorts and t-shirt and was surprised by his appearance. There was something suspicious and a little tragic about him. He told me that he'd been sleeping in a hammock, but it had broken, and since then he'd been sleeping on the ground without a tent and had gotten sick. He thought he had a fever. I told him Rangeley had a clinic and he said he had no money. When I told him there were plenty of lean-tos where he could sleep, he shook his head and said that

189

he couldn't camp with people. I assured him that everyone had bad days and his luck was bound to change. I'd been passing only a few northbound hikers and suggested that he might have the lean-to to himself. He was out of food and I gave him some. As I walked on and heard him cough behind me, I had a growing knot of uneasiness in my stomach. A part of me was really frightened by this guy, and I had a desire to get as far away from him as possible. Another part of me was calm and took him at his word. I hiked over a mile while constantly looking back and stopping and listening. It was a good time to call on St. Bernard, the protector of mountain climbers.

I found a camping place after a tricky crossing of Bemis Stream, whose waters were high because of the recent rains. I found a place where a blown-down tree divided the flow, and I managed to get to the other side by jumping on one of the thick branches and on several rocks. I was camping alone in a spot where people had camped before, but now it was overgrown. I reluctantly trimmed and cleared an area for my tent, telling the small bushes as I whacked away at them, "Sorry, but this is camp maintenance and improvement time." It was dark by the time I finished washing my cooking pot in the stream.

All day I had been thinking about the Native Americans who once lived in this place. I knew it sounded strange, but I thought I could feel their presence and wondered what sounds would come from their camps. I tried to imagine the laughter of the children, the pounding of corn, and the cutting of fire wood. Being alone for so long, the line between my imagination and reality was thin. I decided that the time had come to offer to the spirit of the Native Americans the tobacco that I'd received from my friend Kerry. I gathered some sticks and stones, made a small mound, and sprinkled the tobacco on top. I gave thanks for them and apologized for the changes and death brought by the Europeans. I told them that I was open to any wisdom they might have to offer me. In this low valley between the mountains there was no moonlight, and when I turned off the tiny lamp that I'd hung in my tent after my night prayers, the blackness of the night seemed at its darkest. I tested my vision by moving a hand in front of my face, but could see nothing. There were rocks and pointed objects poking at me from beneath my sleeping pad, and they caused me to think for the umpteenth time, "I've got to get another sleeping system." After a while, I went to sleep listening to the bubbling Bemis Stream.

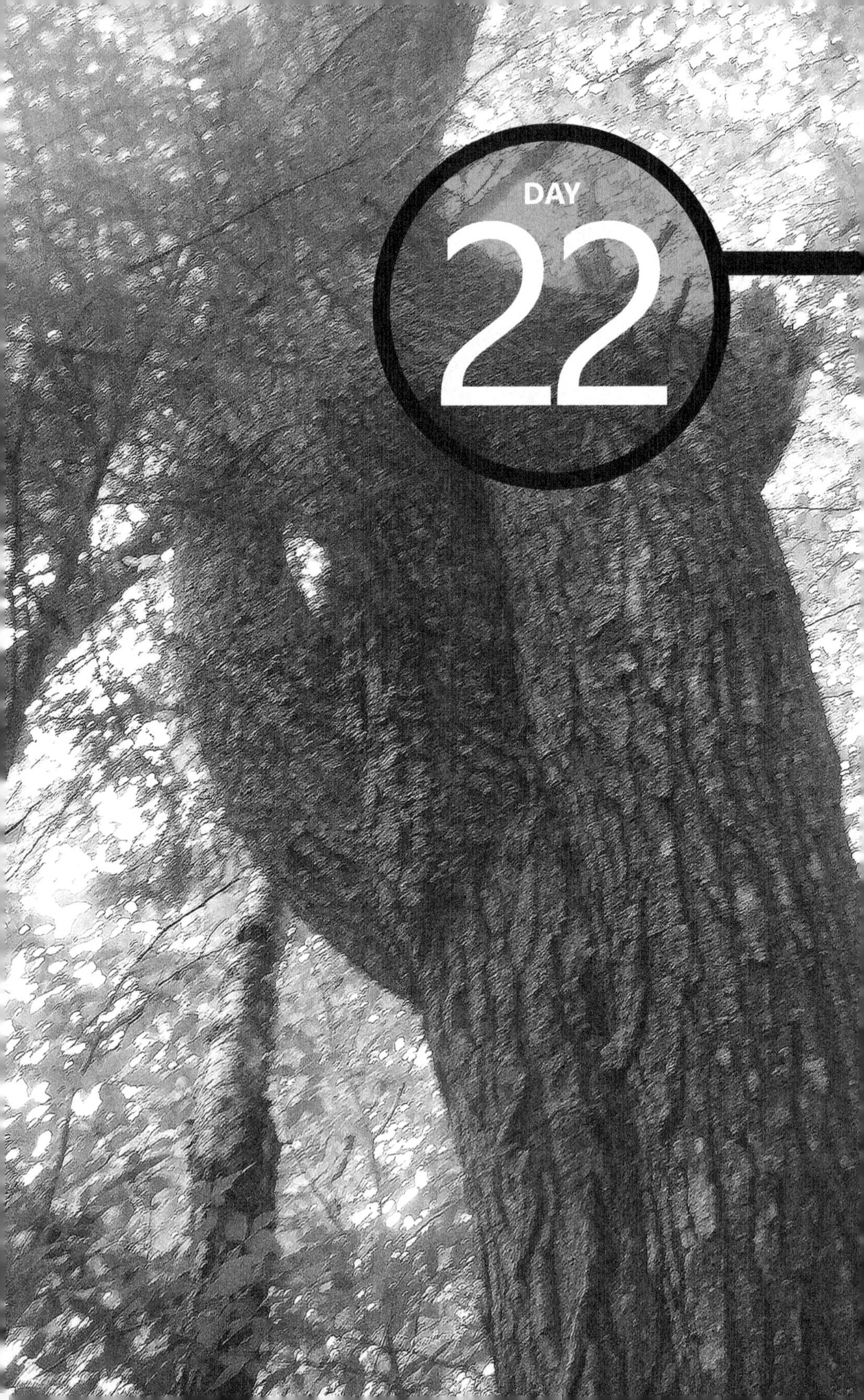
DAY
22

Solitude

**Bemis Stream
to Moody Mountain**

I woke up hearing voices. Who was talking around me? The image that sprang to my mind was of some Native American elders sitting in the campsite and talking in low voices. I strained to hear what they were saying, but I couldn't understand them. Drowsy from a deep sleep, I kept trying to wake myself up. If there were people outside my tent, I needed to be awake. Were the voices from the spirit world? Had I not put the tobacco out? Then I thought that the man I had seen the day before had followed me and was talking to himself, and this sent a jolt of fear through my body. When I was more conscious, I realized that what I was hearing was the sound of the bubbling stream. Was I getting disoriented or hearing ghosts? My rain gear was a pair of pants and a jacket made of some material that felt like paper, and I crammed the set into a little bag and used it for a pillow. When I slept with my ear to the ground, for some reason I was able to hear night sounds from the forest. Some nights I had to change positions so I would not hear the animals outside the tent. If I used my clothes bag as a pillow, however, it muffled the sound rather than conducting it. Having an ear to the ground reminded me that I was sleeping and living in an active mystery.

When it comes to spiritual matters, I wanted to listen to God without all the muffling. When Jacob slept on the ground and used a rock as a pillow he was connected to God's presence. St. Teresa of Avila used a block of wood for a pillow. She saw visions and was connected to the spiritual world, but some accused her of being crazy. Being in the woods for so many days, and being sleep deprived, may have caused me to hear voices, but maybe there were voices to be heard. I fell back asleep and was

193

awakened by honking sounds from the ducks flying over Mooselookme-guntic Lake. I wondered if the fall migration had begun and if the ducks had been flying all night. Soon the loons began to call, and I realized that the air had turned cold. I pulled my toboggan hat down tight to warm up.

Between Elephant Mountain and Old Blue mountain there was a large patch of old growth forest with red spruce trees, which can live more than 400 years. Some trees in this stand have been dated to 1620. Resting among them, I realized that my days in the wilderness allowed me to take a break from the busy world. Gerald May, an American psychiatrist and theologian, calls this "the power of the slowing."[36] Not everyone likes to be alone, but I welcomed solitude. I met another hiker, and he said that when he first started out he was afraid to camp alone at night, but, over time, he'd grown more confident and now enjoyed it. The gift of solitude can be one of the hardest to receive because we often don't want to face ourselves and don't want to be bored. Time alone can be frightening when we live in a culture of distractions. When I was younger, silence was hard to take, but as I've gotten older I've found that silence has its own reward. It gives me a chance to return to the heart—the true center where God meets me. Sometimes prayer has words, and sometimes prayers can be quiet actions where we are simply attentive. It is in solitude where I want to listen not only to nature which echoes God's presence, but to my own thoughts, fears, beliefs, and assurances.

Many times as I hiked in solitude or rested in my tent at night, different anxieties arose, and I remembered the writings of Gerald May. As he was dying, he began to go camping, and in the solitude of nature he learned to give himself permission to accept the nature within himself, whether it was fear, gratitude, imperfections, anger, or love. He named whatever he was feeling and resisted the impulse to run and hide in distractions. In solitude, he came to accept things as they were, including his impending death, without having to judge any of them as good or bad. "Love," he wrote, "is the pervading passion of all things that draws diversity into oneness, which knows and pleads for union, that aches for goodness and beauty, which suffers loss and destruction... Love is the energy that fuels, fills, and embraces everything everywhere. And there is no end to it, ever."[37]

Whenever I felt lonely, I recalled Dietrich Bonhoeffer's words: "Let him who cannot be alone beware of community. He will only do harm to himself and to the community...But the reverse is also true: let him who is not in community beware of being alone."[38] It is in solitude that we learn to receive God's unconditional love, which can be the grounding of our identity, our calling, and our belonging. Without this grounding, we will expect and even demand that others meet our need for approval, a sense of self, and whatever else we are missing. On the trail I tried to rely solely upon God, but had varying levels of success.

As I was hiking up Old Blue Mountain, I chose to accompany a retired couple from Maryland. They had been hiking the A.T. in sections for 15 years. They were slackpacking and each day would exchange car keys with a friend from their hiking club and then meet at a hotel or hostel at night. After being alone for so many days, I was happy to have someone to talk to. At the summit of Blue Mountain, we were surprised to see a row of wind turbines in the distance. We soon came to the South Arm Road and to the couple's car, and they invited me back to the hostel with them for Shepherd's Pie, but I decided to keep going and reenter a state of solitude.

It was good to have people with whom to share the experience, but I just as glad to be alone. I remembered the bright but wounded young man who, after graduating from Emory University, thought life would best be lived in solitude. Christopher McCandless occupied an old rusty bus parked beyond the end of a road in Alaska. After more than a year of living on his own, he felt his season of solitude was over. He packed his backpack and tried to hike to civilization, but was thwarted by a swollen river that became impassible because of spring rains. Stranded in his bus, he now desired community and wrote, "Happiness isn't real unless it is shared." On my hike, I kept coming to the conclusion that solitude is a great teacher, but I wouldn't want to live in it all the time. Often I welcomed it, but after too many days alone, like dead fish, it began to smell bad.

DAY

23

Death and Life

Moody Mountain
to Frye Notch Lean-to

The clearing next to the trail seemed level enough for a tent site, but as I lay in what felt like a bowl, trying to sleep, I wished I had found a flatter spot. Not wanting to limit myself to staying at shelters or to trusting that a place would come when needed, I had found my own spot on Moody Mountain. My hope was to watch a sunset and a sunrise, but the sun had already set when I pitched my tent. Instead of counting sheep, I realized that I was counting the aches in my body: shoulder, knees, feet, hips, finger, and sore throat from constant coughing. I had missed the sunrise, too. When I emerged from the tent after a mostly sleepless night, the sun was already up. I was tired and didn't have much energy when I arrived at Hall Mountain Lean-to some three miles later after hiking a major drop and gain in elevation.

I took a break in a forest thick with fir and birch trees. I set out the bread and wine on a makeshift stone altar nestled among moss. The wind blew lightly and the scent of fir was pleasing. As I meditated on the meal, I was reminded of how the spiritual and material meet in the bread and wine, representing the cycle of life, death, and resurrection. This is a basic cycle for all of life. Several days before at Crocker Mountain South Peak, I had stopped to dry my tent in the sunshine and used the fir trees as a temporary clothesline. It was a gorgeous day, and the sunshine felt good as I looked out at the Sugarloaf Range with its ski runs and antennas. Spaulding Mountain, which I was about to climb, looked awesome and, as usual, seeing my destination across a stretch of valley made it look too far away to reach in a day's walk. I cooked some soup for lunch and gazed at the beauty before me. Then I was startled to notice that closer, on a nearby limb, was the skull of a moose. The animal must have died on the nearby ground and someone hung this part up. An A.T. thru-hiker drowned the month before in Pierce Pond, some 40 miles away. A few years earlier, a female woman hiker drowned while attempting to ford the Kennebec River. Even on the clearly marked trail there is the cycle of life, death, and resurrection. Often at the end of the day, with my knees swollen and my feet sore with blisters, I'd think, "I won't be hiking the next day." But during a night of rest, my body healed itself; so the next morning, I started out again.

The violence in the world and the violence in nature all share the same cycle. The pile of blue feathers I found on the trail, the owl pellet with the teeth and fir—this is the world in which we live. The mushrooms which brought me delight were now covered with white fungus and were deteriorating. Dead trees lay everywhere in various stages of decay. Leaves were changing colors in their annual cycle. Nature mirrored the same natural cycle as the bread and wine. All around me I saw signs of the cycle of degeneration: the mushrooms, trees, feathers, and the very mountains

and streams themselves. Our culture, so fearful and separated from death, would do well to befriend these recurring changes and see them as a natural part of life. Only 10 percent of the American population will die suddenly, in an accident or as a result of a heart attack. The vast majority will die in the cold impersonal rooms of ICUs, hooked up to tubes and machines, rather than at home surrounded by loved ones. One reason is that we fail to face what's happening, and then fail to have the difficult conversations in which we discuss the end of life. As a pastor, I find myself close to people who are in the dying process and I realize how helpful it is to ask, "Do you think you're going to die?" Usually the person wants to talk about death, but is not given permission because family members believe the best way to show their love is doing everything medically possible to extend life. This lack of communication can result in painful interventions that only extend the quantity, but not the quality of days.

According to Dr. Monica Williams-Murphy, an emergency medicine physician, the ER of a hospital is not the place to have these conversations.

If we can welcome death as a visitor to our family's table, we can prepare the kind of legacy we want to leave. We can make decisions ahead of time about the types of medical care we'll receive, the procedures we don't want to undergo, and where we wish to die. In our important conversations with family and friends we can include the phrases, "I'm sorry… forgive me…I forgive you…I love this about you…thank you…it meant so much to me when you…this is what I've learned in my life…and good-bye." Loved ones can give permission to their loved one to leave by saying, "I'll miss you, but it's okay to die." Often such permission frees the dying to let go and have an easier death. By not resisting the natural dying process, we'll be able to have better deaths at the end of our days.[39]

Seemingly unaware of the cycle of life and death were some teenagers I met on the trail from East B Hill Road to the Fry Notch Lean-to. When I got to East B Road, I was worried about running out of food. The teens were playing a game at the creek and just being kids. I left them and hitched a ride to a store for medicine and food and paid a shuttle to take me back to the trail. The group of youngsters were still messing around at the creek, laughing and playing. When they decided to get going again,

I joined them and hiked with different ones over the course of the next several hours. They would get distracted and dawdle, and I would hike on ahead. I was already at the campsite and in my tent saying my night prayers when they arrived, laughing and talking loudly. I was happy for their joy and excitement and covered my ears to block it so I could sleep.

GOOSE EYE TRAIL

GOOSE EYE

SUCCESS POND

AMC

MAHOOSUC TRAIL

(APPALACHIAN TRAIL)

← CARLO COL TRAIL   1.8
← CARLO COL CAMPSITE 2.1

Signs

**Frye Notch Lean-to
to Speck Pond Shelter**

One of the lovely surprises of hiking in Maine is hummingbirds. The first time I saw them was when I was taking off my pack at the edge of Nahmakanta lake and several flew up to check out my yellow sleeping pad bag. As I walked around a pond, I sometimes heard a familiar buzz and wasn't sure if the sound belonged to the many dragonflies or to the hummingbirds. Dragonflies are brightly colored and agile, but hummingbirds brought with them the gift of contagious joy, playfulness and lightness of life, which helped me alleviate my negativity. As tiny as they were, I couldn't help but smile as I watched them. Their long distance flights were impressive and their curiosity and courage made me feel alive. This section of the trail also had many grasshoppers that jumped at my feet and on my legs. At one point there were so many that when I passed it was as if a huge chain reaction, like a wave in a football stadium, greeted me, and I felt part of their world. Peter Levine says that we only feel really alive when our ancient instincts are engaged. In modern times, we rarely have an opportunity for this kind of raw experience in the wilderness.[40]

While hiking up West Baldplate Mountain (elev. 3662 feet), I was followed by a cloud of yellow butterflies, or moths. The granite flows brought Psalm 62:2 and Psalm 18:2 to mind: "The Lord is my rock, my salvation." The smooth granite was secure just as the Divine is rock solid. However, climbing up and down the slanted slopes was dangerous. Afraid, I prayed, "He will not allow your foot to slip; he who keeps you will not slumber" (Psalm 121:3), and, "If I should say, 'My foot has slipped,' Your loving kindness, O Lord will hold me…" (Psalm 94:18), as well as, "My feet almost slipped…" (Psalm 73:2). It was a glorious day and I felt so happy to experience it.

The Psalms of course were not about literal rocks but about staying near to God and the moral life. The Psalmists prayed that they would not slip down a path and fall into sin. But as I took little steps up and down these granite flows, I enjoyed embracing their literal meaning: "Lord, do not let my feet slip! You are my Rock and my Salvation." In Biblical times, there was a curious and comforting belief that each of us has a guardian angel. When Jesus talked about treating children with respect and care, he indicated that the little ones had angels watching over them (Matthew 18:10). There was also the notion that churches had angels or spirits in the heavenly sphere which influenced the earthly congregations (Revelation 1:4). With these beliefs in mind, I built a prayer cairn to give thanks that, so far, my feet had not stumbled. Balancing on the cairn were stones for my children, my church, and myself, and I imagined my cairn refreshing the alertness of our guardian angels, in case they had fallen asleep.

I was enjoying my lunch by the parking lot kiosk in Grafton Notch State Park when a day hiker arrived from the woods. He visited with me and gave me a cold drink to go with my lunch. He told me to climb the fire tower on top of Old Speck Mountain and look down into the Mahoosuc Notch. I'd love it! After I had made use of the trash cans and privy, I began the 3000-foot ascent up Old Speck Mountain and met a woman with bloody and bandaged elbows and legs and terrified eyes. She was being guided by a man with a grey ponytail who reminded me of Gandalf from the Lord of the Rings.

He asked me about my hike, and when I told him about spending 40 days in the wilderness, his response was, "It's a worthy goal."

The woman said, "I hope you have an angel in flesh or spirit to help you through the Notch." She pointed to the man and said, "He's my angel."

He had found her paralyzed with fear and bleeding in the Mahoosuc Notch and was leading her out to Grafton Notch to take a break from the trail. As we parted ways, I thought of the feather hanging from the Green Giant; and I thought of the angels or spirits which come to our aid when we need them.

I debated whether I had the energy to take a side trail to the summit of Old Speck and decided I did. My walking prayer up the mountain had changed from "Peace with every step," to repeating, "I can do all things through God who strengthens me." I reached an overlook, and as I started to take off the Green Giant to rest, the shoulder strap hit my watch and knocked off the small round pin that connected the band to the time piece. It was easy to locate my watch on the ground, but finding the small pin was difficult. I was crawling on all fours, searching for the small, shiny, half inch needle in the midst of gravel, leaves, and grass. "Who is the saint to help find lost things?" I muttered to myself. At the time, I couldn't remember that it was St. Anthony, so I prayed "Saint, you know who you are. Come around. My pin is lost and must be found." To my amazement, I found the pin under a leaf and was filled with a rush of gratitude. The feather swung around as I lifted the Green Giant to my back.

I hiked a little farther to the peak and climbed the fire tower. It was well worth the extra effort, and I was glad I'd taken the side trail. The sun was out and the sky was blue. Gazing down at the Speck Pond Shelter and the Mahoosuc Notch, and across to Goose Eye Mountain on the opposite side was an arresting sight, worthy of a picture postcard. I took a number of photos, hoping to capture the beauty surrounding me. I tried to imagine how notches were created some 15,000 years ago by global warming. Melting ice lakes sent pressurized water and sediment scraping like sandpaper across the rock. Scientists say the ice sheet extended from Maine to Alaska. When the glaciers finally melted, the vegetation was able to grow again into what I was seeing. I was tempted to set up my tent near the fire tower but decided I needed water, and I wanted to give myself as much time as I needed to climb through the notch the next day. In good weather this mountain top would be a great place to see the sun rising and setting, and the Milky Way.

A gentle breeze blew, and I sat contemplating the hike and the shift in my walking prayer. I was too exhausted to pray for peace and the virtues and had begun to doubt I could make this climb on my own strength. It occurred to me that this was the first step in Alcoholic Anonymous: when you realize you are powerless to live on your own, but need a Higher Power. It also dawned on me that around the time I had begun to say the prayer, "I can do all things through Christ who strengthens me" that I also had begun seeing a creamy white moth following me up the mountain. The suspicious part of my brain insisted: This must be the time of year for these creatures to live here. Their presence is not a sign of encouragement from the Spirit world. Your imagination is only making connections of coincidences. The other part argued: If you believe in the spirit world, why not believe that guardian angels are sending a comforting sign that helps you know you are not alone. The white moth could be a confirmation of what I felt about the feather. It occurred to me that I wouldn't take time out of my busy life and wouldn't even contemplate such things if I weren't alone on the A.T. and talking to everything—trees, squirrels, moths. One of the strengths of Alcoholics Anonymous in helping people stay sober is attending meetings where companions and sponsors help keep one from taking a drink. The next time I saw the white moth I grinned and told her, "You can be my sponsor to remind me that a guardian angel is encouraging me."

The hike down Old Speck to Speck Pond was a narrow steep granite walkway with two-foot bushes on either side. I kept thinking, "This is like climbing down Stone Mountain near Atlanta, Georgia, with no steps." By taking small baby steps and sometimes going down sideways, I only fell once.

The caretaker of the shelter was gone for the season, so I didn't have to pay a fee to set up my tent on a platform. The campsite filled and I enjoyed listening to a group of chatty young northbound hikers share their stories. They cooked over a fire to avoid carrying a stove, putting their energy instead, I suppose, into carrying a large food box. Made of tin and shaped like a round ottoman, it doubled as a stool. They discussed recipes and the many ways to spice up Ramen noodles, a trail staple. In contrast, the three men in the shelter who were my age, but from Maryland, were rather quiet. Their notch experience had terrified them. One man said, "We aren't good at jumping boulders. It's outright dangerous." By the time they made it thru the notch, the three lacked the strength to climb up Mahoosuc Arm, and so camped in the woods. They were so exhausted the next day that they only climbed the Arm to the shelter. Back in Maryland they actually worked as volunteers to maintain an A.T. shelter, but this was their first time hiking the trail in Maine, and they found it daunting. Surprisingly, their mood didn't rub off on me. After the last few days of hiking in nice weather, my confidence had grown and I was looking forward to being tested on the toughest mile of the A.T. Perhaps I was eager to prove something to myself.

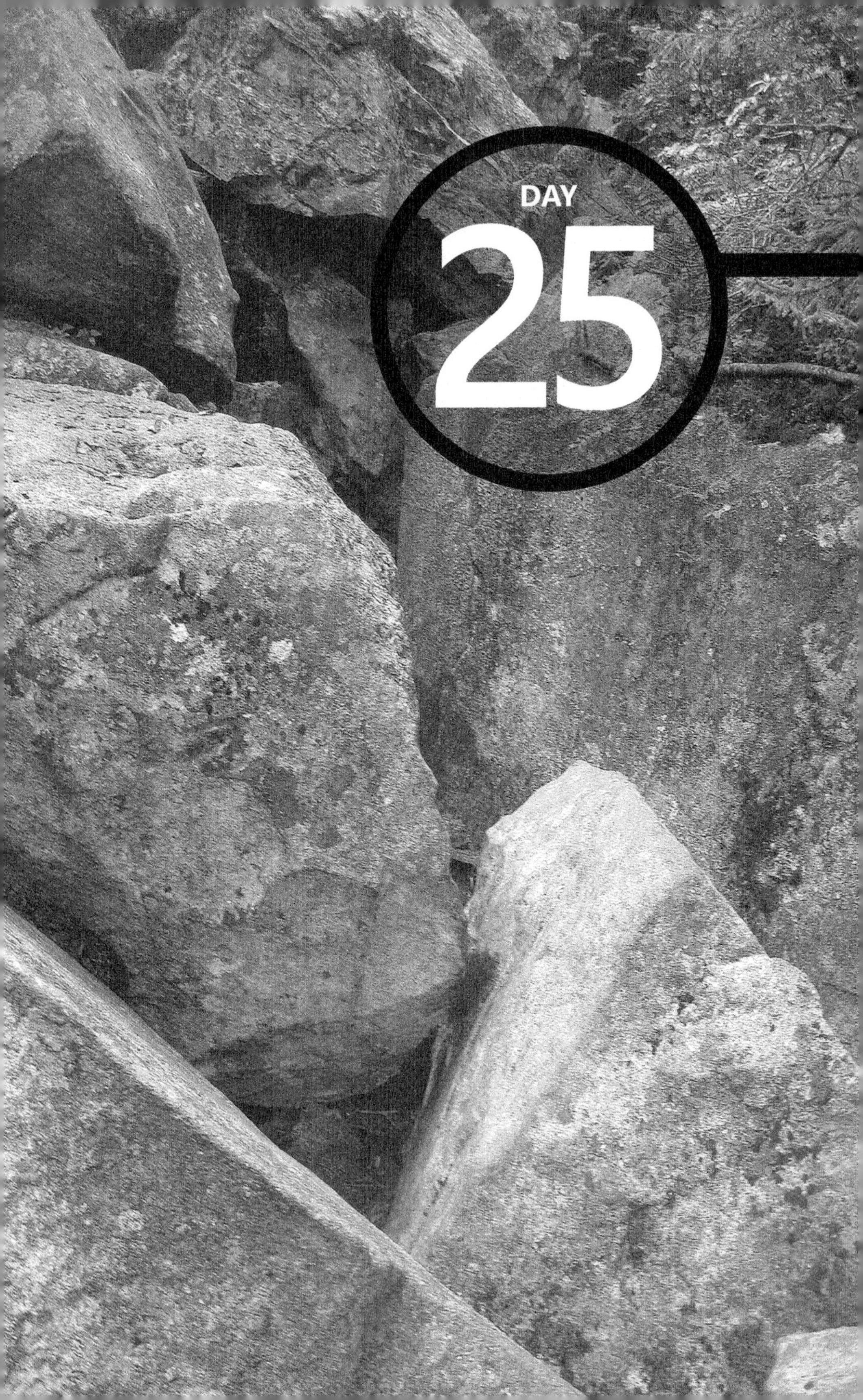
DAY
25

The Toughest Mile

Old Speck Pond
to Carlos Col Shelter

During the night, I slept in shifts. I'd lay on my right side until I woke up with a pain in my hip, then turn to sleep on my stomach, then on my left side, then on my back, and then start the process over again. I felt like I was on a rotisserie, constantly turning. I woke up at 11:30 p.m. and 2:30 a.m., spending a little time reading Annie Dillard's *Pilgrim at Tinker Creek* on my phone before falling asleep again. In the morning, my knees, ankles, and hips were sore, and I packed up as quickly as I could to hit the trail and warm up. At the shelter, other hikers were also getting ready to head out. One of the men from Maryland related the nightmares he'd had about his experience in the notch I was about to tackle. I told him, "I don't need to add your fears to my own," and left before he finished. Another hiker stopped me and suggested I adjust my pack so that my yellow sleeping pad would be on its back rather than underneath it. That way I could sit and slide on my bottom. This turned out to be a very helpful suggestion.

The morning light around Speck Pond was beautiful. The sound of a woodpecker echoed through the forest, and I breathed in the Christmas fragrance of the balsam fir, along with a slight hint of earthy decay. Dragonflies came out to greet me. Everything was fresh and eager to meet the day. Despite feeling energized, it took me took longer than I anticipated to get to the famous Mahoosuc Arm. The trail down the side of the mountain is one full mile of slanted slabs of granite. Like the day before, I took baby steps and sometimes walked sideways to keep from falling. The steady click clack of my walking sticks scraping the rock comforted me.

211

My adrenalin was flowing as I began to negotiate the jungle gym of boulders and holes between two mountains, a pathway notoriously known as the Mahoosuc Notch. I remembered how some hikers encouraged me to relax and enjoy it as you enjoy a playground with an obstacle course. "This is the test—the initiation for the entire trail," one of them told me. I was comforted that I had attached a SPOT Satellite device with an SOS button to the pack strap near my chest. If I did fall and get hurt or stuck, and no one came along to help, I could push the SOS button and a help signal would be sent to a monitoring service, along with my GPS location.

The notch was filled with boulders and 20-foot high piles of rocks that had fallen from the mountain cliffs on both sides. As I started to scramble over them, I realized that getting through successfully would require some flexibility and planning. I had to use trial and error, choosing which rocks to jump over, which to climb, and which to squeeze under or through. When I came to my first major leap, I stopped and took a deep breath. I could hear the running water and feel the chilly air rise from the caverns below. As I stood there, gathering my courage, I thought about Peter, who had a failure of nerve after the crucifixion. He ran for his life and later wept for being a coward. I did not want to be like Peter. I made myself lean forward, saying, "I can do all things through Christ who strengthens me," and jumped. It was like a leap of faith, and the effort was successful and my confidence grew. I began to repeat the prayer over and over again for the next mile as I crawled, climbed, jumped, and squeezed through a number of holes. At times I wondered about the story of these huge boulders. Did they once have eagles build nests on them when they were the high cliffs of the mountain? Did they once feel the weight of a heavy ice sheet? Between the rocks were holes that descended into caves, and I feared falling or slipping through them. That's what happened to Lyman Jackson in 1852 while fishing near Kinsman Notch in New Hampshire. He slipped on a moss covered rock and fell 15 feet down a hole and into what is now known as Shadow Cove. In his case, the story had a happy ending. In his fall, he discovered the Lost River, a 6.5 mile stream in the White Mountains.

All journeys have their difficult stages. In Dante's The Divine Comedy, after descending into the inferno of hell, going through purgatory and climbing the seven story mountain, the pilgrim had to pass through the ring of scathing fire before entering Paradise. I thought of the Mahoosuc Notch as the final purifying test for northbound hikers as they enter the paradise of Maine. Of course, for me, a southbound hiker, it was the testing place that would earn me entry into the White Mountains of New Hampshire. As I traversed the notch, it occurred to me that jumping from rock to rock was familiar. I realized that I'd been preparing all my life for this day, because I've enjoyed climbing and jumping on boulders since I was a kid. This gave me more confidence to take risks. I kept telling myself, "Trust the rocks, trust the rocks, they will hold you up."

When I was not sure how to descend from a boulder, I would sit down on my bottom to slide and catch myself with my feet. The thought of trusting a rock with my bottom made me laugh. As I was finishing

the notch, I met a northbound hiker who was my age, and we talked for about 20 minutes. I would have enjoyed hiking with him, had we been going in the same direction. As I climbed to the South Peak of Goose Eye Mountain my spirit soared. I felt like I had won my own personal victory by completing the notch in three hours, without getting hurt. If David or my family had been there, I would have jumped up and down, shouting with joy.

Full Goose Shelter was a nice place to have a snack and refill my canteens. I had four more peaks to climb before reaching the Carlo Col Shelter. The high mountain bogs above tree level surprised me. There were signs everywhere asking us to stay off the delicate plants, but the wooden bridges were often in disrepair, leaving hikers with no choice but to tread on the fragile vegetation or slosh though black water of unknown depths.. I did the best I could under the circumstances to avoid damaging anything and apologized to the lichen if I hurt them. I arrived at the shelter at 6:30 p.m., just after dark. I had hiked 13 hours. Some hikers greeted me, asking if I had seen the bears. When I told them "no," they said there had been some trouble and I needed to be careful. I set my tent up on a platform, and as I cooked my dinner I wondered if a bear was out there in the night, sniffing and liking what he smelled. When I turned on my light in the tent, I noticed a white moth fluttering inside. I made a mental note to make sure to let it out before I disassembled the tent the next morning.

DAY
26

The Downside of Success

Carlos Col
to Gorham, New Hampshire

The sound of light rain on my tent woke me, and I scrambled out of the sleeping bag. The moth began to stir with me, and I carefully let it out of the tent. Because I didn't want to hike down the granite slopes in the rain, I quickly took down the tent and packed to leave. The morning light sent slanted rays through the forest. A dove was singing its morning call and was answered by another. The confidence I gained from completing the notch lingered on, and I planned to hike to Gorham, N.H. before the post office closed at noon. Not far from the campsite, I stopped in disbelief—the trail was a sheer cliff face. But I would climb it. So, to get a better handhold on the rocks, I removed my wool gloves. The cold weather gave me extra energy, which I quickly expended. I reached a point where I just couldn't navigate up the cliff while shouldering the backpack. After failing to pull myself up over a five-foot section, I decided to take the pack off, toss it up ahead of me, and then follow. It may not have been the best strategy, but fortunately it worked. I repeated the process at another section. This very difficult climb was the "Welcome to Maine" shock that the northbound hikers had told me about, and I was both proud and relieved when I finally made it to the top.

Soon I crossed the state line into New Hampshire. There was a marker indicating that it was not 10 miles to Gorham, but 17! My New Hampshire maps were waiting for me in the Gorham post office, but I wasn't worried about getting lost because on the A.T. all you need to do is follow the white blazes. Of course, it wasn't long before I wished I had a map.

While climbing Mount Success (elev. 3565 feet), I reflected on the meaning of success. A cartoon came to mind of competitive men climbing, trying to get ahead of each other by stepping on each other's necks. When we are young we want to develop our identity through skills, become competent and loving, and to learn to live a moral life. Thomas Merton calls this identity the "false self" because our approval comes from external sources—our accomplishments, degrees, affirmations by others. In this phase we are always trying to become worthy. To build up our ego, we promote, protect, and uphold an idealized self-image, and judge others as good, bad, worthy or unworthy. When we are stuck in this stage of life, we are puzzled why all of our busy activities and hard work don't lead us to joy. Jesus came that we might have abundant life without always having to prove ourselves worthy. According to Richard Rohr, the abundant life happens when we are able to move beyond the "false self" to the "true self." It is a move from the "first half of life" to the "second half of life."[41]

In the second half of life, we discover the joy that God is already within us. We are already worthy and do not have to prove anything anymore. This is expressed in Colossians (1:27): "The mystery is Christ within you—our hope of Glory!" The God within us is called by many names: the soul, the Divine Mystery, Prevenient Grace, or the Truth—the "Truth within us that will be with us forever" (2 John 2). We are a combination of both God and human. Thomas Merton understood this when he wrote, "If I had a message to my contemporaries it is surely this: Be anything you like, be madmen, drunks, and bastards of every shape and form, but at all costs avoid one thing: success…If you are too obsessed with success, you will forget to live. If you have learned only how to be a success, your life has probably been wasted."[42]

With these thoughts in mind, I felt a prayer cairn was needed on Mount Success. For all of us who are driven by ego needs to prove ourselves worthy, I placed on the ground a large brown stone marked with scrapes and indentions. I stacked a stone as smooth as a river rock on top for those of us who use smooth talk and a condescending attitude to put others down. Next came a light colored stone giving thanks for Richard Rohr and other visionaries who help us move beyond the "false self." After looking around, I found a small white pebble which I placed on top to

represent the divine in all of us. I stood for a minute, praying that I would remember, especially when confronted with the challenges of this difficult trail, that there was nothing about myself I had to prove because I was already filled with grace and love.

As I finished putting on the Green Giant, I met a young hiker who had twisted his ankle but was determined to keep hiking in order to be successful. He limped past my prayer cairn without taking notice. Later, I met another hiker who had slipped on one of the many wooden blocks that were fastened into the granite cliffs. He'd been climbing up and fallen, landing on his backpack. He was pretty shaken but still walking. Real success, I thought, is pulling yourself up and continuing after you fall. I noticed that the rain clouds moved on, and the sun burned away the moisture. It turned out to be a beautiful day to hike.

In New Hampshire, the A.T. follows existing trails, and I got confused by this when I came to a sign directing me to leave the Mahoosuc Trail and follow the Centennial Trail. I stood staring at it without understanding

until I got up closer and saw that someone had carved a small "A.T." symbol next to the Centennial Trail. This was my clue to change trails. Both of them would take me to Gorham, but only one was the official A.T. trail. As I reflected upon how confusing these differentiations were, I had to admit that Christian denominations do the same thing. Surely there is a common path to God and salvation, but in our churches we use different images, metaphors, and names for it, and even look down on those with a different approach. No wonder people get so confused and frustrated with religion.

From the path I was on, I saw some wonderful views of the rivers and lakes on the surrounding mountains. The trail I hiked was smooth, but as it wound through forests with old giant trees, I still questioned if I was on my intended route. One of the rivers, the Androscoggin, looks beautiful from afar, but has been badly polluted by textile mills and paper-making factories. The manufacturing plants were considered a success until it was discovered they poisoned the river with mercury and other chemical toxins. I reminded myself not to eat the local fish in Gorham. The trail ended on a dirt road. I wasn't sure of the direction of the A.T., and I wandered up and down until I saw a white blaze and tentatively walked forward.

When I finally reached a paved road, I followed it across a dam on the Androscoggin River (elev. 750 feet) and saw an old power plant. I began to look for the hiker hostel I had heard so much about, and closely observed several houses along the road, looking for evidence of a hostel. Instead, I was greeted by barking dogs. Although uncertain, I kept walking down the road and finally reached a white house with a sign welcoming me to the hiker hostel. It was after dark, and there wasn't a restaurant nearby. After hiking 17 miles over five mountains, I told myself I was too tired to eat anyway. It was the last night that the hostel was open for the season, and inside a group of hikers was celebrating with beer and pizza. I watched their merriment and felt even more alone than when I was on the trail. At least the hot shower brought some pleasure. As I lay down on the bed, I missed my family and remembered the statement of the Alaskan hiker Christopher McCandless, "Happiness is only real when shared."

DAY

27

Rest

Gorham

The hostel served an abundant breakfast around a big table for the last meal of the season, and I was able to visit with some hikers. Then, since the hostel was closing, the host gave me a ride into Gorham to a hotel. I think I woke the hotel owner up because she came to the desk in her housecoat and looked none too pleased to greet me. I knew it was early to check in and offered to leave the Green Giant behind her desk.

She gave it a glance, and maybe smelled it, and said, "I'll go ahead and give you a room."

After I settled in, I decided to look for an 11 a.m. church service and walked through town wearing my Chaco sandals. My feet were happy to be free from boots. I worshiped at an old Congregational church that was preparing to celebrate its past and future with a homecoming the next week. Looking around at the grey-haired worshippers, I hoped it had a future. The interim pastor preached a wonderful sermon and talked about the contributions the church in New England had made throughout American history. He spoke about the pastor and poet Thomas Star King, who wrote about the White Mountains, and about the abolitionist and author Harriet Beecher Stowe, who wrote *Uncle Tom's Cabin*, a classic book about slavery in America.

At the coffee hour following the service, I asked a young man, a fellow visitor who was an intern with the forestry service, if he could take me to Wal-Mart. He wanted to be helpful and offered to wait while I shopped, but I told him I was planning to stay for several hours. I found a pharmacist who suggested a different drug for my cough. I bought it and took some immediately. In the photo department, I uploaded my photos and was told that it would be over an hour before they were ready, which was fine with me. I was in no hurry.

Thoreau said that going to the wilderness gives us a chance to reflect upon what is real and what is trivial. But on this day that Christians reserved for rest, I had left one wilderness for another, the woods for the modern world. Sitting in Wal-Mart and then later in my hotel room in Gorham, I had a chance to reflect on the Sabbath and what keeping it meant, and on how detaching from the world helps us rest in Jesus. "Why is it," I wrote in my journal, "that I wanted to charge forward with the hike and not take a rest day?" The obvious reason was that I didn't have much good sense and was urged on by a myriad of deep-seated fears, including the fear that any deviation in my hiking plan would jeopardize my goal of hiking New Hampshire. So strong was my habit of living a frenetic life that I couldn't give myself permission to rest when one of my goals stood unfulfilled and threatened.

According to Genesis, on the seventh day of creation, God rested and was refreshed. The seventh day is a gift to enjoy and celebrate what God created, and that may be point of the creation. God set aside time simply to be in the presence of creation. Then He bestowed the gift of rest on the seventh day to the Israelites and all of humanity.

Most of us need to be reminded to rest because we are addicted to busyness, which leads us to emotional, physical, and spiritual exhaustion. Technology enables our work to be part of our lives twenty-four hours a day and, for some of us, work controls our sense of self-worth. In order to feel good about ourselves, we must use all of our time being productive at work and at home. Just as businesses argue that they would lose money if they closed on Sunday while their competition remained open, we, too, may worry that we'll fall behind if we take one day off a week for rest and refreshment. In examining new Methodist ministers, John Wesley, the founder of the movement, asked them many questions, including one about how we spend our time: Are you determined to employ all your time in the work of God?... Will you never trifle away time? Somehow, I have taken Wesley's rule more seriously than the Fourth Commandment.

One of my friends attends the services of the Seventh Day Adventists, a denomination that takes the Sabbath very seriously. Our church sometimes hosts a Saturday morning pancake breakfast where neighbors in our community, including my friend, gather to visit and relax. During the week before the breakfast, she'll stop by and prepay for her food. She does this because on her Sabbath she does not carry money, transact business, use the telephone or car, or turn lights on or off. When she greets us, she utters the traditional Hebrew phrase "Shabbat Shalom" to wish us a peaceful wholeness. She often says that our busy lives leave us fragmented and that the Sabbath gives us a chance to take a deep breath and pull our lives together. She likes to explain that rest is not just the absence of work, but a replenishment of the body and soul with good food and sleep. The Sabbath also offers the opportunity to do things that nourish the soul, such as laughing with friends and family and creating some kind of art. The closest thing I can equate to Sabbath is a snow day, when schools, roads and businesses are closed and we are all given permission to relax and play outside.

When I was growing up, my grandparents kept the Sabbath on Sunday. They went to church, ate a meal together as a family, played games, read the newspaper, took leisurely walks or maybe a nap, and visited with family, but they never shopped, hunted, worked in the garden, or mowed the grass.

According to the gospels, Jesus practiced Sabbath rest, but challenged the legalistic interpretation of it when it ignored the needs of the people. In Matthew 11:28-30, Jesus proclaims, "Come to me, all you that are weary and are carrying heavy burdens and I will give you rest. Take my yoke upon you, and learn from me; for I am gentle and humble in heart, and you will find rest for your souls. For my yoke is easy, and my burden is light." For all who carry heavy backpacks, there is a promise of rest. Jesus himself is the resting place. Reading this scripture helped me give myself permission to take a deep breath and be refreshed by the One who is rest.

There is also a certain amount of withdrawal and detachment involved in keeping the Sabbath and focusing on God. Backpacking itself is an exercise in thinking about what is essential and detaching ourselves from daily comforts, and in reflecting upon those heavy burdens which slow us down. With this in mind, walking up and down the aisles and seeing things I wanted but didn't need was overwhelming. In the woods I was satisfied being without most of what Wal-Mart sold. Learning to walk lightly and live simply is a gift, but it may mean that you live without comforts.

I am not the only backpacker who has learned over time to leave chairs, clothes, and hatchets behind. When I first started leading backpacking trips, novice hikers would show up with cans of beef stew and other foods and supplies. I tried to help them by going through each pack and questioning the necessity of every item before we left the parking lot. Now when I lead a backpacking trip, the group has a packing meeting long before we head out. To make what they need to do clear, I hand out packing lists and unpack my own pack, placing an emphasis on lightness and bulk. Of course, there are trade-offs. The lighter your pack, the fewer comforts you'll have at the campsite. But a heavy pack is harder to carry, and can cause more joint pain and injuries, not to mention slow down your pace. On the trail, I continued to trim weight from my pack. Every week I had what I called "a purging" of nonessentials, like the things I'd sent home with Kelly. I'd learned not to take too many clothes, and none made of cotton. When wet, cotton stays wet and won't hold body heat, which can lead to hypothermia; thus the expression, "cotton kills" and "dead man's clothes." Polypropylene clothes are better because when they get wet, they retain body heat while allowing moisture to escape.

I bought a book, *Walking the Appalachian Trail* by Larry Luxenberg, and began reading it in the Subway Restaurant over a long lunch. Then I retrieved my bundle of photos and purchased supplies, and began asking people who were leaving Wal-Mart for a ride back to the hotel. Several looked at me and declined. Then a small man with long pony-tail agreed to give me a lift. Walking across the parking lot with him, I noticed an old car covered with bumper stickers, many of them political in nature. Signs for people running for local offices were stacked in the front and back seats. Just as I was thinking, "Surely, this is not the car," the man pulled out his keys and unlocked it. We left Wal-Mart with me holding political signs in my lap. I was glad he knew where the hotel was because I couldn't see around them to offer any direction. He was delightful and told lively stories about New Hampshire politics from the perspective of a die-hard Democrat.

In my hotel room, I laid out what I had purchased and made two piles. One was the essentials and the other was my "what was I thinking" heap. I decided I needed to go ahead and eat some of the candy so it wouldn't go to waste. In Wal-Mart, I had allowed my "desire" to win out over "need," but I had been depriving myself on the trail, so I felt justified. I wondered if possessing too much stuff was as much a burden in life as it was in backpacking. We become attached to our possessions because so often they are part of our self-image, which we mistake for our essential

selves. Making a conscious and deliberate choice to detach, like purging a heavy backpack and moving forward with what's left, is not an easy task and requires practice and discipline. I have contemplated the statement by St. John of the Cross who says, "If we don't learn to deny ourselves, then we can make no progress in perfection."

If I could practice Sabbath rest each week as the scripture suggests, I wonder if it would both increase the quality of my life and increase my love for God and my neighbors. The desert mothers and fathers of the third and fourth centuries heard the story of Jesus and the rich young ruler who asked what it took to be saved. Jesus told him to love God and his neighbor and to sell his possessions and give them to the poor. These hermits and monks did this because they knew that they could not love

God without loving their neighbor and that they could not totally love God and their neighbor while worrying about the distractions of life. They memorized all 150 Psalms and spent time standing up with outstretched arms reciting these in prayer, making baskets and mats to sell for food, and living very simply like Adam and Eve before the Fall. Streams of persons came to ask their advice and have them settle disputes. They would set a dish with a little money in it outside their door each night in case someone needed it. Choosing to live simply enabled them to have more time to pray for the world and their neighbors. Backpacking forces us to simplify and fully focus on the present moment, and it gives us more time to enjoy God's creation and pray for the world. Backpacking itself is a way of Sabbath living. I have felt guilt for not denying myself enough in my younger years when I was in a stage of trying to make a name for myself. Perhaps I am idealistic and foolish to have this idea, but as I move closer to meeting God, I want to live more simply, keeping less for myself and giving back more to God and the community.

Backpacking can teach us to wean ourselves from our inclination to take only the easy, pleasurable path in our everyday lives. To the Philippians, Paul wrote about people whose highest God was their belly—or feeding their appetites and comforts. We can only learn to rely upon God by eliminating our reliance on these lesser things. Part of spiritual growth comes by wading into the river and going against the strong currents and saying "no" to our unworthy desires. It is a tiring activity and can only be accomplished with strength of will and with the support of God and others. By detaching ourselves from the things we lean on, we have a greater chance to lean on God and experience Jesus as rest. By slowing down and taking a deep breath for a period of time, we have a chance to reconnect the fragmented parts of our lives and seek wholeness and peace.

For supper I treated myself to salmon in the restaurant across the street from the hotel. I hoped it didn't come from the local waters, but decided not to ask. I kept nursing my cough with hot tea and fell asleep.

DAY

28

Entitlement

Gorham
to Carter Dome

It was chilly that morning when I dropped my key into the night box of the hotel office. The patrons of the McDonald's across the street stared at me as I hefted my pack and left. I could see my every breath as I walked to the post office. I retrieved the box of food I had sent ahead and mailed home the photos and the book. As I began hitchhiking to the trail, I wondered who might be my morning angel. It would not have surprised me to see an old car with political stickers stop. After a while, a couple picked me up. They were taking a vacation day hiking in the mountains and knew the location of the trailhead.

The sun shining on the gently sloping trail from Highway 2 South along the Rattle River warmed things up. I was delighted to walk on a carpet of red and yellow leaves and hear them crunch with each step. The Rattle River gurgled along and the mist rose from the water as it rushed by and over the rocks. At one point the trail crossed the river, but I missed it and kept walking on the path that ran along the river's side. After a while I realized I had not seen a white blaze for quite a while. My heart began to beat faster and I calmed myself saying, "You're not lost, just retrace your steps and you'll find the trail." Slowly I backtracked and found the spot where the A.T. crossed the water. I took off my boots and socks, put on my Chaco sandals, and forded the river.

It was a glorious morning for a hike, but a nagging experience with a thru-hiker at the Hostel in Gorham kept going round and round in my mind. A young man with a thin brown beard loudly made fun of section hikers to a room full of people. Music was playing and some folks were dancing, and he shouted out in a shaky high-pitched voice, "Excuse me,

I'm a section hiker. I have to hike five miles." Then he did a slow, mocking, old man's shuffle dance to the music. He insisted that thru-hikers should always have precedence to stay in the shelter and that section hikers should plan to use their tents. I'd heard similar concerns from other thru-hikers who did not carry tents, but their comments were not laced with such an angry sense of entitlement. The young man also spewed negatives about his mother. Apparently she had ruined his hike by sending food and supplies to locations off the trail.

The next morning at breakfast he continued to blame others for the bad times he was having. It all but ruined the meal for the rest of us, who listened patiently. I bit my lip, but I wanted to say, "The trail is trying to teach you something. You are not entitled to a space at a shelter any more or less than anyone else. What can this adversity teach you about patience? What gifts are in store for you as your path takes a detour to get your packages? The trail owes you nothing. This is a life lesson. If you don't like the way your mom is sending you stuff, get the food yourself and send it from place to place yourself. Stop expecting others to make you happy and give you peace. Stop the whining, it's annoying." But I didn't say those things. I knew that, sooner or later, he would be brought down by failure and ashes and have the opportunity to develop compassion; I suspected, though, that it would happen later rather than sooner.

Generally, people did treat thru-hikers differently than section hikers. When asked if I was a thru-hiker, I experienced more respect when I answered, "I started at Katahdin" than when I said, "I am hiking Maine and New Hampshire." That led me to think about entitlement, and I had to admit that I too have felt entitled. Sometimes I've felt that because I've prayed, sacrificed, given to the church, or was "good," I was entitled to a good life. But God does not owe me anything. God is not making deals with me; I am making deals with God. I was talking to someone about this, and he said, "Well, what use is your God if you don't get the goodies?" I replied, "There are the rewards of believing God has put us here to help birth a better world that is life enhancing. My walk with and to God has given my life meaning and purpose. It has given me membership in a caring community and enlarged my world. But if I think I deserve to get my way, then I'll be disappointed."

Even knowing this, I still carried the heavy burden of "the whiner" for six miles, from 760 feet all the way to the top of Mt. Moriah (elev. 4049 feet). The name of the peak means "bitterness," and it matched my mood. Signs along the trail alerted hikers to bear activity. A swipe of a bear's paw could take out an eye. In the book *Bear Attacks of the Century*, the story is told of a black bear picking up a hiker by the head and swinging him around and around. If that happened to me, I would be bitter.

As I looked for bears, I tried to clear my mind, but I couldn't stop thinking about the angry young man, and I carried the weight four more miles past Middle Carter Mountain (elev. 4710 feet) until I decided I needed a new strategy. On an overlook on North Carter Mountain, I took off the Green Giant and built a prayer cairn for him and all of us when we feel bitterness and entitlement. I looked at the white moth that fluttered nearby and told her that I wanted to be free from this burden and get it out of my system. I noticed the shell still hanging with the feather on the Green Giant and said, "I'm ready for new birth and transformation."

As I began to ascend Carter Dome, I found a flat space to camp and set up my tent. The water wasn't clean, so I used a coffee filter to try to get the debris out and treated it with chemicals to eliminate the bacteria. I didn't want to add giardia, a nasty stomach bug, to my cough. I was glad it was dark and I could not clearly see the water as I drank it. I knew the young whiner would be pleased I hadn't taken a spot in a shelter from a thru-hiker who didn't carry a tent. My knees were swollen and my feet and back ached, but I was determined to refrain from feeling entitled to better treatment than others. I took some Advil and said my night prayer with the new flashlight I had bought in Gorham. Then I listened in the darkness. There were no sounds, nor was there any light from the moon or stars. I saw and heard nothing as I went to sleep.

DAY

29

Dark Night of the Soul

**Carter Dome
to Pinkham Notch**

Having camped on top of a ridge between two peaks near the bluff, I had hoped to see the sunrise. But when the darkness receded and I emerged from my tent, the fog was so thick the trail had disappeared. I packed up my tent, wet from the mist, and expected rain. "It's coming," I said to the trees. It occurred to me that I hadn't seen anyone since the previous morning. After climbing up Mount Hight and Carter Dome, I began the mile long descent to Carter Notch Hut, one of the huts run by the Appalachia Mountain Club (AMC). Coming down the trail, I came upon a surprising view of two small high mountain lakes and a hut compound. I was so shocked that I stopped in disbelief—I simply was not expecting to see a lake or a series of buildings here in the mountains.

I met a young hiker who was without a pack and seemed to be out for a stroll, but he wasn't interested in chatting. I'd heard that the caretakers of the huts were also responsible for making sure that hikers camped in designated campsites and not in the woods, and I wondered if the unburdened young man was one of the AMC enforcers. I made my way to the hut by hiking along the giant rocks near the small lake. I went inside, hoping for some hot coffee, tea, or someone to talk with, but the place was deserted. Though the water on the stove was not hot, I used some of it to make a warm chocolate drink. I read a wall poster and learned a little of the history of the notch and hut, and that the lakes and the large boulders were the result of a landslide in 1886. The boulders created a natural dam for the two lakes. The first shelter here was a cabin built in 1904. The existing hut was constructed in 1914. The main room served as a dining room, and a counter separated it from the small kitchen, which appeared to consist of a propane stove and a water heater. The old wooden walls and rafters were darkened by wood smoke. An open door revealed a messy office with a cot and sleeping bag. The place smelled a bit stuffy and old. I was a tourist, so I walked to see the bunkhouses, but they were locked up and had their mattresses turned on their sides—closed for the winter.

During the summer, people pay around $100 for a night's stay. This includes a bed, supper, breakfast, and the joy of being with others who like this kind of vacation. If there's room, thru-hikers are allowed to sleep on the floor of the bunkhouse and eat leftovers in exchange for an hour of work. It being out of season, Carter's Notch hut was now in "self-service" mode, although I suspected a caretaker was around somewhere. It was early in the morning and I thought I should keep hiking to avoid the rain. I signed the trail book and used the composting toilet. When I returned, I found a hiker repacking his pack on the bench outside the front door. He asked me if I knew that a big storm was coming. Three to four inches of rain were expected. He added "It's going to be a monster." I decided I didn't need all my food and offered him some tuna fish, which he accepted, and some instant oatmeal, which he declined. I placed the oatmeal in the hiker box in the hut. The air seemed to hang in stillness as if in anticipation of something serious. As I climbed up Wildcat Mountain Peak, I listened to thunder clapping in the distance. The cool air began to swirl around me, sending leaves and debris into the air.

My map showed five Wildcat Mountain peaks, and they looked like they were close together. But as I anxiously walked, it seemed as though I was in a time warp; I was going as fast as I could but didn't seem to cover much of the distance between the peaks. When fat drops started landing like blobs everywhere, I put on my rain suit. Although I prayed "Peace with every step," I felt no joy, peace, or contentment. In the past few weeks, I had repeated it so many times, it often seemed to pray itself. The words almost became a hum, and whether I was muttering or humming, the resulting joy would be the same. But not on this day. I tried to pray, "I can do all things through Christ who strengthens me," but it also seemed to fall flat. I tried the beautiful Jesus Prayer that is so popular in the Russian and Greek tradition: "Lord Jesus Christ, have mercy on me." I repeated it over and over again, but I felt only uneasiness. I was like the disciples who had spent the entire night fishing but caught no fish. When Jesus came to them in the morning and told them to fish on the other side of the boat, they dragged in a huge catch. I was waiting for Jesus to come, but my nets remained empty. St. John of the Cross, a 16th-century Carmelite friar and poet, called this dry period of prayer the "dark night of the spirit." He said the soul on the journey of love toward union with God will go through periods of darkness and trials so profound that they are difficult to understand or describe. The soul longs for God like the deer pants for water, but the sweet water is unavailable (Psalm 42:1). The life of prayer is similar to hiking the trail. Some days are rewarding and full, whereas others feel empty, lonely, and torturous. In this case, my mood was determined by the storm.

Finally, the trail began to go near a ski lift area on the top of Wildcat Mountain. It was raining steadily, and as I made my way down the steep slope I wondered if I was on a surface that became a black diamond run during the ski season. The guidebook says, "This trail might be dangerous when wet or icy: several sections are steep and rough."[41] I can confirm that coming down polished granite slopes in the rain is more treacherous than climbing up.

At one point, I stepped on a rock that was slanted downward and my boot slid off. As I started to fall to the right of the trail, I tried to grab a tree and did, but it wasn't strong enough and broke, sending me to the left, where I landed on a boulder, which bounced me downward and back to the right. Here I was able to grab a fir tree that was a foot in diameter, and I regained my stability. I felt bounced back and forth like a ball in a pinball machine. My pants were torn, my legs were bleeding, and I felt sore from bruising my side. I couldn't believe that I wasn't hurt worse and thanked God for this miracle. When I regained my composure, I noticed that a white moth was struggling to fly in the rain. Inspecting the Green Giant, I noticed that the feather was still dangling under my rain cover but that where the shell had been was an empty string. It must have smashed into

pieces in the fall. I climbed and slid down the remaining two-mile stretch before finally being deposited onto a relatively flat surface where patches of soil greeted me and I could rest.

These miles were the longest I endured on the trail because my confidence was shaken. I struggled with not hating the whole experience. I longed to have a companion with whom to slog down the mountain. I noted how quickly the joy of solitude can turn into the agony of loneliness. The groaning sounds of tree branches scraping against one another expressed my feelings well. I was amazed that a white moth flew a ragged path through the rain with me. The trail had become, in effect, a stream complete with waterfalls. As I was climbing down the boulders, often the only footholds I found were places where water was gushing. I would step where I could and allow the water to flow into my boots. I was battered but determined to get down the mountain. My descent took me three hours in the pouring rain, and I will remember them as some of the most frightening hours in my life.

I was looking for Highway 16 and came to a sign indicating that it was one tenth of a mile away. My heart sang as I anticipated arriving in Pinkham Notch, where I could get out of the rain. But when I got to a stream and saw the highway on the other side, I knew something wasn't right. Wearing my already sodden boots, I forded the swollen, rushing water and climbed over the guard rail. I looked for the lodge but saw nothing. I crossed the road, climbed over another guard rail, and walked to a parking lot kiosk where a mounted map showed that I was one mile away from the Visitor's Center. I also saw that I had gotten off the A.T. at the sign. Back at highway, I looked at the swollen stream and decided that I wouldn't be a purist today, hiking only on the A.T., but would follow the yellow center lines to the Visitor's Center and Joe Dodge Lodge. I held out my thumb when cars and trucks passed, but no one stopped to pick me up. I didn't blame them. The rain continued to come down in sheets, and I was obviously soaked.

I finally made it to Pinkham Notch, which is at the bottom of a U-shaped valley that was created during the Wisconsin Ice Age some 75,000 to 10,000 years ago. I was glad that the lodge accepted credit cards. I took a hot shower and put on dry clothes, and then turned up the heat in the hiker's room. I hung my equipment to dry on wooden pegs and inspected the Green Giant. The red feather and I both missed the shell that had accompanied us for so many miles. I looked at the empty leather string and wondered what it meant that this symbol of rebirth and transformation had shattered. Jesus told a parable of ten virgins who were waiting as bridesmaids or torchbearers on the bridegroom. Some were prepared for the procession and had oil while others did not. The oil, which would illuminate the darkness and show the way, symbolizes being ready for transformation on the inside. This is why the oil is not something which can be shared. The shell was only an outer symbol, and I hoped that inside of myself I had a store of oil, so I could be transformed. My prayer, "I can do all things through Him who strengthens me," had been sufficient. My confidence was shaken, but making it to the lodge put the drama of the dangerous hike in the past.

I took my wet clothes back to the shower stall and wrung them out as best as I could. There was a heater in my room with a curtain rod above it that I could use as drying rack, so I hung my clothes there. I was surprised to see sparkling granite flecks sticking to the cloth and wondered what fragments of my experience would stick to me. At dinner, along the large family style tables, I met a number of vacationers who came to stay at the Joe Dodge Lodge each year and hike in the White Mountains. There were families, couples, singles of different ages, and all were comfortable in the cafeteria. There was a wonderful camaraderie among them. As the storm raged outside, we visited and shared stories. I learned that the notch was named after Daniel Pinkham, who worked for two years to build a road only to see it washed away in a flood in 1826. When he finally opened a toll road through the notch, deep snows discouraged his customers. The obstacles I had encountered in one storm had left me feeling beaten up, but his toils lasted for years and his investment never paid off.

In spite of the relaxing atmosphere, my mind could not hide from my body the trauma it had experienced in the frightening falls. We know that the body reacts with either "fight or flight" under such fearful circumstances, and now my mind and body were both almost ready to call it quits. I vacillated. Should I fight on or give up? Should I finish the hike or go home? Getting out of the storm at the Joe Dodge Lodge helped me feel safe and secure. Telling my story of falling, and admitting that I was frightened and rattled, helped me find healing. The encouragement of those I met empowered me to keep going. Had I just found refuge in a lonely tent in the storm, I doubt I would have found the courage to keep going.

After describing my frequent tumbles to others, I received the trail name, "Falls-a-lot."

Frogs and Wind

Pinkham Notch
to Madison Spring Hut

When I woke up the next morning, I was still on the fence about whether or not to continue the hike. I knew that the Concord Bus left Pinkham Notch Visitor's Center at 8:24 a.m. on its way to Boston and that I could be on that bus. I could take the bus, visit my niece and her husband, and the next day take the train to Portland, where a flight would take me home. No more rainy hikes, no more sore muscles or frustrating mountains. I had a list of reasons why I should quit. My wife and family needed me. I've been out for 30 days—surely that was enough! On the other hand, I had set a goal to be in the wilderness for 40 days, and I only had ten days to go. The White Mountains are difficult, but beautiful. At breakfast I learned that the rain had stopped and only scattered showers were expected. The woman at the information center sensed my hesitation and assured me that I could get to Madison Hut. So as the bus pulled away, I was packing my pack to summit Mount Madison. Was I prepared? Could I do it? Did I want to do it? All these questions haunted me and my mind remained cloudy. Did I want to quit? Yes. But I kept telling myself to stick to the plan. Trust the plan. For some reason God had placed the goal of 40 days in my heart and mind. Jeremiah 29:11 has always given me hope: "'For surely, I know the plans I have for you,' says the Lord, 'plans for your welfare and not for harm, to give you a future with hope.'" So I said to the voice that urged me to quit, "Listen, I've got a goal and a calling. I'm doing it."

In the Bible, Peter gave up when he tried to walk on water. He took his eyes from Jesus and began to sink. There are always times in our lives when we want to walk away from our commitments. "Follow Peter,"

243

say my head and heart, which are not into continuing; but my gut says, "Stay the course." We stay because, in the bigger picture, staying is the right decision. Sticking with the plan would be keeping my eyes on Jesus, who called me to pray in the wilderness for 40 days. Sometimes commitments look and feel like a journey toward death, but they really are the way to life.

As I began climbing, the path was often underwater from the rains that so challenged me, but the rushing waters also gave me energy. I experienced an abundance of nature's sounds—croaking, trilling, muttering—were all around me, competing with the bubbling streams. Looking around, I couldn't find where the sounds were coming from. Then, in the chaos of the water soaked mountainside, a host of frogs appeared and the source of the cacophony became clear. Greeting them with a happy "Good morning" was fun, and some were trusting enough to allow me to take their photo. Whether they were underwater or on land, they all seemed to watch me with their big eyes.

The frogs and toads I saw along the A.T. ranged in sizes and kinds. These amphibians have delighted God far longer than humans have existed; in fact, they've been around for 190 million years. As a child, I remembered looking for tadpoles in the creek behind our house and being amazed at their transformation. Summer nights were filled with their guttural sounds, and walking around a pond would always bring plops into the water. While camping, my friends and I even went frog gigging one night and fried up a few frog legs, enough for each of us to have a taste and decide they were too icky to eat again. I needed some frog energy on this wet hike, and the ability to adapt between water and land. Their leaping ability would also have helped. I thought of the story of the frog who asked a princess to give him a kiss. When she finally did, he turned into a handsome prince. The power of love to transform ugliness into beauty gave me hope.

I reminded myself once again that I wanted to walk "gently upon the earth," which meant treating plants and animals with respect. In my lifetime there has been a shift in our attitude toward nature, moving us away from thinking that humans are the only ones that matter. I think this change in our perception is necessary and good. In the Old Testament story of Noah and the flood, it was not only the humans who were saved, but the animals and birds, as well. I've often wondered if this story is one way of telling us that we are not the only things that matter to God. Why would animals, frogs, and birds matter? Because individually and collectively, they reflect the presence of the Divine. Humans are relative newcomers in creation. If frogs matter, so do the dogs who guard our homes, and the bats who eat insects, and even the snakes who eat the mice, not to mention the rivers, streams, ponds, marshes, trees, shrubs and flowers. All of creation delights God.

I enjoyed the first seven miles of the trail up Mt. Madison, named for our fourth president, but I encountered a different world when I climbed out of the forest. The boulder-covered area was wild and untamed, the beginning of a 13 mile, above-tree-line section of the A. T. that ran through the Presidential Range. One difference between the southern mountains

and the mountains of New Hampshire is the lack of soil on the latter. At a certain elevation, the peaks are mainly fields of boulders and slides of rock. Before my hike, Jean, a friend who grew up in the shadow of the White Mountains, told me that I may have to crawl across Mount Washington. I asked her why and she said: "Because of the wind. They have the worst weather on earth."

Until I arrived here I couldn't conceive of crawling across a mountain. I was shocked at the power of the wind. My eyes teared up, and the gale force gusts blew the tears away from the surface of my face. I wanted to wipe my nose with my bandana, but my hands were too busy grasping rocks as I crawled forward. My eyesight worsened on that day and I wondered why. When I realized that cleaning my glasses didn't restore my vision, I took a closer look at the lenses and saw that they'd been thoroughly scratched, as if they'd been sandblasted. It took new lenses to restore my sight. Later on, a hiker told me that the same wind blew his fleece hat from his head and his water bottle from a pocket of his pack. The next day I asked the ranger on Mount Washington what the wind speed had been on that day and he said 60 mph. The more I thought about it, the more it made sense that when we get close to the wild, untamed Almighty God in the wild, untamed uncontrollable creation, a good posture is bowing low and crawling on all fours. The Holy Spirit, one of the names for God, is symbolized as wind. Spiritual encounters may be wilder than we expect, but despite their danger, all are vehicles of God's grace. At Pow Wows, Native Americans sometime sing, "You can't stop the Spirit, She is like a mountain, old and strong, she goes on and on and on." As I reflected on the power of the wind, I concluded that they knew something long before I did.

There is no camping allowed on the Presidential Range above tree level, but a White Mountain hut caretaker I had met at Pinkham Notch told me that under the Madison Hut there was a crawlspace that was available as an emergency shelter for people stuck on the mountain in bad weather. He said I could stay there since the hut was closed, that it would save me from having to hike off the mountain to a campsite.

I saw the hut long before I was able to do a combination of crawling and walking to get to it. I found that as soon as I got below a certain elevation, the wind decreased, allowing me to walk again. After opening the jail bar gate to the crawlspace, I saw one four-by-eight foot piece of plywood that I could use as a bed. Feeling a bit like a trespasser, I walked around to locate the flowing spring. Not wanting to cause a fire and burn the hut down, I took my denatured alcohol stove and food and found the least windy place in my immediate environment to set up my stove. I huddled by the outside corner of the building and built a wind shield with rocks, but the wind repeatedly blew out the stove's flame. When it finally stayed lit, it never heated the icy water above a warm temperature. My dream of a hot meal became in reality just a warm supper, but I ate it anyway.

The howling wind blew through the gate and openings under the hut and into the space I was occupying. I put on all the clothes I had and hunkered down in my sleeping bag and wrapped my ground cloth around me. But I was still cold. I tried to lull myself to sleep by thinking about the fact that I was on the Presidential Range and had not quit. And not only that. I had made it to Mount Madison through strong winds. I felt a sense of accomplishment and pride that made me happy. But I was still cold.

DAY

31

Protect Nature

Madison Springs Hut, Mount Washington to Mizpah Springs Hut

I woke around 6 a.m. and climbed out of the sleeping bag. I was not exactly hyper-charged, definitely not ready to jump up and down, but my heart and mind were thrilled, and I left Madison Hut with enthusiasm for what was ahead. I could see my breath, and the little water puddles on the trail had turned to ice. The sun had not yet crested the ridge, but the fresh eastern light gave Mount Madison a halo and made the top of Mount Adams glow. Across the valley below me, white puffy clouds extended for miles. A heavy frost was on the rocks, bushes, lichen and high elevation vegetation. The air was crisp and I was excited about reaching the summit of Mount Washington (elev. 6288 feet) on a clear day.

After rounding Mount Jefferson, I could see the high peak named after the first president of the United States and the expansive buttresses that shored up the northeastern slopes. It looked close, but it wasn't. I had first spotted Mount Washington from Gorham, New Hampshire, and it looked daunting. Indeed, it was. The mountain has taken dozens of lives. I passed several signs warning hikers not to attempt to summit if the weather was threatening. Although the weather remained clear and cold, the sun was rising higher as I crossed the Six Husbands Trail. I later learned it was named for the six successive husbands of Queen Weetamoo, of the Pocasset Wampanoag tribe, who lived from around 1635 to 1676. This tribe was reputed to have celebrated the first Thanksgiving with the Mayflower Pilgrims, although the story is probably apocryphal. As the number of Puritans increased, the numbers of her tribe decreased. Weetamoo's first husband, who took the English name of Alexander, was a leader of his tribe and was invited to have a meal with the Puritans. The story goes that he was poisoned and died. Her sister was married to the chief of the Wampanoag, Metacom, who was also known as King Philip. Weetamoo sided with him when he went to war with the colonists over their practice of displacing and annihilating the natives. The Christian pastor Increase Mather fanned hatred toward Philip by claiming that he was one of the "heathen people among whom we live and whose land the Lord God of our Fathers hath given to us for a rightful possession."

King Philip's War was the bloodiest conflict fought on American soil, and both sides committed horrific atrocities. When the English finally gained the upper hand, they killed Philip and captured his wife and son and sold them into slavery in the West Indies. Queen Weetamoo was in hiding with only 30 remaining warriors. When an Indian informer led a group of militia to capture them, she said she knew of the "tender mercies" of the Christian whites and preferred to flee rather than surrender. During her attempted escape across the Taunton River, she lost her footing and drowned. The Puritans mutilated her body, and cut off her head and displayed it on a pole. Reverend Mather showed anything but Christian charity when he mocked the grief the native people felt over

the death of their queen. When I learned about such evil masquerading as pure and holy, I better understood why Weetamoo put her trust in the harshness of the rivers, mountains and woods, rather than in the Puritan Christians.

I climbed through the fields of boulders for five and half miles. Many had ice on them, making them slippery. Others were loose and rolled when I stepped on them. There wasn't a trail, just cairns showing the way. I watched the puffs of smoke of the cog railway as it slowly climbed and descended from the peak. The three-mile track was completed in 1869, and President Ulysses S. Grant and his family were among the first passengers on the train. When I got closer, I heard the train whistle and resisted the hiker tradition of "mooning" carriages. I'm not sure why the tradition started. Perhaps those who climbed felt more than a little contempt for those who sat comfortably in passenger cars that were pulled to the top. When I finally reached the summit, I went inside the visitor's center. I was salivating at the thought of having a cheeseburger and milkshake for lunch. There was a day room downstairs for backpackers to sort or dry their stuff, but trail hikers were not allowed to spend the night on the summit. I went into the bathroom and looked at myself in the mirror. My ears were sunburned and, to my surprise, the bottom of my ear lobes had sores. Unfortunately, the diner didn't have milkshakes or cheeseburgers and I had to settle for a chilidog and Sprite. They tasted good, too.

The place was bustling with tourists who had ridden up on the train, and I spoke with a ranger behind a desk just to talk to someone. In the gift shop I laughed at the postcards and T-shirts showing the view from Mt. Washington on a cloudy day—all white. Others proclaimed the peak as having the worst weather on the earth, with the highest wind speed ever recorded—231 mph. I stood in line and had someone take my photo at the Mt. Washington summit sign and then toured the three-room hotel museum and imagined what it would be like to be snowed-in in such a small space and with cold wind coming through the walls. It was a beautiful day and I could see for miles. My eyes rested on the barren, rocky surface of the Presidential Range above the tree line.

Waves of mountains beyond mountains with their forested lower elevations stretched as far as I could see.

Benton MacKaye, the American conservationist, originally proposed Mt. Washington to be the northern terminus of the A.T. in 1921. I was glad it was now set aside for the public but knew that this only happened because of the vision and hard work of people long dead. In his journal of June 3, 1861, Thoreau wrote, "New Hampshire courts have lately been deciding if it was for them to decide whether the top of Mt. Washington belonged to A or B…but I think the top of Mt. Washington should not be private property; it should be left unappropriated for modesty and reverence's sake, or if only to suggest that earth has higher uses than we put her to."[43]

Having played the role of tourist, and read some history and eaten, I had nothing else to do but keep walking. A little way down the path, I stopped and made a prayer cairn giving thanks for my successful summiting of Mt. Washington. Two days before in Pinkham Notch, I doubted I would make it at all, and here I was. I had endured the high winds and the coldest night of my trip, slept in a crawlspace on top of a mountain, and climbed for hours through fields of boulders. These were accomplishments of both will and grace. As I slung the Green Giant onto my back, the feather was still hanging from its side.

Looking down, I noticed my pack belt buckles were getting closer, indicating that I had lost weight. When I got to the Lakes of the Clouds hut, which sits on the southern shoulder of Mt. Washington, the caretakers were pulling mattresses out onto the porch to close up for the season. Like other caretakers, they do keep open what they call the "dungeon," the crawlspace underneath, as an emergency shelter for hikers. The A.T. follows the Crawford Path, the oldest continuously used hiking trail in the country. Having read about it, I knew that it had been built by Abel Crawford and his son Ethan Allen Crawford in 1819. The Crawfords were pioneers. They opened their home to tourists and brought them up the trail to see Mount Washington. Ethan later converted the trail to a "bridle path." When I first read the words "bridle path," a place for weddings

came to mind, but I knew that didn't make sense and remembered that bridles were used on horses. In fact, Ethan turned it into a trail for tourists on horseback. I could imagine that in the 19th century, riding on horseback would certainly have been the way to go. The notch was later named after the family, too.

As I made my way south, I thought about the many people—including poets, presidents, preachers, and naturalists—who had walked the trail. It may seem crazy, but knowing we walked the same path and saw the same sights somehow gave me a mystical sense of connection to them across time and space. At some point I stopped and looked back at Mt. Washington. As impressive as it was, the Psalmist says that mountains will melt before the Lord (Psalm 97:5). I laughed and thought I wouldn't want to be around for that event. The power, strength, and awesomeness of God are beyond my imagination.

There was a trail to reach the summit of Mt. Monroe, and I considered climbing it, but decided I had scaled enough mountains for one day and was ready to put the Presidential Range behind me.

I met a backpacker taking a break, who was also hiking south to Mizpah Hut. He was lying on the ground with his head on his pack and eating a giant candy bar.

I said, "You deserve that candy bar after hiking up Mt. Washington." We laughed and I kept going.

The A.T. goes around Mt. Franklin and Mt. Clinton rather than over their summits, an unusual omission, but I knew we were following the bridle path of the Crawfords. There were signs everywhere warning how dangerous this trail was due to unpredictable weather. "Beware!" I said to myself. "Many people have perished on this mountain!"

Finally, the Crawford trail brought me below tree line, and I took the Green Giant off to take a break. I found a candy bar I had stashed in my food bag, and I ate it while sitting in complete silence, overlooking a vast evergreen forest. I realized I hadn't heard songbirds for a while. The absence of birds on one part of the trail makes their presence on another even more noticeable. My birder friend John Ehinger once told me that he became interested in identifying birds while hiking the A.T. According to John, there are so many different birds along the trail, you have to be really self-absorbed not to notice and want to identify them.

That reminded me of Wendell Berry's observation that the fish in the rivers and animals and birds on the land in Kentucky, where he has lived for over half a century, have been greatly reduced in numbers. He was surprised that biologists haven't noticed or studied the shift. Since the 1960s, scientists have been noting a world-wide decline in various populations and have surveyed avian populations to determine why a half-billion birds have been lost. The razing of large tracts of forests and the diminishing of wintering grounds with adequate food in Central and South America are popular theories. Some birds require 25 acres of woods to provide food for their family, and with roads, malls and suburbs being built, they simply can't find places to breed and live. I carried with me a haunting poem by Drew Dellinger, "Hieroglyphic Stairway," which passionately and achingly questions our poor stewardship of the Earth. In my tent at night, sometimes I couldn't help but fish it out from my pack and reread it.

By the time I staggered in to Mizpah Springs Hut, I had played leapfrog with the candy bar hiker several times, and I was the first to ask the caretakers if I could stay there for the night.

When they said they could only use one hiker, I protested, "But I know there is one other hiker coming, and I don't want to take his place."

A young man wearing a black toboggan spoke up, "I can use him at the Nauman tent site, don't worry about it."

I immediately liked him because he acted as though he liked hikers. I thought, "Now this is someone who understands what I've been through." I didn't get the same impression from the staff of the Mizpah Hut. Perhaps they were ready for a break after a busy season. There were only three customers at the hut that night, and they weren't very social. Usually at the huts, a sense of community prevails as people tell jokes and the enthusiastic staff offers talks about the nature and history of the area, but none of that happened. I was happy to eat some leftovers and, for my hour of work, wash dishes and make a good attempt to replace aluminum foil in the gas ovens. I felt most of the staff were condescending, with the exception of a young woman who asked about my hike.

After my short answer she said, "You don't seem confident you're going to finish."

I responded, "No, after Wildcat Mountain, my confidence is shot."

When I was done with my chores, I withdrew to the room they called the library, where I had laid out my sleeping mat and bag on the floor. I debated whether I had a greater need for social contact or for sleeping indoors and decided that I could endure the cold weather and hardships, if I had someone with whom to share the experience. We could laugh about it and it would lighten the burden. My sore muscles ached, and I was grateful for Advil and my spot on the floor, even though I was surrounded by rooms of empty bunks. And I was thankful that the hut was warm and dry. Although I had no interest in prayer that night, habit took over and I prayed:

> *Keep watch, dear Lord, with all who work or watch or weep this night, give your angels charge over those who sleep: Tend the sick, we pray, and give rest to the weary; soothe the suffering and bless the dying; Pity the afflicted and shield the joyous. Guide us waking and guard us sleeping; that awake we may watch with Christ and asleep we may rest in peace. Amen."*

DAY

32

Alone or with God

Mizpah Springs Hut
to Zealand Springs Hut

The rain suit bag I used for a pillow was stained with blood when I awoke. Confused, I headed to the bathroom and noticed that the bottoms of my ears had dried scabs. I wasn't sure how to protect my ears, but I got ready to head out on my own, anyway. Having told the staff the night before that I would be leaving before breakfast, I slowly closed the front door so I wouldn't disturb anyone. Mist hung heavy in the air as I eased my way from the hut and noticed the tents were still quiet at the Nauman site. The air didn't smell of rain, but of fir and decay. I scanned the woods for any movement and listened for birds. Why hadn't I seen any deer in New Hampshire? Now the primary sound I heard was the click of my hiking poles. I had read in the trail guides that for some hikers Mount Webster and Webster Cliffs were their favorite part of the trail, and I was looking forward to the view. For three miles I hiked and tried, off and on, to pray, but the words seemed empty. I said the Jesus prayer, "Lord Jesus Christ, have mercy on me" but I felt far from God.

I was longing for some sort of assurance of God's mercy and guidance, and without it, my thoughts were not clear. The unease I felt may not have been a spiritual deficiency, but, instead, the result of being sleep deprived. Suffering unfulfilled prayers was not a new experience for me. It helped me be even more grateful for the many times I actually had felt close to God. Perhaps God now thought it was time for me to leave the nest, to stand on my feet, to walk on my own. I laughed to myself for thinking I had outgrown my baby shoes, spiritually speaking, but I was feeling on edge.

As I emerged from the woods at an exposed overlook, I was shocked, and I hesitated as the full sun hit me. The moving cars on the road below appeared tiny from my elevation, and the railroad track that stretched on the mountain opposite me looked as if it belonged in a toy store. Consulting the map confirmed that I was looking at Crawford Notch. Looking down, I also realized that if I fell off the trail, I would plummet hundreds of feet. I carefully made my way down the steep, and often exposed, Webster Cliffs, giving thanks that it was not raining. Several times my hiking poles saved me from falling. I was doing well when I met a day hiker about my age, who had a great deal of hiking experience. He asked me how things were going and I surprised myself by saying, "I've decided today to leave the trail and go home." He shook his head and said, "The toughest fight on the trail is mental, not physical." When he asked me how I planned to leave, I shook my head and said I didn't know, and moved on.

The truth was I had finished talking to him and was embarrassed to have confessed to a complete stranger about a weakness. But I didn't tell him all. It was homesickness that led me to the decision to leave the trail. As I walked on, I devised a plan. I would hike down to Crawford Notch, stick out my thumb and hitchhike to a town. I'd take a bus, or several buses, to Portland, and from there, fly home by the next day. Wondering if my plan was a nudging from God, I wanted some guidance from someone I trusted. Was my desperation just a result of homesickness or was this a spiritual sign? A little later I checked my phone and, to my surprise, had one bar of signal—I had not had a signal for four days. I called Kelly. When I got her answering machine, I said, "Kelly, I need to talk to you. I just want to come home," and began to cry. I didn't know I was going to cry. I was surprised and embarrassed and hung up thinking that I would call back when I pulled myself together. Irritation that she hadn't answered combined with alarm that she would hear my tears and fear that I'd been hurt.

I kept hiking and checking my signal, but none showed. For the three miles down the mountain, I cried on and off and kept praying about whether I should quit or continue. I felt no indication from God. This irritated me because I wanted a sign. "Why will God not give me a sign?"

I cried. I wondered whether God was failing me, or if I was just allowing my emotions to block my path to Him. I knew I didn't want to be a quitter.

When I got to Crawford Notch and Highway 302, I watched a car approach, but I didn't stick out my thumb. I had decided that I wasn't going to abandon the plan and run. I crossed the road and kept hiking. After a half mile, as I began climbing toward Zealand Falls Hut, I prayed for guidance again and a clear voice said to me, "Your church has given you a wonderful gift to see this beautiful place. Do not miss the gift. You are with your family in Alabama at all times. Finish the 40 days!" Something clicked within me and I was not homesick anymore; a flood of assurance and mercy overcame me. I took off the Green Giant and the feather was still dangling. I took it as a sign that God gave me the assurance I looked for and blessed my decision, and I was amazed at my change of attitude. From time to time, I suspect, we all have a secret wish to throw in the towel. Maybe the most important way to be faithful is simply to refuse to run away. I prayed a word of thanks that God had not given up on me. The

faith and hope which returned to me so quickly confirmed for me that it was a gift from God. Paul was right in Ephesians 2:8 and Romans 12:3. Faith and grace are gifts from God. They did not come from me. I simply kept walking with an outstretched hand, hoping that God would take it, and He did, pulling me up.

I found out later that the phone call that I had made in my despair had left Kelly feeling uncertain and helpless. Unsure if she should send out a search and rescue team or simply wait for further instructions, she called one of my close hiking buddies. Fortunately, he reassured her: "It sounds like Dale has hit the wall, but he can take care of himself in the woods."

When we fast, we usually think it's a time of not eating or drinking, but it's really a period of ascetic commitment that prepares us to receive profounder truths. When Jesus went to the wilderness for 40 days, he examined at a deeper level what was to be the purpose of his life. When he left the wilderness, he had a new consciousness. Jesus appeared four times to the disciples after the resurrection, in what the church calls the 40 days of Easter. A common theme in these stories is that the disciples didn't know Jesus when he reappeared. Was it their self-pity and nostalgia that kept them from recognizing him? Or had Jesus transformed to such a degree that he was no longer familiar to them? As I thought about my own homesickness, I realized that I, too, was trapped in the past and couldn't see what was before me. Mary recognized Jesus when he called her name. Then he told her, "Do not cling to me." Mary had to learn to let go if she was going to recognize Jesus.

A number of day hikers joined the A.T. for a short while on their way to the Arethusa Ripley Falls. They told me how fabulous these falls were, and I debated making a detour to see them. I left the A.T. and walked for 15 minutes, or so, down what I thought was the right trail, until I realized that something wasn't right. I decided to turn around and press on to the Zealand Falls hut. It was three muddy, uphill miles to the Ethan Pond Shelter. As the trail skirted the large pond, there was evidence of flooding. Following the North Fork I was excited to see a short side trail to Thoreau

Falls and took it. I could hear the falls long before I saw them. They were impressive. The water drops a total of 80 feet, with each section cascading about 15 feet, with some wading pools in-between. As I stood above them, I was careful not to get too close because I could imagine slipping and sliding all the way down to the bottom. I wondered if Thoreau had actually ever come here.

The place seemed to call for a prayer cairn to give thanks for Thoreau's vision of wanting not to just see and observe nature, but to experience it in a mystical way, and I began with a base rock. In gratitude for God's grace, I placed another rock on the cairn. Like the gushing waters, grace is not stagnant but dynamic and flowing throughout the world, bringing wholeness, reconciliation, justice, and healing. Through forgiveness we are brought closer into the likeness of Christ. Just as I did nothing to contribute to the beauty of the falls, I cannot earn grace. It is unmerited and unconditional. Just as the falls flowed for the benefit of all creation, God's grace and love flows over, under, and around all of creation. The love of God is known best through relationships between ourselves and God and through us to the world. Just as the power of the water can carve a canyon, overturn rocks, and carry debris downstream, grace and love are also life-changing energy. "May I be changed into Your likeness," I prayed as I put another stone on the cairn.

As I sat looking at the falls, and breathing the cool air, I was overwhelmed with thankfulness. It was such a gift to be in this amazing spot. I remembered that as a child I visited my great Aunt Lola, who had a prized conch shell on the shelf of her simple, small, four-room house. She had never seen the ocean, but the shell had been passed down in our family as a prized possession. She told me that if I held the shell up to my ear, I could hear the ocean. Like my aunt, I'd never seen the ocean either and was amazed to hear the mysterious roar in the shell. The memory told of a mysterious world which, although out of sight, surely existed. I placed a stone on the cairn, acknowledging the invisible spiritual world surrounding us. As I walked the remaining two and half miles, I felt supported by the grace and prayers of those I loved. What I didn't know at the time was

that after receiving my message, Kelly had begun praying for me and asked others to pray for me, as well.

When I climbed onto the porch of the Zealand Hut, one of the caretakers greeted me and told me to take off my pack and come in and visit. Inside, the volunteer at the counter greeted me as if we were old friends. The staff supervisor's trail name was "Quilt," and she had completed the whole A.T. in four months. Another staff person had hiked half the trail before dropping out. They gave me some pans to scrub with steel wool, and I did my hour of work. The hut was full of energetic patrons who sat around the large tables for supper. While they ate some yummy roast and vegetables, I was served the leftover pancakes from breakfast, which I enjoyed. Thru-hikers and the staff only eat the left-overs from the paying guests. After supper, several day hikers surrounded me to ask me questions about my experience. After an interesting nature program, I moved the large table over and made myself at home on the floor for the night.

I found Nathaniel Hawthorne's story "The Great Stone Face," published in 1850, in the library and read about the "Old Man of the Mountains." I was excited that I would be seeing this famous site in two days, when I got to Franconia Notch. The staff and others staying at the Zealand Hut offered me encouragement. When I prayed my night prayers, I was truly thankful for the gift of community. Kind strangers were no substitute for my family, but their care answered my need. The feather on the Green Giant was now dry and seemed to be shimmering in the low light.

DAY

33

Interdependence

Zealand Springs Hut
to Mount Lafayette

Gloves and toboggan hat and warm clothes felt good against the chill as I quietly closed the door to Zealand Hut. My ear lobes had again bled during the night, but I knew it was not life threatening. I noticed that the huts generate their own electricity and that Zealand uses solar, wind, and hydropower and was glad the warmth I enjoyed was clean. Before I left, I wanted to see a little of what the staff had described the night before. To my surprise, I was not the only one awake at that early hour. Quilt, the staff leader, came to me as I was packing Green Giant and said, "If you give yourself to the trail, the trail will take care of you. You can trust it." "Giving yourself" was akin to the trust advocated in Psalm 37, "Trust in the Lord." Her kindness almost made me cry, and I wanted to give her a hug, but I just thanked her for her encouragement. When I walked out and looked at the cascading Zealand Falls, I was impressed by how simple it seemed to harness the force of the flowing water. The power is there if we can just appropriate it. Then to my surprise, I saw the white moth flying along the trail. Tears came to my eyes and I considered why I was so emotional. I had given everything I had to this adventure for 33 days and had less than a week to go.

The morning fog was not solid, but as I began the long ascent to Zealand Mountain and the Twin Mountains, the higher I climbed, the more it thickened. It was Saturday and there were many people on the trail. I met a weekend hiker who had stayed at the Guyot Shelter and bragged about the beautiful views they had the afternoon and night before. After conquering the Twin peaks, I stopped at Galehead Hut for lunch. I bought a bowl of warm soup and piece of bread to supplement my Gorp and sat at table with some Asian runners who were training for a marathon. They were from Boston and had already run 17 miles, but had that many more left to go. They were impressive athletes, but they were not enjoying the mountain terrain.

The sun had overcome the mist, and I lingered on the Galehead Hut porch soaking in its warmth before I headed out again. A young hiker wearing a green handkerchief on his head sat down and our conversation turned to masculinity. He was hiking to explore being a man. An uncle had told him to join the army, but he was not sure becoming a warrior would give him what he was seeking; although he felt he had primarily feminine characteristics such as mercy, tenderness, and patience, he wanted to develop more masculine traits such as strength, assertiveness, decisiveness, and power. We talked about how boys nowadays rarely have the opportunity to do physical work with their fathers, and discussed how sometimes our masculine qualities can become numb. We laughed at that—our manly muscles certainly felt alive that day. Learning that I was a Christian pastor, he asked about masculinity in the Bible. I told him that to our knowledge, Jesus didn't have traditional masculine roles such as husband, father, and athlete, although he was a carpenter by trade; but he was calm in a storm, acted decisively toward critics, and showed courage when facing death. He became an angry man with warrior energy when he overturned the tables of the money changers in the temple. Yet he was tender toward children, merciful to the needy, and unusually respectful toward women.

The young man said, "So Jesus showed both feminine and masculine tendencies."

I explained that the Bible was written in a time when there were very strictly defined gender roles that gave men power, ownership, and control over women, so we cannot look to the Bible to answer all our questions. I doubted God approved of this cultural arrangement that dominated the environment when the Bible was written. Some guidelines can come from the Bible, such as the command "Fathers, don't provoke your children," which tells us that men's anger, power, and provocative language caused more harm than good in families. We also have the command to "stay clear of seductive women, power, riches and pride," which reminds us of common struggles men face. Images of military strength and athletic feats are used to inspire the faithful. Judges and Joshua said, "Be bold, be strong," and Paul tells us to "run the good race, adding in his letter to Corinthians to do everything with love (1 Corinthians 16:13-14). As we left to hike in opposite directions, the young man thanked me for the good company and new ideas to ponder.

As I meditated, the image of intertwined roots of trees stretching across the trail came to my mind. They allowed the trees to support one another in a tangled web of interdependence. The mountains of Maine and New Hampshire didn't have much soil, so the trees figured out how to thrive together. Part of God's gift to the world was to give it the capacity to reproduce, change, and adapt. The trees, lichens, and flowers are examples of this transformative ability. A second part of the revelation was that I am a part of this web of interdependence. I belong to creation. I thought about how weeks ago I stopped cursing the roots, and trees and rocks, and began to thank them. When I stepped on a root that might either send me sliding or keep me from slipping, I would thank it. When I held on to trees as I was moving up or down the mountain, I expressed my gratitude. My shell symbolizing transformation may have been gone, but this concrete change in my behavior had stayed with me. I realized that if I can remember what I've learned, I can take the transformation with me.

There's a line in my daily morning prayer, "Stir up within me a desire to serve you, to live peaceably with my neighbors and all creation." When I began to thank the trees for helping me, I felt I was taking a step toward living in peace. In one of my night prayers, there is a portion of confession, "I confess I have sinned against you this day; some of my sin I know, and some is known only to you." While hiking I would think of this and wonder what my sin could be, since I was rarely interacting with other people. Then one night it hit me that my sin is when I am walking only for myself and not for the common good of all of creation. I was sinning when I did not regard the animals, trees, and plants with respect. I was sinning when I used them without realizing that they are an important part of creation. A gift of the Body of Christ for the world is offering an embrace to welcome all creation.

Walking the A.T. was an experiment to pour myself out to God. I tried to give up my big ideas about myself: my image of being a pastor and of thinking the church and world were relying on me and my self-appointed place of privilege. Everyone on the trail is equal; no one has any privileges. I and other people give one another space to hike and camp in solitude. For much of my journey, I hid behind my armor, not touching others and not allowing them to touch me. But in the end, I poured myself out and became vulnerable.

One of the challenges to spirituality for Americans in the 21st century is our separation from the Earth. Many people no longer have direct contact with it. Although many children are learning to become whizzes at using technology, they don't have an opportunity to walk a winding path through the woods to see a waterfall or mountain, or even spend enough time in the woods to know what it is they're seeing. Children have more opportunities to plug into their virtual world than to see a newborn calf or make a fort of sticks. One fourth grader, when asked why he preferred to play indoors, he replied: "That's where all the electrical outlets are."[44] When a hiker from Denmark asked me why I was hiking, I told him, "I want to be surrounded only by the things God created." He laughed and said he felt the same way and acknowledged that he felt an emptiness and sense of incompleteness in the city. Our souls have something in common with the wilderness, and being surrounded by it can bathe, refresh, and heal us at a deep level, and fill a void.

The A.T. followed the steep Garfield trail up to the 14th highest peak in the White Mountains. It went up and down and was difficult because of the slick rocks, dirt slides, and precariously tall steps between rocks. A hiker had told me that he had camped at the peak by laying out his sleeping pad and bag under the stars in the remains of what once was a fire tower. He said it was beautiful because he could watch the sunset and the sunrise, although it could be dangerous if the weather was cold or wet. I was happy to climb to the square foundation on top of this peak. I took off the Green

Giant, sat down, and drank in the beautiful views to the south and north. However, I didn't last five minutes before the icy wind drove me to look for my toboggan hat and gloves. I debated whether to stop there for the night to catch a sunset and sunrise, but the shivers running up my spine made the decision to leave easy. Below the tree line, where I wasn't exposed to the elements, would be a better place to camp. I asked some hikers if they'd seen places to pitch a tent and was assured there were several options. I descended the mountain and a few miles later found a site where the trail began to climb Mt. Lafayette. There was no water, but I found a flat space for my tent. I could smell the rain coming and was grateful I was not on top of Mt. Garfield. It had been a good day. To my surprise, when I turned on my phone I had service. I was excited about touching base with home, so I called Kelly and she answered. She was relieved to hear that I hadn't fallen off a cliff and that I'd moved through the crisis that had frightened her earlier. After explaining to her about my homesickness, she said she was glad that I missed them because they certainly missed me. Talking together gave both of us the sense of security about our relationship that we needed. The next day's hike to Franconia Notch Visitors center would be only eight miles. Once there I would retrieve a supply box, take a shower, and sleep in a real bed. I went to sleep dreaming about a cheeseburger and a milkshake.

DAY
34

Anticipation

**Mount Lafayette
to Franconia Notch**

It rained most of the night, and I was so excited about having someone to meet at Franconia Notch—friends of a friend—that I kept waking up, like a child on Christmas Eve. At 5:30 a.m. I began packing, waiting for daylight. Around 6 the rain stopped, and I brushed my teeth in the dark and broke down my wet tent. At 7 there was enough light to see the trail despite the fog, and I started to hike. I made sure I had my pack cover on and wore my rain suit. The strong winds made it difficult to scale Mount Lafayette (elev. 5260 feet), the second most prominent mountain in New Hampshire and the highest along the Franconia Range. The trail followed ridge after ridge in an alpine zone above the tree line. The clouds and fog seemed to flow across the sky like a river. The whistling of the wind in the trees below and through the rocks provided a constant stereo accompaniment. Through occasional breaks in the clouds I saw what I thought was the peak of Mount Lincoln, but I only got the briefest of glimpses before the white cover closed again.

My adrenalin was flowing because I was going to meet Ed and Mary Bagley, who lived in Littleton and would take me into their home for the night. It was fortifying to know someone was expecting me. Following Mount Lincoln was Little Haystack, and I wondered how its name had sneaked in among all the presidents and other historical figures. I later learned that Mt. Lafayette had been "Big Haystack" but then was renamed to honor the French general who helped General Washington and the Continental Army. General Lafayette visited New Hampshire on the 50 year anniversary of Bunker Hill in 1824-1825 as part of a celebratory tour. So perhaps one day, Little Haystack will be named for another

President or foreign leader who comes to our country's aid. Several hikers had told me that Franconia Ridge was their favorite stretch on this part of the A.T., but the fog and biting cold wind made it hard to walk on the exposed sections, and I couldn't see much. When I got

farther south, the clouds scattered to reveal a lovely view of the valley and surrounding mountains.

As I tried to pray my walking prayer, "Peace with every step," and the other mantras which had brought me close to God weeks ago, the words would not come. I wondered if I was just too tired or if there was something else going on. I tried to repeat the name of Jesus, but it didn't feel right. Augustine and St. Thomas Aquinas taught that prayer was a mental activity of reflection, thinking, and memory. I'd been using this method over the past weeks as I reflected upon roots, rocks, frogs. But in the past few days the mental approach to prayer was not working for me. I recalled the anonymous English mystic who wrote *The Cloud of Unknowing* and taught that prayer is not a mental activity and shouldn't be forced by an effort of will. In prayer we are responding to the mysterious appeal of God who is hidden in the clouds beyond our comprehension. I was walking in the wind and fog, unable to pray, using words to the Creator God who is beyond words.

As I simply tried to be in God's presence, beyond any images or word, from somewhere inside I began to hum. I was surprised, but it felt right, so I just continued. It wasn't a tune, though I was tempted to turn it into one, but refrained. The hum continued, and as my throat opened up, I felt open and connected to God. I could imagine the shock on my congregation's face if on a Sunday morning when it came time for the Pastoral Prayer, I just began to hum. Yet I knew that if I desired God, and my desire came from the heart, God would honor the desire, and I continued humming off and on across Franconia Ridge.

It was a Sunday and I was thinking about the worship services in my own church when I saw rocks which, from a distance, actually looked like a church. It stirred my feelings of home and I felt joy. As I got closer, it turned out to be just a pile of rocks, and I was disappointed. Another unique stack of rocks called the Eaglet was more impressive. For centuries eagles nested and raised their young there. I knew I was back to a more Augustinian, mental way of prayer because I began remembering the mountain top where Moses, close to death, watched a mother eagle teaching her eaglets to fly by flying underneath them, flapping her wings to give them an updraft. I thought of the popular song, "Wind beneath My Wings," and the inspiring text from Isaiah 40:31, "Those who hope in the Lord will renew their strength. They will soar on wings like eagles. They will run and not grow weary; they will walk and not be faint." This was a verse I needed for the last week of the hike. I remembered that the eagle represents the Holy Spirit in some Native American traditions and announces the full presence of Creator God.

Although the eagles are no longer on this mountain, in 1981 environmentalists introduced peregrine falcons here to make their nests and raise their young. Since then, the falcons have moved from the status of "endangered" to "threatened." The mountain climbing community temporarily limits its routes over nesting places to help in this repopulation effort. The falcons mate for life and catch their prey in midair. They can fly at a speed of 200 miles per hour, making them the fastest members of the animal kingdom. I kept looking for these birds, but didn't see any.

I continued my descent on what appeared to be a very popular and well maintained trail in the Franconia Notch State Park. After crossing a bridge over the Pemigewasset River, the A.T. turned right, but the visitor's center was another mile to the left. I thought, "What's another mile or two" and began walking down the combination of paved paths, trails, and Highway 3 until I found my way into the busy visitor's center. I called Ed and Mary Bagley and told them I had arrived. They are the

relatives of a friend of mine who had arranged for them to let me stay at their home for a night. A helpful woman retrieved the supply box Kelly had mailed to me. In the snack bar, I ordered a cheeseburger and bought some milk and ice-cream to make my own milk shake. Before I could finish eating, the Bagleys arrived and found me without too much difficulty. I guess I stood out among the clean weekend tourists. My hosts were delightful and took me to the see where the famous "Old Man of the Mountains" rock formation had been before it collapsed on May 3, 2005. There was a park where you could stand in a certain place and, with the aid of a metal silhouette, see what the formation once looked like. The "Old Man of the Mountains" is a symbol for New Hampshire and its image is on the state's quarter and license plate. I thought about the disappointment that citizens of New Hampshire must feel that their state's symbol is no more. Its disappearance reminded me that we are all part of an interesting, changing, and dynamic earth and universe.

In the Bagley's home, I took a shower, looked in a mirror at my body, and weighed myself. I had lost 15 pounds and my hips were covered with big brown bruises. Because of the blistered sores, my ears looked like I wore earrings. My knees and feet were swollen. I wore some of Ed's clothes while mine were being washed. The Bagleys took me to four stores until I found the supplies I needed, and fed me a boiled New

England dinner. In one large pot, Mary boiled corned beef, cabbage, onion, carrots, potatoes, parsnips, and seasonings to make a filling and tasty meal. Ed showed me the place in his yard where he fed animals who visited regularly, including bears, raccoons, deer, and sometimes, a porcupine. I dried my tent and then repacked everything with my new food and a full supply of denatured alcohol. I had added PowerBars to my list of snack foods. I dabbed my bleeding ears with Neosporin and took medicine for my cough. Before going to bed, I carefully spread out my handkerchief and some paper towels on the nice clean pillow so my ears would not bleed on it. The next morning I was pleased to discover that my plan had worked.

DAY

35

The Nature of Water

Franconia Notch
to Gordon Pond (Mt. Wolf)

Mary Bagley treated me to a huge breakfast before she and Ed drove me to the Franoncia Notch State Park. Ed had hiked this part of the trail up to Lonesome Lake and said I would love it. They couldn't have been more encouraging, and I gave them hugs to express my gratitude before I walked back to the A.T. At 7:30 a.m. the air was crisp, and I could see my every breath. The trail followed alongside the Cascade Brook, a rushing torrent of small cataracts and gushing streams pouring into streams. Signs warned hikers not to cross it during times of high water. I was able to hop across on several rocks and continue up the mountain beside what seemed like a half mile of cascading waterfalls, With the help of blocks and metal rungs that had been attached to the cliff, I was able to carefully climb the slick granite slopes. Several times I thought that if I were with a group, we'd be using safety harnesses and ropes to prevent injuries if someone slipped or fell. My tumbles on Wildcat Mountain were not far from my mind. Probably every A.T. hiker could tell their own polished granite nightmare story. A few times, a block gave way, so I checked every one to make sure it was secure before I trusted it with my weight.

Hiking beside the powerful, noisy, crashing water gave me energy. It reminded me of the ways water is used as a metaphor—justice flowing like waters, the river of life, living water, and quiet waters bringing comfort and empowerment. The waters next to where I was climbing were flowing with freedom and abandon. Just as I was drawn to watch and listen to the bubbling, dancing waters cascading down the hills and mountains, people were drawn to Jesus. We sometimes think the path to God is a matter of climbing upward, like the vision Jacob had of a ladder to God, or rising like the chariot of Elijah, but Jesus also shows us a path of descent. The first three Beatitudes are a call downward: "Blessed are the poor in spirit...blessed are those who mourn... and blessed are the meek" (Matthew 5:3-5). The movement downward roots us in the soil from which we were created. In soil science, the Latin word "humus," or soil, refers to mature compost of soil organic matter, and it's the stem for the words humility and human. Water loves the lowest point, and it's in the sacrament of baptism that those being baptized descend, allowing an elder to guide, handle, and control them as they are ritually cleansed and reborn. It's no small thing to hand yourself over to someone and have him put you under the frightening water.

The downward path of this backpacking trip had put me in the vulnerable position of needing and accepting help and charity from others. Most of us wear protective armor for a variety of reasons, many of them practical. Armor can help us deal with intolerable anguish or endure the many stresses of life. But while the armor shields us from pain, it can also separate us from our emotions.

After hiking for two hours, I arrived at Lonesome Lake and met a large family who had spent the night there to celebrate a birthday. The children, teenagers, parents, and grandparents were all in high spirits as they were now slowly hiking back to their cars.

I asked a child who looked to be eight years old, "Did you have fun?"

The joy in his eyes and his relaxed smile spoke volumes as he said, "It was awesome!"

When I reached the hut, I marveled at the way it was spread out with decks and entrances to different sleeping rooms and an open kitchen with a long counter. An added feature was a nice view of the lake. I used the privy and signed in at the trail register. There were muffins and breads for sale, but I had a full pack of food. Heading out again, I hiked with John from Boston, who was taking his time hiking to Hanover. He said we were lucky because the Appalachian Mountain Club (AMC) now maintained this section of the trail with stepping blocks and metal rungs, something I'd already learned to appreciate. Some years earlier, John had broken four ribs in a fall and had stayed inside his tent for two days before he could sit up and hike off the trail.

After hearing his story, I glanced at the feather and said, "Thanks."

I'd been told that the north and south rims of Kinsman Mountain were steep and brutal, and in the hours I spent on its slopes, I had to admit that I had not been misled. At one point the clouds covered the mountain and it began to hail. During my descent, I met a young northbound thru-hiker who was carrying a jacket in one hand. We talked for a while and he said it couldn't fit in his pack. He was bringing it to a friend who had left it behind. I couldn't imagine climbing up these mountains without having the use of both hands and feet. He said that if it had been his jacket he would have already thrown it off the mountain, but this was a really good friend and he felt obligated. Seeing the hardship the jacket had caused him over the past few days, and his loyalty, almost brought tears to my eyes. I told him he was a very good friend and moved on. After 10 minutes of climbing down the mountain, I thought of the large red twist ties I had on my pack, which I used to fasten socks or shirts to my pack so they could dry as I walked. He could lash the jacket to the outside of his pack with them. Turning back, I looked at the steep grade trail and knew I couldn't catch him and wished I'd thought of my solution earlier.

It was about a 1500-foot drop from South Kinsman summit to Eliza Brook Shelter, and all along the way there were rushing tributaries that seemed to meet and join forces. It was not unusual to see standing water in the trail, but I was surprised to see a white moth had gotten stuck in the water. I'd been trying to capture a white moth for days, but it was like me, always in flight. Yet, every time I needed some reassurance, it seemed to be around. I took out my camera and took a photo of the water logged moth. Then I used the tip of my hiking pole to gently lift it out of the water and set it on the ground. I watched as it began to crawl and shake. It must have been tired because, for a while, it stayed at rest, just slowly raising its wings up and down. I wanted to encourage it to fly, but knew it had to find its own way. I left it there, drying its wings, fully expecting to see it fly past me soon.

The trail was not well maintained, and I had to skirt one mud hole after another. I stopped to sit on a log beside a stream for lunch and to build a prayer cairn. I placed rocks for my family, for Ed and Mary Bagley, and for the hiker with the coat, who was such a loyal friend. The world was a better place because of them. It was 3:00 p.m., too early in the day to stop, when I passed the Eliza Brook Shelter and kept walking. There seemed to be a number of logging roads that crossed the path as I climbed the East Peak of Mt. Wolf. The mountain was wooded and I began to hear songbirds. When I stopped to watch a pair of bluebirds, one dodged behind a tree, then came out and looked at me, then hid behind a rock. I enjoyed the game of hide and seek before they flew off.

I began to look for a campsite after Mount Wolf. The rules stated that hikers are not to camp within 200 feet of the A.T. There was a trail down to Gordon Pond, and I hoped to find a stealth campsite, which is an undesignated, flat place where people have camped and sometimes leave a fire ring, sitting log, and a flat rock for a stove. When I didn't, I found a fairly flat surface and made a stealth campsite for myself. For supper I enjoyed hamburger meat and vegetables, and hot tea. As I read my night prayer in my tent, I heard animals moving around me. It occurred to me that the Gordon Pond trail was a thoroughfare for the local animals, and I tried to cover my ears so their traffic would not wake me.

DAY

36

The Breadth of God's Love

Gordon Pond (Mt. Wolf)
to Mt. Mist

I had gone to sleep thinking about animals walking near the tent and then was awakened in the middle of the night by the sound of grunting. It could have been a bear, but the clomping sounded more like the step of a moose. "I'm just a guest in its home," I said to myself. The heavy-footed steps came near my tent and stopped. My sense of hearing became hypersensitive to every leaf blowing and twig breaking. My mind flashed on horror stories I had heard about human and animal encounters. At a campsite next to Bear Claw Lake in the Grand Teton National Park, a grizzly bear ripped up a tent and the backpacker barely escaped. Then there was the moose who didn't like the yellow raft in a lake and chased the father and son who paddled it as fast as they could. When they got to shore, they ran, and the moose stomped the raft to pieces. What if the moose outside didn't want a green tent here. If he kicked and stomped, could I exit quickly enough and climb a tree? I tried to remember what trees were nearby. I turned on my flashlight and began getting out of my sleeping bag when the large animal tromped on down the trail. Eventually, I went back to sleep and woke to the sound of honking ducks.

The hike down to Highway 112 in Kinsman Notch was uneventful, but the climb up Beaver Brook Cascades was one of my favorite ascents. At the top I took off the Green Giant and took a break, meditating by the waterfalls. The water that was surging on a downward path into various pools reminded me of how God poured out His love through the energy of Jesus' love. It occurred to me that God sent a part of Himself to the earth to show us His true nature. Humanity responded with violence, but the crucifixion did not cause God to love less. God is love. This idea

283

is different from the notion that Jesus died because of our sin. I prefer to think that he sacrificed himself to demonstrate the cascading love of God. Loving is what God does. I wanted to live this kind of loving life. There was power and energy in the gurgling, rushing water, and I imagined that I was one of the pools being filled with God's grace and love, which overflowed and spread to others down the path.

The trail followed the cascading brook for what seemed like a mile. At places where the polished granite was too steep, wooden steps and rebar hand rungs had been attached to the rocks. There were also a number of rock steps to assist the hikers. A sign warned that in icy weather the trail could be dangerous. It seemed fairly dangerous to me on a nice day. Like the day before, the energy of the rushing water seemed to give me energy as well.

I had been told that Mt. Moosilauke (elevation 4802 feet) was the last of the giant bald mountains I would have to climb before making my descent to the Vermont border. Because I had a good night's rest and eaten plenty of good food, I was ready for the challenge. I read that backpackers burn 6,000 calories a day and was sure I had calories to spare. It was a beautiful day to hike because the sun was shining. When I reached the alpine zone above the tree line, I unexpectedly saw a grassy meadow with the trail cutting through it and signs asking hikers not to venture off the trail into the fragile zone. As I continued to climb, the grass turned into a clear, open boulder field, exposing over 100 acres of alpine tundra and rocks. The mountain's name, Moosilauke, means "high bald place" in the Pemigewasset Native American language, which was fitting. When I reached the peak, I built a prayer cairn and had a fellow hiker take my photo with the Moosilauke sign and view. Because of the angle of the sun, in the photo I appeared as a shadowy silhouette. The cold wind was so strong that many day hikers huddled next to the remnants of a building foundation to eat their lunch. The bricks belonged to a hotel called the Prospect House, which had been built there in 1860. Later, it became the Tip Top House and operated until it burned down in 1942. When I arrived in Hanover a few days later, I saw several photo books about Moosilauke, also known as "the gentle giant," and read that it was one of the most loved mountains in New Hampshire. I was surprised to learn that Dartmouth College owns a good bit of the side of the mountain and that the Dartmouth Outing Club had adopted the Tip Top before it burned.

The hike down the Moosilauke Carriage Road, a broad trail that had been built to bring tourists to the hotel, was not steep. There were a number of hikers walking up and down this side of the mountain, and for a while I joined a man from Vermont who had taken a day off from work for a day hike. The trail passed through a mature forest of old trees with diverse species and not much undergrowth, and I enjoyed listening to a variety of birds. I got some water from the well at the tidy Jeffers Brook Shelter and signed the trail register. Then I got off the trail somehow, came to highway 25, and had trouble finding where the trail crossed the road. Without a guidebook, I didn't know that southbound hikers were supposed to turn right and walk along the road for .6 miles to rejoin the trail. After wandering back and forth for a while, I finally found the right spot.

At "Hairy Root Spring" a large tree had fallen, exposing an eight-foot sized disk of roots with a spring underneath. The root mass indicated that the roots had grown sideways rather than downwards. Trees have a quiet dignity. Their roots usually go deep into the ground to anchor them and bring nourishment. The tree, which we see above ground, is balanced by a whole root system beneath. It seems to achieve a wonderful balance between its inner and outer life. Seeing the fallen tree made me ask, "How can such a tall straight tree fall victim to the winds?" Appearances can hide problems. Upon investigation I saw that just under the surface of the ground, the roots had begun to rot. I don't know what happened to this tree, but I do know what happens to people when we fail to develop an inner life that receives constant nourishing at its depths. We become out of balance and tend to become addicted to superficiality.

When some friends and I were in Ireland on retreat at Glenstall Abbey, I spent some time with Bro. Anthony, who leads a very popular Day Set Apart called "Mystagogy of the Forest." We talked about Job 38-40 where God asks Job, "Where were you when I laid out the foundations of the world?" Brother Anthony asked me what I thought the writer meant by "foundations of the world?" He suggested that God was talking about geology. In the British Isles some rocks are as old as 425 million years.

He said, "You know, we often think that God didn't begin a relationship with the earth until 4000 or 2000 years ago, but the Trinity—Father, Son and Holy Spirit—has been in relationship with the universe since the foundations were laid."

We think that real history is human history, and if it isn't in our Bible, it must not have happened.

"We have to believe," Brother Anthony said, "that God through the Holy Spirit is at work in the world, revealing aspects of holiness."

God's glory is written all around us. Nature is God's first Bible, and is certainly much longer than the one we know and claim as our own. It would be silly to think that God didn't care about other parts of creation than our small recent portion. We do know that in the Noah story God insisted on saving every living creature on Earth, suggesting that He cares about more than just us two legged beings. God must have gotten pleasure from His relationship with the creation prior to humans.

When talking with Brother Anthony and discussing the prayer walks I lead, I also told him about an exercise in which I invite people to get centered and still and then to look around to see if they are drawn to some part of nature—a rock, bark, bird, tree, flower, insect or squirrel. I encourage them to meditate on the object's character or life and ask if it speaks to them. For example, when I chose to watch a squirrel busily collecting and storing nuts, which I assumed means it is preparing for the future or maybe the winter, it sparked my imagination to ask if I need to spend time preparing for the future. Brother Anthony described that as a conscious endeavor. He challenged me just to allow the forest to work its magic on its own. Simply by experiencing the forest we can be blessed unaware—in an unconscious way. I think he was trying to tell me that there is a spiritual healing power in nature when we gain a new appreciation for the natural world. Our bodies and souls surprise us and fill us with joy and we bless and are blessed—we are connected to God, unaware.

About a mile beyond the spring, on the edge of Mt. Mist, I found a camping site overlooking Wachipauka Pond. I hoped I was the required two hundred feet off the trail. I celebrated passing the 400 mile marker this day with roast beef hydrated with Merlot, potatoes, and green beans for supper. I also had a toast with the leftover half cup of Merlot. Then I got out the bread and wine, the communion elements I had carried, and wondered if it was time for Holy Communion, but decided to wait.

The quietness of the evening was interrupted by the howl of coyotes. They were moving and traveling around the pond. Then I heard turkeys as they moved. I had not been asleep long when I woke to flashes of lightning and booms of thunder. The smell of rain filled my nostrils. I wondered why, earlier in the evening, I had missed signs of its impending arrival. It rained throughout the night. I woke up hourly and shined my light around the tent, looking for leaks. I stayed pretty dry, but the air was wet and chilly.

DAY

37

Gaining Perspective

Mt. Mist
to Smart Mountain Fire Warden's Cabin

When I got up, it was still raining I stuffed my sleeping bag inside the compression sack and then put it inside two Ziplock plastic bags. I knew that if I went outside in the rain and returned into the tent, I would get everything wet. So, I packed the pack first and leaned it against a tree while I brushed my teeth. Then I took down my tent and got going. At the overlook where I had had a nice view of Wachipauka Pond the day before, white mist hung in the air like an impenetrable curtain of white. Somehow I had misplaced my watch, and so didn't know what time I left the campsite. In the cloudy rain and fog, I couldn't see the morning sun and felt disoriented. The climb up Mt. Mist was pretty steep. Fortunately, the descent to Road 25 C was more gradual, and from there, it was five straightforward miles over Ore Hill to Road 25A. Along the way, I saw sugar maples that had begun to change colors, and I could tell it was going to be a beautiful fall, even if my day was wet and muddy.

I had been warned not to trust the drinking water around Ore Hill and the Ore Hill Brook. From 1834 until 1915, the area was mined for heavy metals, and piles of waste rock laced with arsenic, cadmium, copper, iron, lead, mercury and zinc had polluted aquatic life downstream for nearly a century. The old mine became the property of the federal government as part of the White Mountain National Forest in 1937, and the A.T. had passed the abandoned eyesore for decades. To improve the view, the Forest Service planted red pines, but they did not survive. Then in 2006 and 2007, it moved the trail a few hundred yards away, and excavated and cleaned and reseeded the area with wildflowers. My map showed an Ore Hill Shelter, but it had burned down a few years earlier, leaving only tent sites. I wondered if a camper had caused the destruction by building a fire too close to the shelter.

In the afternoon my aching muscles told me that the climb up the Cube Mountains was as difficult as any I had yet experienced. By the time I made it to the Hexacuba Shelter trail, I was tired. It was still rainy and, tired or not, I decided to push on and spend the night in the Smart Mountain fire tower. For years I had been wanting to sleep in a fire tower and here was my chance. Throughout the history of Christianity, there were individuals who tried to live a holy life on a rock pillar. The children's game "Simon Says" may have been named after one such holy man, St. Simeon Stylites, also known as Simon the Elder. He lived in the fifth century and spent nearly 40 years of his life on a 45-foot high pillar near Aleppo (now in modern Syria), standing, sitting and sleeping, and day and night, exposed to the elements. He was not only considered holy, but wise, and his pillar became a pilgrimage site. People would come from miles away to seek his wisdom and blessing. So revered was he that his words were taken as the gospel truth. St. Daniel prayed as he

was ascending his pillar near Constantinople in the fifth century, "May this manner of life teach me to lean on You alone….Strengthen me that I finish this painful course; give me grace to end it in holiness."

I've never wanted to live on a column, but I did pray that God would give me the strength to finish the hike. My body ached and I still was missing home. I don't think that sleeping in a fire tower would make me holy, but I hoped that it would be a great place for me to watch the sunset and sunrise and to look at the stars. I also thought that since I was nearing the end of my hike, it would be a good place to have Holy Communion with a 360 degree panorama view. It was 4:00 p.m. when I reached the bottom of Smart Mountain, with four miles to go to my destination at the top. It would be dark at 6:15, so I knew I needed a 30-minute mile pace. I got out my phone and listened to the Michael W. Smith worship albums for two hours and arrived just at dusk. I had two bumps on my forehead, mementos from running into trees branches that hung across the trail, while I was looking down at moose poop. I was worshiping in my heart, but did not bow before the Lord.

Smart Mountain (elev. 3240 feet) was shrouded in fog, rain, and clouds, and a strong, cold wind blew across the summit. I found the Fire Warden's cabin and kept looking for the Fire Tower, which the New Hampshire Forest Service used as a lookout from 1915 until 1973. When I located it, I climbed the stairs and popped open the trap door leading to the small cabin on top. My heart sank. Some windows were broken, allowing the chilly rain inside. I tried to imagine what the view might be if I could see farther than 10 feet. Climbing back down the ladder, I had to laugh. Cloudy white scenery was not what I had had in mind as a view.

It was completely dark by the time I made it down the trail to the Mike Murphy Spring to get water, and my hands and knees were shaking from the cold. Fortunately, the fire warden's cabin was completely enclosed and dry. The rhythmic beating of the rain on the tin roof was comforting. Since I was the only visitor, I stretched out my clotheslines and hung up my wet tent and clothes. I had a candlelit dinner for one, with Sesame Chicken as the entre and a snickers for desert. I hung my food so the mice couldn't reach it and snuggled in my sleeping bag. I thought about St. Daniel's prayer, "I lean on You alone. Give me strength to finish this painful course." His prayer became my night prayer, "Give me grace to end it in holiness." This desire for holiness was my longing. It occurred to me that life, like this hike, has holy moments, but those moments when I felt really connected to and "in tune" with God never lasted long. I could name my unholy moments as well as my holy ones. When I look at the lives of the saints, I overlook their human foibles. I trust God will overlook mine as well and grant me the ability to be at peace with them.

DAY

38

Using Our Gifts

Smart Mountain
to Etna Hanover Road

It took a while to get packed and going in the morning. During the night, the temperature had dipped into the high 20s, and I was moving in slow motion. The privy near the Smart Mountain tent site was unique in that it had an open back. Because of the rain, I didn't want to leave my pack on the soaked ground and ended up taking it inside with me. I felt both exhilarated and vulnerable sitting on a privy exposed to the woods. It was 7:45 before I started down Smart Mountain.

When I passed a sign indicating that the Vermont border was 26 miles away, my heart was filled with excitement; I realized with certainty that my goal was attainable. Planning the hike on my deck at home, I had overestimated my abilities. Then, I had projected traveling a distance of 500 miles, some 50 miles into Vermont; on the actual trail, however, my pace was slower and the length of my trip grew uncertain. As I hiked I often doubted I could even make it to the Vermont state line. Everyone I met told me, "After the Whites, it is all downhill to the Connecticut River on the Vermont Border." Unlike them, I found it difficult going. My sore feet and tired muscles, and the constant rain, mud, and slick rocks tested me. But now I had the end in sight.

In a shelter journal I had read hikers' recommendations to stop at the home of Bill, the ice cream man, who offers "trail magic." Although in a hurry, I decided a short break for ice cream would be okay. A side trail led to a house with Tibetan prayer and peace flags hanging on the front porch. The door opened before I could knock, and Bill ushered me into the dining room, where he began asking me about my hike. He had a kind, engaging manner and recorded my name in the register he used

to track how many hikers had stopped by during this season. He asked about the most difficult aspect of my journey, and I told him homesickness and isolation from people. He nodded and said, "Yes, the mental struggle is the hardest obstacle. It takes great mental as well as physical strength to complete the hike. But you have a whole congregation of people who are supporting and cheering you on."

I confessed that I'd worked hard to separate myself from my work, and I realized that I kept forgetting the gift of a big group of people rooting for me.

As I was leaving and passed the Tibetan prayer, I told Bill of my prayer mantra, "Peace with every step."

He affirmed that prayer and offered another, "Peace everywhere."

I appreciated his tender care and, as I walked away, a hundred questions came to mind that I wished I'd asked him. He was the first person in many days with whom I'd actually had a conversation, other than saying hello. Later I learned from a newspaper article that he'd been a professor at Harvard and then a psychologist in private practice. In his "retirement" he had become a very special giver.

Not far from Bill's house was the Trapper John Shelter, named after the fictitious character from the television series *Mash*, who had graduated from Dartmouth. Thinking about him and that show made me smile. A fence along Holt's Ledge, where the outcroppings are home to nesting peregrine falcons, kept me from sliding off when I lost my footing on a wet rock. I made it safely down and realized with pleasure that the steep 4,000-6,000 foot climbs were finally over.

The rain continued to come down steadily, but I was grateful it was not a downpour. The leaves were changing colors and, occasionally, the sun tried to poke out for a few minutes before rain clouds descended again. I walked by the first fields I had seen since beginning at Katahdin. Large ferns dotted the ground of the beautiful hardwood forest. Along the more open roads and fields were trees with thick tree branches that grew close to the ground as well as up near the crowns. "These trees have an easier time gathering light than others that struggle to raise their branches above the canopy," I thought, and I reflected on the difficult lives some people have just to survive, when others seem to have it easy. In the lifecycle of a forest there is competition, leaving some trees under less stress than others. Each step made a muted crunching sound on the wet leaves which had fallen. I was able to pray my walking prayer, "Peace with every step" and found it most meaningful when I prayed it for different family members and others. I felt as though I was surrounding them with a blanket of peace, joy, love, grace, community, Jesus, smiles, hope, forgiveness, and strength.

My pace was quick, and I arrived at the Moose Mountain shelter (elevation 2290 feet) at 4 in the afternoon and immediately cooked supper. The water source at the shelter had dried up, and so the caretaker had purchased a few five gallon jugs of water and carried them up them up the mountain for hikers. I appreciated his gift of trail magic. It was windy and I kept shivering even after putting on all the clothes I had. I didn't want to spend another freezing night on top of a mountain if I had a warmer option. My map indicated that I would cross a road five miles farther down the trail. My A.T. guidebook listed a hiker hostel called

"Tigger's Tree House." The owners preferred hikers to call a day ahead to stay there. The battery on my phone was almost dead, but I called the number and left a message saying, "I am at Moose Mountain Shelter, and I want to get off the mountain and get out of the cold. I would love to stay at the hostel." I gave my phone number and turned off my phone to save the battery. As I packed up I looked at the feather on Green Giant and said, "Okay, I'm going to trust that I'm going to get a little help here," and prayed that something would work out.

I hiked as fast as I could and made it to the road, narrowly beating darkness. I had walked 19.5 miles in one day. When I turned on my phone, I was overjoyed to hear a voicemail from a woman named Karen who said, "Just call us when you get to the road by the cemetery, and I'll come and get you." It took me a while to find the cemetery and call. The ground was wet, and as I stood waiting I thought about how in the One Hundred Mile Wilderness I was hesitant to accept anything from strangers. Now, I was seeking help and going to a stranger's home. About 20 minutes later, a car pulled up and a woman's broad smile welcomed me into her car. Karen was of medium height and build, and smartly dressed in a casual way, as if she would be equally at home in the White House gardens or volunteering at the food bank. She stopped by a country store for me to get food, but I figured with only 6.5 miles to go I didn't need to replenish my food supplies. Besides, I had already eaten a good supper at Moose Mountain Shelter. Tigger's Tree House turned out to be a camper in the couple's backyard. I took a shower, washed my clothes, cooked a frozen pizza in their basement, and ate some ice cream. I could have eaten more, but then I remembered how disgusted I had been earlier on the trail when I saw a young women eat a half gallon of ice cream. I realized I could easily do that now myself, but I refrained. The camper wasn't heated, but it was heaven to be there. My excitement to finish the hike kept me from sleeping well. The next morning, Karen drove me back to the trail and recommended I eat breakfast at Lou's Bakery in Hanover, New Hampshire.

DAY

39

The Red Feather

**Etna Hanover Road
to the Vermont Border
September 28, 2012**

An occasional fern dotted the open forest floor between the huge, sparsely spaced hardwoods. For the first few miles past the Etna Hanover Road, it was a beautiful place to walk. Attractive wooden bridges crossed over bogs, and it seemed as though I was walking in a neighborhood's backyard. I barely noticed the light rain under the canopy of the trees. Still, rocks, roots and mud made the miles drag on as I anticipated getting to Hanover. I was beginning to feel sorry for myself when I felt a moment of resistance before landing on the ground. My pack had snagged a branch and had quickly lost the tug of war. I felt like I'd been thrown back by a slingshot and laughed at how the trail even now continued to humble me. I was tired of climbing mountains and disappointed when the switchbacks began under the hemlocks and pines on the way up the Velvet Rocks Ridge.

Once again, I was fighting the trail rather than accepting it as it was. I gave myself a scolding, "Have I learned nothing over these 40 days?" The shell on the Green Giant was smashed. I wondered if I would be like the woman in the parable who carried a jar of flour from the market to her home without realizing that in the journey the handle had broken and the flour had begun to leak out. By the time she got home, the flour was gone (Gospel of Thomas: 97). I thought it would be sad for me to discover at the end of this hike that my heart still had such a long way to go in the transformation.

There were swamps, stream crossings, and several steep ridges to climb before finally reaching the Velvet Rocks Shelter. I guessed the name

"Velvet Rocks" came from the moss-covered granite scattered long the spine of the ridge, which seemed to extend for several miles. I hadn't met another thru-hiker, or even a section hiker in several days, and was tired of the isolation. I had pushed my body hard for six weeks. My forehead was red from bumps, my knees were bloody from falls, my hips had large bruises from carrying the Green Giant, and my legs were trembling. I didn't stop to examine the shelter, which had been built in 1936 on the Dartmouth campus to recruit members to the Dartmouth outdoor club. Then it was relocated here. Two more miles and I would be in Hanover for breakfast. The rain was coming down pretty hard and the raindrops were dripping from my hat, making it difficult for me to see out of my scratched up glasses. When I finally emerged from the trail onto a gravel road beside a sports field, the rain was pouring down in sheets. It took me a while to find Lou's Bakery because I mistook the white reflectors on the utility poles for white trail blazes and had to consult my map. When I finally got to the restaurant, it was packed with clean, well-dressed, talkative people. I left the dripping wet Green Giant near the door and ordered the "Big Green Breakfast," made from locally grown food. The pancakes, muffins, bacon, and fruit were more than I could eat.

It was the Friday of homecoming weekend for Dartmouth College, and there were signs welcoming the alumni back to different events and gatherings. Dartmouth is the ninth oldest college in the United States. It was started in a one-room cabin in the pine woods to educate the youth of the Indian tribes, and others. Reverend Wheelock, the first teacher, had four students. I think I would have felt more at home at the old college than the new. I was the only wet dirty smelly backpacker on the streets of this Ivy League town. I went into the exclusive Hanover Inn lobby. The hotel staff was kind and allowed me to check the Green Giant and gave me information about the bus stop and schedule. I walked across the campus and down the sidewalk on the busy street to the Connecticut River and Vermont border. I crossed the massive bridge and took photos of the "Welcome to Vermont" sign. At 407 miles the Connecticut River is the longest waterway in New England. I watched how the pouring rain mixed with the swirling current. I had imagined sitting on a bench here to contemplate what the past 39 days had meant. I wished I had a ritual way to end the hike. When I couldn't have communion at the fire tower, I hoped to have it here at the river, but decided against it. Hikers going north place rocks on a huge cairn on Baxter Peak of Mount Katahdin, but standing the river alone in the pouring rain, with cars rushing by, did not make for a good contemplative setting.

After I thought of it, the water itself symbolized new birth and renewal. We are nurtured in the water of the womb, and I was finishing my goal in the middle of the Connecticut River (elev. 400 feet) at the lowest point on my journey, and one day this water that had traveled down from the mountains would be in the ocean, and some would turn to mist and ascend to the sky. The bridge had a large granite wall with columns spanning its length, acting as a balustrade. I contemplated the lessons I had learned during the past thirty-nine days. Determined to take my own photo with the "VT" marking on the bridge, I squatted and took several selfies, adjusting the frame each time.

I had hoped to go into a thrift store to buy some old clothes that I could wear as I returned to civilization, but Hanover around Dartmouth had none that I could find. Did I belong to this world, or the world of being in the woods? When it came time for the bus, I retrieved my pack, stored it in the compartment underneath, and was happy to sit down for the ride to Boston. I felt sorry for the lady who sat next to me. She was polite and never mentioned my appearance, or my smell. After hiking in the rain for three days, I was happy to have completed the 443 miles of the A.T. and proud of the accomplishment. I was not returning home rested in body, but I was much richer in spirit. I was aware that I did not do it alone. It would've been inappropriate to just say, "I did it," and more honest to say, "Thank God, I did it."

It seemed strange to watch the fields and mountains fly by outside the window. Once I arrived in Boston, I navigated the metro to visit my niece Amy and her husband Aaron. In the crowded subway car I got overheated and had trouble holding on to my backpack while wearing my warm hiking clothes. A man must have noticed because he kindly offered me his seat. I took it and quickly stripped off my wet fleece. I caught a bus to get to my niece's apartment not far from Boston College. After cleaning up, we walked to a pub for dinner. I ordered a green salad, the first in weeks, and it tasted heavenly. The futon in their apartment felt like paradise, too.

DAY

40

Communion

Portland, Maine

The next morning the three of us took a bus to Portland, where Amy would run her first marathon. After she registered, I shopped for Maine souvenirs and some clothes. I used my last cash for a taxi to take me to a hotel near the airport, where I took yet another shower just because I could. I unwrapped the bread and wine I had carried up and down the mountains for 443 miles and carefully laid them on the desk. The words of Bishop Kenneth Goodson came to my mind, "It is no small thing to hold in your hands the body and the blood of Christ." It was no small thing to carry the presence of God on this journey. God was just as present in the noisy city, in the hotel room, as he would have been in a church. The rite of the "Eucharist," first held by Jesus at the Last Supper, means thanksgiving. Sometimes we call the liturgy "The Great Thanksgiving," where we recall God's love which is so reckless that it led to Jesus being crucified on the cross. We remember that love has the final word through the resurrection.

I pulled out a bag of different colored and sized stones and laid them out in a spiral formation on the desk. In the center I put some large rich colored stones. One represented Mt. Katahdin, another signified my struggle up White Cap Mountain. A smooth black stone represented David's injury and having to leave the trail. A brown flat stone symbolized spending the night on Chairback Mountain. A pencil shaped stone denoted my fall and my injured finger, which was still swollen. A dark stone stood for my burned or uncooked food. A smooth stone represented the bumps on my head from the times I hit it on a tree branch that extended across the trail. A scallop looking stone recalled my falls down Wildcap Mountain. A stone with holes, yet smooth from rushing water,

307

epitomized fording dangerous streams and rivers. A solid rectangle stone symbolized the Mahoosuc Notch. Another stone represented crawling across Mount Madison, and a black rough stone signified Mount Washington. I placed a small white stone designating the moments I was homesick and wanted to give up; and another stone, reddish in color, for my sore muscles and swollen knees. A stone that I imagined look like a raindrop, suggested the wet and foggy days. Between these stones in the spiral I began to place smaller stones, lighter in color, which represented the moments of peace and joy I felt as I prayed my walking prayers, and later hummed as a wordless prayer. They also represented my church community, which was praying for me. Some were for friends and family, who were also remembering me in their prayers. Others were for the people I had met who encouraged me. And still others were for people who had offered trail magic. There were stones for people who gave me rides when I was hitchhiking, and for the Bagleys, who offered hospitality and support. There were far more light colored stones than dark, and the spiral created a labyrinth symbolizing the past forty days.

I went to the Green Giant and unfastened the red feather. I began on the outside of the labyrinth and slowly moved the feather through the path to the interior, silently giving thanks that, indeed, the God of love had accompanied me throughout the journey. God was there throughout, even when I was desperate to feel His presence and did not. God could be trusted. The feather came to the center, the place where traditionally, persons who pray in the labyrinth imagine union with God. I turned the feather upside down and stood it up with the help of some rocks. It reminded me of a flame. And there it was—in the center of the grace and trials, pain and love—the "Living Flame" of God's love. The light in the room seemed brighter. I broke off some bread.

Tears began to fall down my cheeks as I lifted the bread and dipped it in the plastic cup of deep dark wine. I silently thanked God and prayed that this bread, wine, and hike would make a difference in my life and, in so doing, make a difference in the world. I wondered if I was finally beginning to understand Psalm 121, "I lift up my eyes to the hills from where my help comes. My help is in the Lord."

Epilogue

On the plane ride to Alabama, I closed my eyes and played scenarios over in my mind about how best to express my joy at coming home. I imagined getting off the plane, kneeling, and kissing the ground. I had done that once before, when I returned from living in Europe. This time, it was not the American soil I wanted to kiss, but my family, pets, home, and church. I was looking forward to the sweet smell of the honey house, where we process honey in the backyard, and the twittering bluebirds and cardinals. I wondered if the pileated woodpeckers and hawks would be nearby when I arrived, or if I would have to seek them out. Kelly had told me that she'd redecorated our bedroom and that I would love it. At that point, any soft place to stretch out was welcome. It's funny how we don't realize the depth of our love until it has been absent, or almost lost.

After we landed, my stiff legs ached as I pulled them from under the seat, and I grimaced in pain as I walked through the tunnel to the gate, and then to the end of the terminal. Waiting there were a smiling Kelly and Laurel, holding green helium filled balloons and a "Welcome Home, Dad" sign. Tears of joy filled our eyes as we hugged and exchanged kisses. When I hugged Kelly again, this time more deeply, I felt my shoulders let down and relax.

"Okay, let's move on, don't embarrass me," Laurel said as she watched us exchange a long kiss.

In the car on the way home, she commented, "Dad, your beard is long and you need a haircut. You smell, did you shower?" I was surprised because I had showered, and I'd washed my clothes and was wearing a new shirt.

"Really?" I asked. "I don't smell me, but I know I've smelled much much worse."

Kelly thought it was funny that I didn't notice the lingering sweat and odor. Later, my niece Amy told me that I had smelled in Boston, too, but she didn't want to mention it at the time. Kelly suggested we eat anywhere I wanted and I chose a favorite Mexican restaurant.

When we entered the house from the backyard, I could see Buddy, our lab/chow mix, bark and repeatedly leap up the full height of the back door, while our smaller black dog, Yoda, twirled around in a happy dance. When we opened the door, they burst inside, filling the room with boundless energy and barking. Yoda greeted me with siren-like yips. Petting and talking to them didn't calm them down—it took food to do that. Francisco the cat took note of the homecoming with studied disinterest from the back of the sofa. He stood up, stretched, yawned, and wandered into another room to resume his nap without interruption.

I was still hobbling and feeling exhausted as I began my first week of meetings and hospital visits, an appointment with an eye doctor, and repeatedly answering the question "How was your hike?" My body was rebelling and telling me that I had pushed it too hard, so at first, I answered that it had been real hard, and I was glad I made it. When a dear grandmother asked, "Was there anything you liked about it?" I realized that instead of letting my words come from my overall positive experience, I was letting my sore muscles speak. Thereafter, I began answering the question with the promise of doing a program, complete with slides, in which I'd tell them all about it.

The congregation welcomed me back in worship with a standing ovation. I felt them sending me so much love it brought tears to my eyes. I had prayed over and over that they would have peace, love, hope grace, joy, strength, community, forgiveness, and Jesus with every step, and now it felt as though they were overwhelming me with an abundance of these same virtues. My heart moved up to my throat as I looked into the faces of those who had surrounded me with prayers for safety, love, and renewal. My emotions got the best of me, and I had to take several breaths before I could begin the sermon, which was structured around parts of the daily prayer I used on my hike. I shared how I had meditated for days on different words in my morning or evening prayers, such as "devote," as in "stir up within me a desire…to devote this day to you, O Lord." I asked the congregation to ponder with me the question of how we devote our energy, time and resources, and how our lives might be different if we truly devoted each day to God. There was a practical reason why I chose this topic. Giving in the church had dropped while I was gone, and there were bills to pay. When I recently reread that sermon, I was struck by the relaxed, easy-going flow of the words as I illustrated my points using the different sights I had experienced on the trail.

That Sunday afternoon we had a "blessing of the animals" service on the front patio of the church. It was a warm, sunny day with a cool breeze. I was delighted to meet the pets of our community and offer each one a prayer, and receive a blessing back from them. Several women who had brought pets with illnesses were in tears as I offered a prayer of healing. After the service, church members and neighbors were carrying their birds back to their cars, wishing they had not brought their pesky cats, and were allowing their dogs to smell around the flower beds and bushes, and one another. A woman approached me and said, "This hike changed you. You are more at peace than I've ever seen you." I took a deep breath and her words felt true.

For several weeks I worked on typing up my journal and assembling a PowerPoint presentation of photos from the hike. To my surprise, on the Wednesday night of the program, the fellowship hall was packed with joy and energy not only from members of our church, but curious neighbors as well, eager to join me on my journey. They laughed when I described my terror of losing my eyesight only to realize that my glasses were scratched up. I shared my anxiety when I showed them the photo of the beaver dam I had been afraid to cross. They smiled as I confessed how fighting the trail only brought on suffering. They oohed at the stunning, above-cloud sunrise photos from Mt. Madison. They were horrified that I had slept in the crevice of a cliff during a storm, but laughed with me as I described the squirrel's surprise at seeing me at dawn. They asked many questions about how I cooked, packed, and used my walking poles, and wanted to hear about my loneliness. They didn't seem as surprised as I was that my biggest obstacle was being homesick. It was a wonderful celebration.

It took several months before I felt rested enough to want to hike again. Since then, I have discovered a passion for helping others, especially young people, learn to love and feel at home in the woods. Our family hiked 200 miles on the Camino de Santiago pilgrim trail in Spain in the summer of 2013. Both of my daughters have shown an interest in back-packing. Laurel, her cousin Amy, and Amy's husband Aaron came with me to hike a section of the A.T. in Vermont in 2014. Sarah, my oldest daughter, has enjoyed camping and hiking with college friends and called to say, "Dad, I need a tent and a backpack."

In 2015 Kelly and I hiked the Maryland section of the A.T. with a group of thru-hikers. One of them, a young man with the trail name "Thor" decided my trail name, "Falls-a-lot," needed to be altered. He talked it over with his friends and changed my trail name to 'Sir Falls-a-lot."

Each year now, some friends and I are leading groups of young people on their first backpacking trips and on day hikes. Every month someone shows up at my office wanting to try out backpacking and seeking advice on gear and where to go, and I often loan out camping equipment to them.

The trip has also lessened my anxiety about facing tasks that seem monumental. "We can tackle large problems," I tell people. We can scale mountains that seem impossible by taking our time and climbing one step at a time. On several occasions, I have gone on trips without making hotel reservations, knowing that if I take my pack and tent, all I really need is a small patch of earth to be happy. This confidence has empowered me to live life with less anxiety and more gusto. When a friend said he thought I was full of "grit and vinegar," I laughed out loud. I had never thought of myself in that way. Strength and determination are not traits I would not have put on my list of gifts prior to my hike.

Another thing I learned was how much the support of my family means to me and how to ask for what I need. My wife and kids have responded enthusiastically, and our greater openness in communicating our mutual needs has resulted in stronger relationships. Kelly and I have grown closer each day of our 31-year marriage and this 40-day pilgrimage in the woods, while seeming to cause me to take some steps backwards, accelerated the growth. While being apart was laden with fears and anxiety on both sides, the return home to my family and to our marriage accomplished what a time of leaving home can do for both of us. So I might even add that the second half of our marriage has been fortified for the inner journey. This leaves me hopeful that we can not only endure but thrive and share with those under our care the blessing of a healthy marriage.

I want to keep in mind the voices and faces of people who offered unselfish and joyful love on and off the trail, and model myself after them. Many offered gifts without knowing they did—the store clerk clucking as he told a joke, the waitress offering encouragement. Others are more deliberate about their gifts of love—the unseen angels who maintain the trail, the friendly shuttle drivers, the practitioners of trail magic. I would like to think that because they unselfishly show love to strangers, they live a larger and deeper life and will have their own reward. I want to be like them.

Remembering is a challenge, and something that continues to help me is the words of my morning prayer. By saying, "All day long, God is working for good in the world," I am reminded to work with God on bringing good into the world. This is especially helpful when there is disappointment, suffering, and pain around us. Looking for the silver lining helps me to find it or accept that it is there, even when I can't see it. As the prophet Isaiah proclaims (Isaiah 40:31 selected): "Those who wait for the Lord shall renew their strength…they shall walk and not faint." On the trail, when I was in need, I cried out to the Lord for help and depended upon God to be with me. It even worked when I prayed without words or images, but simply hummed and acknowledged emptiness. Remembering that His strength is available to me in many forms has been a blessing many times since the hike.

* * *

In April, 2015, almost three years after my 40-day trek, three friends and I hiked the Appalachian Trail just north of the Great Smoky Mountain Park. As we began, I felt once again a rush of excitement. Since my time in Maine and New Hampshire, the manufacturer had repaired my green giant pack, and replaced the tent poles and the fly of my tent, which had become sticky. The boots I had worn in 2012 had fallen apart and I had broken in new ones, but much of my gear was the same, making me feel a bit sentimental.

Added to my emotions was the awareness that in my pack I carried a portion of the ashes of my hiking friend Michael Stewart, who had died suddenly of a massive stroke at the age of 60. He had loved this section of the A.T. and especially the bald section on Max Patch. It was to him my wife turned when she was worried about me after I left a message on her phone saying I wanted to quit.

The rich smell of the woods was invigorating. The unbridled abundance of early spring wildflowers was breathtaking—rhododendron, trillium, blood root, toothwort, trout lily, shooting starts and Indian pink thickly carpeted the forest floor and mountain sides in a riot of white and purple and yellow and red blossoms.

"Michael would love this" I said to my friends.

While waiting for slower hikers in our group to make it up the mountain, I tried to dry out my tent and ground cloth. We watched a storm quickly move from south to north. The wind shifted and soon the fog and rain enveloped us. After about thirty minutes, the wind pushed the rain cloud past the mountain top. I took Michael's ashes out of my pack and said: "Ashes to ashes, dust to dust, earth to earth. We thank you, O God, for giving Michael to us, now we give him back to you, on this place he loved. Rest in peace, friend. Amen" The wind spread the ashes across Max Patch bald. By the time we were ready to keep hiking, the sun was shining once more and the fog had burned away to reveal a distant view of mountain ridges beyond mountains ridges. Some were in shadows, and some were in sunlight.

End Notes

1   Jennifer Pharr Davis, *Called Again. A Story of Love and Triumph*, Beaufort Books, New York, 2013

2   Thomas Merton, *Mystic and Zen Masters*, Dell Publishing Co., New York, 1967, p. 92

3   John Neff; *Katahdin: An Historic Journey*, Appalachian Mountain Club, 2006, p. 16

4   Henry David Thoreau, *The Maine Wood*, Bramhall House, New York, p. 277

5   Ibid, p. 274

6   John Neff; *Katahdin, An Historic Journey*, Appalachian Mountain Club, 2006, p. 50

7   Thoreau, *The Maine Wood*, p. 270

8   V. Collins Chew, *Under Foot, A Geologic Guide to the Appalachian Trail*, Appalachian Trail Conference, 1993, pp. 159, 164

9   Thoreau, *The Maine Wood*, p. 277

10 Richard Rohr, *8 Principles of the Center for Action and Contemplation*, Franciscan Media, Cincinnati, 2013

11 Thomas Merton, *Mystics and Zen Masters*, Farrar, Straus and Giroux, New York, 1967, pp. 94, 112

12 Levine, *In An Unbroken Voice,* p. 92

13 Henry David Thoreau, *On Man and Nature*, Peter Pauper Press, Mount Vernon, p. 8

14 Robert Bly, *Iron John*, Addison-Wesley Publishing Company, Reading, 2008

15 *Appalachian Trail Guide to Maine*, 15th edition, p. 71

16 Zara Renander, *Labyrinths: Journeys of Healing, Stories of Grace*, Bardolf & Company, Sarasota, 2011

17 Urban Holmes, *A History of Christian Spirituality*, Seabury Press, New York, 1981, p. 154

18 Leonard Sax, *Boys Adrift: The Five Factors Driving the Growing Epidemic of Unmotivated Boys*, Basic Book, 2007

19 Bill Irwin, *Blind Courage*, WRS Publishing, p. 11

20 Ronald Rolheiser, *Sacred Fire: A Deeper Human and Christian Maturity*, Image, New York, 2014, pp. 25-27

21 Carlo Carretto, *Letter's from the Desert*, Orbis Books, New York

22 *Appalachian Trail Guide to Maine*, 2009, p. 104

23 Mark Ellison, Hiking *Research.wordpress.com*, "Kalevi Korpela Discusses Finland's 'Power Forest' for Well-being an Emerging Research," posted on December 16, 2013

24 Richard Rohr, *8 Principles of the Center of Prayer and Contemplation*, Franciscan Media, Cincinnati, 2013

25 Henry David Thoreau, *A week On the Concord and Merrimack Rivers*, 1849, 10:443

26 Wendell Berry, *Hannah Coulter*, Shoemaker and Hoard, 2004

27 Thomas Merton, *Mystics and Zen Masters*, p. 133

28 Levine, *In An Unbroken Voice*, , p. 276

29 John Phillip Newell, *Listening to the Heartbeat of God*, Paulist Press, Mahwah, p. 34

30 *The Appalachian Trail Guide to Maine*, Fifteenth Edition, 2009, p. 97

31 Larry Mueller and Marguerite Reiss, *Bear Attacks of the Century*, The Lyons Press, Guilford, 2005

32 Annie Dillard, *Pilgrim at Tinker Creek*, Harper and Row, New York, 1974, p. 198

33 Henry David Thoreau, *Walking*, 1851, p. 206

34 Robert Benson, *A Good Life: Benedict's Guide to Everyday Joy*, Paraclete Press, Brewster, 2004, p. 31

35 John Phillip Newell, *Listening to the Heartbeat of God*, Paulist Press, Mahwah, p. 76

36 Gerald May, *The Wisdom of Wilderness, Experiencing the Healing Power of Nature*, Harper Collins, San Francisco, 2006, p. 15

37 Ibid., p. 15

38 Dietrich Bonhoeffer, *Life Together*, Harper and Row, New York, 1954, p.77

39 Dr. Monica Williams-Murphy and Kristan Murphy, *It's Okay to Die*, MKN, Huntsville, 2011

40 Levine, *In an Unspoken Voice*, p. 276

41 Richard Rohr, *Falling Upward, A Spirituality for the Two Halves of Life*, Jossey-Bass A Wiley Imprint, San Francisco, 2011, pp. 8-15

42 Thomas Merton, *Love and Living*, Harcourt, Orlando, 1979, pp. 11-12

43 *Appalachian Trail Guide New Hampshire-Vermont*, p. 72

44 Richard Louv, *Last Child in the Woods: Saving Our Children from Nature-Deficit Disorder*, Algonquin Books, Chapel Hill, 2008, p 10

Bibliography

AMC White Mountain Guide, 25th Edition, Boston, Mass., Appalachian Mountain Club, 1992

Robert Benson, *A Good Life: Benedict's Guide to Everyday Joy*, Paraclete Press, Brewster, 2004

Wendell Berry, *Hannah Coulter*, Shoemaker and Hoard, 2004

Bly Robert, *Iron John*, Addison-Wesley Publishing Company, Reading, 1990

Bourgeault, Cynthia, *Wisdom Jesus: Transforming Heart and Mind, Boston*, Shambhala Publications, 2008

Bonhoeffer, Dietrich, *Life Together*, Harper and Row, New York, 1954

Carretto, Carlo, Letters from the Desert, Orbis Books, New York, 1972

Clem, Dale; *Winds of Fury, Circles of Grace*, Abingdon Press, Nashville, 1997, and Bardolf & Company, Sarasota, 2011

Chazin, Daniel, Editor, *Appalachian Trail Data Book 2012*, 34th Edition, Harpers Ferry, Appalachian Trail Conservancy, 2011

Chew, V. Collins, *Underfoot: A Geologic Guide to the Appalachian Trail, 2nd Edition*, Harpers Ferry, Appalachian Trail Conference, 1993

Daloz, Laurent A. Parks, "Mentoring Men for Wisdom: Transforming the Pillars of Manhood," Chapter 8 in *Adult Education and the Pursuit of Wisdom*, New Directions for Adult and Continuing Educators, Wiley Periodicals Inc., Fall 2011

Daloz, Laurent A. Parks, *Mentor*, Jossey-Bass, San Francisco, 2012

Dante, *The Divine Comedy*

Davis, Jennifer Pharr, *Called Again: a story of love and triumph*, Beaufort Books, NY, 2013

Dellinger, Drew, "Hieroglyphic Stairway"

Ellison, Mark, "Kalevi Korpela Discusses Finland's "Power Forests" for Well-being and Emerging Research" on Hiking Research website, *https://hikingreasearch.wordpress.com/* posted December 16, 2013.

Fendler, Donn, with Joseph B. Egan, *Lost on a Mountain in Maine,* Beech Tree Paperback Book, New York, 1992

Holmes, Urban, *A History of Christian Spirituality,* Seabury Press, New York, 1981

Horn, H.S., *The Adaptive Geometry of Trees,* Princeton University, 1971

Irwin, Bill, with David McCasland, *Blind Courage,* Waco Texas, WRS Publishing, 1993

St. John of the Cross, *The Collected Works,* Translated by Kieran Kavanaugh, O.C.D. and Otilio Rodriguez, O.C.D., ICS Publications Institute of Carmelite Studies, Washington, D.C. 1991

Krakauer, John, *Into the Wild,* Anchor, 1996

Levine Peter, *In an Unspoken Voice: How the Body Releases Trauma and Restores Goodness,* North Atlantic Books, Berkeley, California, 2010)

Louv, Richard, *Last Child in the Woods: Saving Our Children from Nature-Deficit Disorder,* Algonquin Books, Chapel Hill, 2008

Matthew, Iain, *The Impact of God, Soundings from St. John of the Cross,* Hodder & Sloughton, London, 1995

May, Gerald, *The Wisdom of Wilderness: The Healing Power of Nature,* HarperCollins, New York, 2006

Merton, Thomas, *Mystics and Zen Masters,* Farrar, Straus and Giroux, New York, 1967

Merton, Thomas, *Contemplative Prayer,* Darton, Longman, & Todd Ltd, 1973

Merton, Thomas, *Love and Living,* Harcourt, Orlando, 1979

Miller, Cynthia Taylor, Editor, *Appalachian Trail Guide to New Hampshire-Vermont, 12th Edition,* Appalachian Trail Conservancy, Harper's Ferry, 2012

Mueller, Larry & Reiss, Marguerite, *Bear Attacks of the Century,* The Lyons Press, Guilford, 2005

Murphy, Kristan and Dr. Monica Williams-Murphy, *It's Okay to Die,* Huntsville, Alabama

Neff, John W., Katahdin, *An Historic Journey*, Appalachian Mountain Club Books, Boston, 2006

Newell, J. Philip, *Listening for the Heartbeat of God, A Celtic Spirituality*, Paulist Press, Mahwah, 1997

Oliver, Mary, "The Messenger" in *Thirst*, Beacon Press, Boston, 2006

Pollack, William, *Real Boys: Rescuing our Sons from the Myths of Boyhood*, Holt, NY, 1998

Plotkin, Bill, *Nature and the Human Soul*, New World Library, Novato, 2008

Rohr, Richard, *Falling Upward: A Spirituality of the Two Halves of Life*, Jossey-Bass, 2011

Rohr, Richard, *8 Principles of the Center for Action and Contemplation*, Franciscan Media, Cincinnati, 2013

Rolheiser, Ron, *The Holy Longing: The Search for Christian Spirituality*, Doubleday, 1999

Rolheiser, Ron, *Sacred Fire: A Vision for A Deeper Human and Christian Maturity*, Image, New York, 2014

Rolheiser, Ron, *Spirituality and the Two Halves of Life, A video workshop*, Oblate Media and Communication

Ronan, Roy, *Appalachian Trail Guide to Maine*, Maine Appalachian Trail Club, 15th edition, 2009

Sax, Leonard, *Boys Adrift: The Five Factors Driving the Growing Epidemic of Unmotivated Boys*, Basic Books, 2007

Sylvester, Robert, Editor, *Appalachian Trail Thru-Hikers' Companion*, Appalachian Trail Conservancy, Harpers Ferry, 2012

Thoreau, Henry David, *The Maine Wood*, Bramhall House, New York, 1950

Thoreau, Henry David, *A Week on the Concord and Merrimack Rivers*, 1849

Thoreau, Henry David, *On Nature and Man*, Peter Pauper Press, Mount Vernon, 1960

Tolkien, J. R.R. *The Hobbit*

THE END

CPSIA information can be obtained
at www.ICGtesting.com
Printed in the USA
LVOW04s2031160416

483725LV00003B/3/P